JUSTICE, JUSTICE

Justice, Justice

HISTORY OF
SCHOOLS &
SCHOOLING

Alan R. Sadovnik and Susan F. Semel
General Editors

Vol. 40

PETER LANG
New York • Washington, D.C./Baltimore • Bern
Frankfurt am Main • Berlin • Brussels • Vienna • Oxford

ERRATA

Cover art courtesy of Robert F. Wagner Labor Archives,
New York University, Sam Reiss Collection.
Photograph by Sam Reiss.

Library of Congress Cataloging-in-Publication Data

Perlstein, Daniel.
Justice, justice: school politics and the eclipse of liberalism /
Daniel H. Perlstein.
p. cm. — (History of schools and schooling; v. 40)
Includes bibliographical references and index.
1. Community and school—New York (State)—New York—History—
20th century. 2. Schools—Decentralization—New York (State)—New York—
History—20th century. 3. Educational equalization—New York (State)—New
York—History—20th century. 4. African Americans—Education—
Social aspects—History—20th century. I. Title. II. Series.
LC221.3.N38P45   370'.89'96073   2003004776
ISBN 0-8204-6787-1
ISSN 1089-0678

Bibliographic information published by **Die Deutsche Bibliothek**.
Die Deutsche Bibliothek lists this publication in the "Deutsche
Nationalbibliografie"; detailed bibliographic data is available
on the Internet at http://dnb.ddb.de/.

Cover design by Lisa Barfield

The paper in this book meets the guidelines for permanence and durability
of the Committee on Production Guidelines for Book Longevity
of the Council of Library Resources.

Daniel H. Perlstein

Justice, Justice

School Politics and the Eclipse of Liberalism

PETER LANG
New York • Washington, D.C./Baltimore • Bern
Frankfurt am Main • Berlin • Brussels • Vienna • Oxford

For Arlo and Reuben

Tho' much is taken, much abides

Contents

Acknowledgments

My interest in the 1968 school crisis originated when I worked in New York City with teachers and students who maintained their faith in schooling and social justice despite the impossible conditions in which they worked. They provided the inspiration and suggested the dilemmas that have shaped this study.

As I pursued my research, countless teacher and community activists shared their time, memories, personal papers, and insights. Passionate in their commitment and generous in their disagreements, these activists embodied what is best about America's civic life. In making its archives available to friend and critic alike, the American Federation of Teachers and its New York local demonstrate the contribution of teacher unions in enriching public debates about schooling. I owe particular thanks to AFT archivist Dan Golodner at the Walter P. Reuther Library in Detroit and UFT archivist Lucinda Manning at the Robert F. Wagner Archives in New York. Every effort was made to secure permissions for protected material. If any rights holder feels that material was not properly credited, please contact the publisher.

Students and faculty at the Stanford University School of Education sustained my study of and enthusiasm for public education. In particular, David Tyack and Larry Cuban demonstrated how historians of education can contribute to democratic schooling as scholar-citizens. This work is stronger for their examples as well as their insights. So too the willingness of students and colleagues at the University of California, Berkeley's Graduate School of Education to hear my ideas and challenge them has deepened my understanding of the politics of American schooling. Laura Schulkind has supported this work and shared her own ideas back and forth between New York and California.

Authors often credit colleagues for any virtues in their work while absolving others of its flaws. I might say the same of my parents, Norman and Norma Perlstein, whose pursuits of justice, even when I have taken a different path, have been models for my own. Scholarship, like democracy itself, is a collective project. This book is the better for all those who have worked to inform it.

Chapter 1

Worldviews in Collision

*There's liable
to be confusion
in a dream deferred.*
—LANGSTON HUGHES[1]

he problem of the Twentieth Century," as W. E. B. DuBois famously predicted one hundred years ago, would be "the problem of the color-line."[2] It continues to perplex and divide Americans in the twenty-first century as well. And in few endeavors have race relations been more contentious than in education. This book recounts the ideas and efforts of teachers and educational activists at the epicenter of America's racial politics. Like many books, this one has more than one theme. It explores the reshaping of America's political life and the central role of schooling in that transformation. In this sense, the book seeks to illuminate the roots of ideas that continue to shape schooling and school politics today. Still, social and political life pulls us in more than one direction. This text also explores how teachers and school activists with differing visions have defined the goals of schooling and attempted to actualize their ideals in a changing and inevitably ambiguous world. That is, in addition to exploring the current state of schooling, this study offers a range of alternatives suggested by educators and activists.

The book focuses on New York in the 1960s, when teacher unionists and black community activists engaged in a bitter struggle over efforts to reorganize the city's mammoth school system. While the United Federation of Teachers (UFT) saw this "community control" of ghetto schools as a threat to due process, job security, and unbiased, quality education, black activists saw it as a prerequisite to democratizing school governance, to eliminating racism in education, and to opening school jobs to African Americans.

The New York school conflict centered on the creation of two neighborhood boards governing a number of schools in Harlem and Ocean Hill-Brownsville.[3] After the Ocean Hill-Brownsville Governing Board ordered nineteen teachers and administrators out of the district's schools, the UFT launched a series of three 1968 strikes against community control. In its campaign against black activists, the teachers' union invoked the standard of race-blind equal treatment, which had been a hallmark of the African-American civil rights movement. Not until they had effectively destroyed community control did the teachers return to work.

The conflict over community control was the climactic chapter in a long struggle to achieve racial equality in New York's schools. It left a residue of bitterness, alienation and distrust that would mark students' and teachers' lives for decades.[4] It served as the benchmark for discussions about centralization and decentralization and about the racial politics of schooling, not only in New York, but also across the United States.[5] Even decades later, both proponents of Afrocentric schools around the country[6] and Chicago activists demanding the creation of individual school councils saw themselves as completing "the unfinished business" of New York's struggle over community control.[7] Moreover, the impact of the New York conflict extended beyond classrooms, school organization and governance. By convincing significant numbers of liberal whites that black advance could come only at their expense, the 1968 conflict marked the eclipse of liberalism in America's political life.

Rarely have teachers and community activists played as dramatic and central roles in the history of American education as they did in 1968. Although academics,[8] political leaders,[9] foundation officials,[10] business elites,[11] and the media all brought their own perspectives to the school conflict, it was the clash between black community activists and white teacher unionists that transformed decentralization from an experiment aimed at increasing parent participation and improving school efficiency into a shattering struggle for the redistribution of political power.[12]

The school crisis was so explosive because it reflected both enduring themes in American history and the changing political and economic contexts of American life. The dilemmas that activists confronted in 1968—separatism and integration in the black quest for racial justice, professionalism and trade unionism in teachers' efforts to gain dignity in their work, and the relationship of race and class in American society—were not new. At the same time, declining industrial production in American cities and the growing gulf between expanding white suburbs and decaying urban neighborhoods did much to reshape American politics and circumscribe the possibilities of meaningful school reform.

Still, the social conditions that restrict our actions do not dictate them; the ways activists understood and responded to the school conflict were by no means predetermined. Both blacks and whites assessed the politics of education in a variety of ways. This book explores the political visions of white teachers and black activists, the efforts that their beliefs catalyzed, and the process through which their conflict became a linchpin for the transformation of beliefs about race, class, schooling, and social justice.

The struggle for racial equality in New York's schools took off when pressure from black leaders and the Supreme Court's 1954 *Brown* decision led the city's Board of Education to announce its intention "to devise . . . a plan which will prevent the further development of . . . segregated schools, and . . . integrate existing ones as quickly as practicable."[13] The school board recruited Dr. Kenneth Clark and other prominent New Yorkers to a Commission on Integration.[14] In the decade following the *Brown* decision, the school board would often reiterate its commitment to desegregation. Still, it vetoed the integration commission's recommendations for changes in teacher assignment and school zoning policies, and behind the scenes, board members and administrators discouraged other integration policies.[15] The schools became increasingly segregated.[16]

By the late 1950s, leadership of the school integration campaign began to pass from elite commissioners to grass-roots organizers. The integration movement achieved its most massive expression in a February 3, 1964 boycott organized under the leadership of Brooklyn Rev. Milton Galamison and civil rights leader Bayard Rustin. Over 450,000 of the system's one million students stayed out of school. Still, few white liberals supported sending white children to ghetto schools, and the boycott was no more effective in winning integration than earlier actions.[17] Following the protest, New York's civil rights movement splintered, and activism shifted increasingly from citywide organizing for integration to neighborhood activism for Black Power.

A new Harlem intermediate school, I.S. 201, was the focal point of the emerging protests. Intermediate schools had replaced junior high schools in New York in order to facilitate school desegregation,[18] but the school board elected to build the windowless structure at a site that made integration unlikely. Although the board promised an integrated school offering state-of-the-art education, when officials first attempted to open I.S. 201 in April 1966, it was understaffed and segregated. Writer Martin Mayer has suggested that historians would

> have no difficulty dating precisely the moment of the decision that the New York schools could not be significantly integrated. It happened on the Sunday after Labor Day in 1966 when the president of the Board of Education . . . announced that the new Intermediate School 201 . . . would not open . . . with the rest of the city's schools.[19]

The movement for school integration had been fueled both by the belief that it would win educational resources for black children and by blacks' dreams of becoming full participants in American life. In response to the Board of Education's acquiescence to school segregation, parents boycotted I.S. 201 and argued that if they could not get an integrated school they should at least have more power in running the segregated one. They talked of appointing a black principal. Like Martin Mayer, Harlem Parents Committee head Isaiah Robinson attributed the black turn toward community control to white New York's thwarting of integration and dated the change to the opening of I.S. 201.[20]

In Brooklyn, too, increasingly militant school activists turned away from the integrationist hopes that had sustained earlier protests. Echoing national calls for Black Power, community activists argued that decentralization would allow blacks to gain the control over their lives that integration struggles had failed to deliver. By 1967, Ocean Hill-Brownsville had surpassed Harlem as the center of militant school organizing.

Calls to reorganize the city's mammoth school system mobilized a wide range of New Yorkers in addition to black activists. The United Federation of Teachers saw in initial calls for decentralization a way to increase both parent commitment to the schools and teacher authority in educational matters.[21] Policy analysts, often relying on models of corporate organization, argued that the centralized school administration created massive inefficiencies.[22] Liberal reformers saw decentralization as a way to encourage citizen participation in schooling and in politics more generally.[23] Both radicals who saw racism as a primary obstacle to organizing the American proletariat[24] and business and political elites seeking to preserve municipal tranquillity promoted decentralization.[25]

In April 1967, under pressure from black activists, the Ford Foundation and the UFT, the Board of Education authorized the election of experimental neighborhood school boards in Harlem (I.S. 201) and Ocean Hill-Brownsville, together with a third district in Manhattan's Lower East Side. In Ocean Hill, community control began functioning with teachers, parents and neighborhood residents all serving on the governing board. Still, with so many different actors seeking to influence school policy, disagreements about the nature of proposed reforms remained unresolved, tensions signaled by the competing labels attached to school reorganization: "decentralization" and "community control."

The lack of consensus about the purpose of school reform reinforced opposing efforts by educators and community activists each to define school reform according to their own visions and to see betrayal in the other's efforts to do so. Ocean Hill-Brownsville activists began organizing a local school board election. As the Urban League noted, when organizers asked the Board of Education for the lists of parents' names and addresses—which only the board had—they were told they had to pay two Board secretaries to go through the files. When they got the money up to pay for these secretaries, they were told the secretaries were on vacation and no one knew when they would be back.

The Urban League saw in the unavailability of the lists "small, mean-spirited behavior, so obviously meant to wreck an experiment that everyone had agreed to support." Despite the Board's actions, a quarter of eligible voters participated in the August 3, 1967 election. Activists were pleased with what they considered a high turnout. The Board complained that not enough parents had participated.[26]

Growing tensions divided Ocean Hill-Brownsville activists from the UFT as well as from the Board of Education. The 1967 governing board elections were held during the summer vacation, and teachers felt they were being squeezed out of meaningful participation in the experiment. Then, teachers went out on a city-wide strike at the beginning of the 1967–68 school year. Convinced that its demands coincided with the interests of New York's students, the UFT asked the governing board to put its own efforts on hold and support the union's illegal strike.[27] Seeing the walkout as a threat to the fledgling experiment in local control, the governing board declined to support the union.

The governing board's hiring decisions furthered tensions. It chose as unit administrator black educator Rhody McCoy rather than Jack Bloomfield, a white junior high school principal who had helped organize the demonstration district. Then, at McCoy's recommendation, the governing board appointed five new principals, three blacks, one Puerto Rican and one Chinese. The five all had New York State principal's certification but were not at the top of the New York City eligibility list. Black activists felt that for the first time, sensitivity to community needs was a primary criterion in the selection of principals; in the eyes of many teachers, race had replaced merit in hiring. A mass exodus from the district, aided by the relaxation of rules restricting transfers, began. J.H.S. 271 principal Jack Bloomfield, a third of the teachers, and five secretaries transferred out of the district, and all twenty-one of the district's assistant principals applied to leave.[28]

In the wake of the teachers' strike and the principal appointments, tensions continued to escalate. The teachers resigned from the governing board, saying that they had been forced out by black extremists. "At this point," in the view of the Urban League, "many UFT teachers in the district began to deliberately sabotage the work of the school district." Absenteeism among white teachers rose alarmingly. Black teachers charged that white coworkers were deliberately letting the kids run wild in order to discredit the experiment. White teachers, on the other hand, complained of "systematic and sadistic harassment, intimidation and humiliation."[29]

Amid deepening antagonisms, the Ocean Hill-Brownsville school board met in executive session on the evening of Wednesday, May 7, 1968. The board's personnel committee had recommended that fourteen teachers, five assistant principals and one principal be removed from the district. The governing board was considering the recommendation when, as it was described in its minutes, "the community walked into the meeting." The matter was decided.[30]

The next day, the teachers and supervisors received registered letters informing them that the governing board had voted "to end your employment in the schools of this District." The letter continued. "You will report . . . to Personnel, 110 Livingston

Street . . . for reassignment."[31] The letter to one of the notified teachers, who was black, was withdrawn, and School Superintendent Donovan told the others to ignore the notice. Nevertheless, the school conflict moved into high gear. Whereas Ocean Hill argued that the transfer of unwanted teachers was common in the school system, the UFT argued that the nineteen had been fired. Reiterating an earlier threat to oppose any assault on teachers' rights, UFT President Al Shanker promised a city-wide strike unless the nineteen white educators were reinstated.[32]

Like the supporters of community control, the UFT's backers included a wide range of groups, with sometimes competing goals. Jewish organizations saw black demands as a cover for anti-Semitism, and organized labor saw them as a threat to municipal employees' ability to organize. Social democrats saw in community control an effort by elite institutions such as the Ford Foundation to manipulate black activists and to divide the working class. Many whites saw in community control the beginning of a black take-over of the city.

Over the summer of 1968, all efforts to negotiate a compromise between teachers and black activists failed, leading the UFT and the Council of Supervisory Associations to go out on a strike, with almost 90% of teachers and administrators honoring picket lines. Although the strike seemed to have been settled when teachers returned to work after two days, a second strike began two days later. After two weeks a second agreement was reached, but it too broke down, beginning a third, bitter strike that lasted for a month.[33]

The conflict between the UFT and black activists brought to the surface extraordinary levels of racial animosity. Teachers picketing ghetto schools reported hearing "Honky," "Jew Pig," "White motherfucking, dirty Jew bastards," and "You will all make good lampshades."[34] For their part, black activists and their white supporters heard "Nigger" and "Nigger-lover."[35] New York City Human Rights Commissioner William Booth was called "Black Hitler" and given the Nazi salute by picketing teachers at Francis Lewis High School.[36] "It's going to be a hard and a brutal settlement," one teacher threatened, "but there's one thing these people are going to have to learn—we outnumber them, ten to one."[37]

Ocean Hill-Brownsville unit administrator Rhody McCoy promised, "Not one of [the transferred] teachers will be allowed to teach anywhere in this city; the black community will see to that."[38] The African-American Teachers Association, headed by Ocean Hill assistant principal Al Vann, editorialized, "How long shall the Black and Puerto Rican communities of New York sit back and allow the Jewish dominated United Federation of Teachers to destroy our every effort to rescue our children?"[39] Meanwhile, the UFT stereotyped black community control as "mob rule" enforced by "terrorism and threats." A "sort of hoodlum element," warned UFT President Al Shanker, "had gained control over several schools."[40]

The union agreed to end its strike only when the transferred teachers were returned to their classrooms and a state-appointed trustee took over control of the

Ocean Hill-Brownsville district. The strike solidified the UFT's power in municipal affairs. "Six months later," UFT founder and AFT President David Selden recounts,

> the UFT and the city signed the famous "Christmas tree" contract, which provided spectacular increases in salaries, fringe benefits and working conditions for a three-year period. When he finished reporting the terms to the delegate assembly, Shanker said, "Some of you wondered why it was necessary to stay out so long last fall when there seemed to be no salary or other economic issue involved." He paused for dramatic effect, and then concluded, "Now you know."[41]

In the spring of 1968 the UFT spent hundreds of thousands of dollars to block a strong decentralization bill in the New York state legislature.[42] The "decentralization" law that was finally enacted in 1969 abolished community control and, in the view of the *New York Times*, made the UFT the "dominating force" in the new "community" school districts.[43] The legislation, echoed one-time New York City school superintendent John Theobald, "negates any possibility of local control over the professional staff."[44]

White teachers paid a substantial price for their victory in the school conflict. Their organized clout, coming at the expense of the movement of racial justice, discouraged interracial coalitions for better education, subverted the notion that schools could help construct an equitable society, and exacerbated feelings of demoralization in teachers' daily school work. Although the school crisis fostered the creation of a few autonomous black schools and other institutions, the vast majority of black children, consigned to demoralized classrooms, fared no better than white teachers. In the years after the 1968 school conflict, white teacher unionists and black activists continued to jockey for power within the schools, but with the passing of community control, hopes for fundamental change in New York's schools faded, and bitterness became ever more firmly entrenched in the schools.

In the decades before the school crisis, politics in New York and throughout America had been shaped by a liberal ideology that wedded the promise to free individuals from ethnic encumbrances and other "traditional" social distinctions with state intervention in social welfare and the economy. This dual commitment united social scientists and elite reformers with union organizers, civil rights activists, and enough of the citizenry to create what Steve Fraser and Gary Gerstle have labeled "the New Deal Social Order."[45]

Nowhere was the American commitment to liberalism more pronounced in the mid-twentieth century than in New York City. A predominantly white, industrial city, it led the United States in public hospitals, mass transit and public housing. Its unparalleled system of public universities offered higher education to generations of the poor. New York pioneered the urban development projects that defined American cities in the two decades after the World War II.[46]

Ironically, these very projects helped undermine the regime that produced them. From the 1940s through the 1960s, over two million New Yorkers—the vast majority white—left for the suburbs, while urban renewal and highway development destroyed hundreds of thousands of working-class homes. Such developments as the 1962 addition of a second level and new approach roads to the George Washington Bridge and the 1964 opening of the Verrazano Narrows Bridge fostered real estate booms in New Jersey and Staten Island, even as they required the razing of blocks of urban homes. Meanwhile, the city's industrial job base declined steadily. In the garment industry, for instance, two thirds of jobs disappeared in the second half of the twentieth century, replaced by employment in corporate headquarters, restaurants, and the like. At the moment when the number of black and Latino New Yorkers was growing, government responsiveness to the poor was shifting to responsiveness to business interests.[47]

Much, of course, has changed since the late 1960s, and New York, like all American cities, was in some respects unique. Still, the conflicts and crises of its history epitomize those of urban America. In New York, as elsewhere, school conditions reflected not only the impersonal social forces of deindustrialization and poverty but also the political activities and choices, whether wise or shortsighted, of those interested in schooling. In New York, as elsewhere, whites demonstrated their unwillingness to support black equality in schooling. In the face of the white repudiation of integration and racial equality, blacks in New York and elsewhere moved from the belief that schools were failing in their mission to educate all youth to the belief that schools were succeeding in their intended job of miseducating blacks.[48] Finally, New York in the 1960s, like much of urban America today, had a substantial population of new immigrants who defied simple racial categories of black and white. Still, the politics of education in New York then, as in urban America today, revolved to a significant degree around what were seen as black-white conflicts.

The battle over community control, together with the virulent ethnic and racial tensions it unleashed, reshaped the New York's liberal politics. It not only exposed growing strains in the political coalition that had promoted racial justice and decent working conditions since the New Deal; it gave voice to ideologies that justified liberalism's eclipse. It both reflected and propelled declining liberal hopes that schooling and other government programs could foster equality and promote a harmonious society.

Sociologist Jonathan Rieder's ethnographic study of Brooklyn's Canarsie neighborhood documents how the school conflict convinced significant numbers of previously liberal working- and middle-class whites that black advance could come only with the loss of their own foothold on prosperity.[49] Similarly, historian Godfrey Hodgson argues that the school crisis precipitated a shift in the balance of political power in New York "from liberal to conservative" as a large numbers of liberal whites "swung away from their traditional emotional and voting alliance with the blacks and the poor."[50]

Disenchantment with liberalism was not limited to New York and did not begin with the 1968 school conflict. The Vietnam War, black protest and white backlash, together with growing economic concerns, figured largely in the splintering of the liberal coalition. Nationally, this resurgence of the right was marked by Richard Nixon's 1968 election to the Presidency. If, however, the New York school crisis was not the cause of the declining place of liberalism in American life, it was more than the reflection of a process created elsewhere. Educators and activists around the country looked to New York, and its school crisis served as a benchmark of urban American life. The 1968 conflict, in Godfrey Hodgson's phrase, was "the classic instance" of America's racial politics, through which white workers were "captured" by conservatives and "yoked to the service of a cause that was not their own."[51]

Examination of the school crisis has the power to illuminate enduring issues in the politics of American education because New York teacher unionists and community activists both were and were not typical of teachers and activists elsewhere. Just as the city was home to an array of government programs and liberal activists rare in American society, the ideological commitments that shaped teacher unionism in New York, as historian Wayne Urban has rightly noted, were hardly the norm across the United States.[52] Indeed, New York's leading teacher unionists and community activists were far more interested in ideological concerns than many of those who followed them.

Still, educators and activists around the country looked to New York's lead in school affairs because the racial and economic inequalities faced by New York activists shaped urban education across the United States.[53] Indeed, the very atypicality of New York led its teacher unionists and community activists to articulate with unusual force and clarity visions of public education that framed the way others discussed schooling. Following the 1968 school crisis, UFT leader Al Shanker was for three decades among the most influential voices in American education. Black teachers and activists prominent in New York achieved national recognition as proponents of Black Power in education. However unusual their circumstances, New York's community activists and teacher unionists were able to articulate their political perspectives in ways that can continue to enrich and clarify debates about the purposes of education in a racially troubled nation.

Intense hopes and hatreds animated the school crisis, and ambivalence and ambiguity shaped activists' beliefs. Nevertheless, ideologies framed activists' dilemmas and conflicts, gave content to their rage, and shaped their dreams of democratic schooling. This book presents the visions that shaped school activism.

The body of this book is divided into two sections. The first examines the ways white teachers understood school politics; the second explores the thinking of black activists.[54] Each chapter recounts the perspective of a group of teachers or civil rights activists, and each represents a significant ideological thread not only in the school conflict but also in American politics more broadly. Each, moreover, continues to help define American visions of schooling today.

Chapters Two through Five explore the ideas and efforts of white teachers. Chapter Two traces the activities of Albert Shanker and other UFT leaders. They argued that only a race-blind movement of poor and working people could transform urban schools and society. Until the mid-1960s, this social democratic ideology placed UFT leaders among the strongest allies of black equality in the labor movement, but by the end of the school conflict, the UFT was widely held by civil rights activists to be the bitter enemy of black New York. Arguably no development in American race relations since the 1960s is more significant than the transformation of race-blindness from a means of opposing racial inequality into a means of justifying it. This chapter recounts the role of New York's teachers in that transformation.[55] Moreover, how teachers made sense of race relations shaped how they understood their place as educators. Teachers across the United States continue to wrestle with the competing claims of trade unionism and professionalism that emerged in New York.

Chapter Three examines a second shift in America's political culture heralded by the 1968 school conflict. Most of New York's teachers were Jewish, and charges that anti-Semitism motivated black demands contributed much to the bitterness of the school crisis. In the course of the conflict, the same teachers who belonged to the UFT, with its ideology of universal rights, also joined the right-wing Jewish Teachers Association, with its appeals to distinctive Jewish interests and identity. Whereas Jews had been seen in the decades before the school conflict as the epitome of an assimilationist American liberalism, in the course of the school conflict they came to epitomize a newfound pride in ethnic identity among white Americans. Rather than contributing to a spirit of pluralism, the new invocations of ethnic identity served to undermine liberalism and to justify racial inequality. Although today schools often rely on "multicultural" celebrations of ethnic identity as an antidote to racist attitudes, the school conflict suggests the need for a more nuanced perspective.

Teachers often call for parental involvement in education, but feel ambivalence about parents' presence in schools, especially when poor and minority parents are involved. Chapter Four focuses on Teachers for Community Control, which sought to convince educators that black self-determination was compatible with teachers' rights. The dilemma that TCC faced—how to convince whites that they had an interest in black equality—has occupied a prominent place in American social science and social reform. Chapter Four examines the roots and trajectory of TCC's call for an alliance of white teacher unionists and the black community.

Finally, Chapter 5 explores the efforts of young white teachers who saw in community control an opportunity to participate in radically democratic communities. These teachers were convinced that bureaucracy and centralized power, as much as economic inequality, distorted American life. Echoing Deweyan calls for schools to revitalize individual autonomy, community bonds and democratic commitments, they possessed utopian hopes that schools could model humane, democratic communities for the wider society. Such dreams continue to inspire many teachers and echo in recent school reform ideas.[56] Chapter Five examines the ambiguities of such hopes in the face of the social divisions of American life and white teachers' own ambivalence about their role in urban schools.

School activism and debate took a different form among blacks. Within labor unions and community organizations as well as schools, African Americans had long debated the possibility and desirability of integration and black self-determination. These debates reemerged with heightened force in 1968. Focusing on the school activism of Bayard Rustin, Chapter Six examines black efforts to sustain an alliance with the labor movement. Rustin argued that poverty had displaced racism as the crucial issue confronting African Americans and that no institution was more committed than organized labor to challenging economic inequality. Despite Rustin's long record at the forefront of the African American freedom struggle, in 1968 he urged blacks to ally themselves with the UFT and the labor movement, rather than be tempted by empty promises of community control. While Rustin's analysis of race relations mirrored that of the UFT leadership, he shared none of its complacency about the prospects for black equality. Rather, a profound and troubling pessimism characterized Rustin's vision. The issues he faced—about the ideal of racial integration in a society that had repudiated it, about the relative power of race and class in shaping black life—continue to perplex Americans of good will. Rustin's stance serves as a reminder of the profound obstacles facing those who rely on race-based politics and school reform in the quest to create social justice for urban youth.[57]

Unlike Bayard Rustin, most integrationists believed that community control could actually further the creation of a just and integrated society. Chapter Seven explores the career of one such activist, Rev. Milton Galamison. In the decade that preceded the emergence of community control, Galamison led the movement to integrate New York's schools. Even after demands for desegregation began to fade, he continued more than any other New Yorker to articulate the dream of integration. Traces of such hopes were an essential element in the emergence of community control. Today, one rarely hears calls for the integration of American schools and society among educators, policymakers or politicians. Our national life has been impoverished by this abandonment. This chapter explores the trajectory of the integrationist ideal that propelled Galamison's activism and that of the countless New Yorkers whose energies he catalyzed.

Chapter Eight focuses on black militants who saw community control as a model of black autonomy and as an opportunity to foster a black identity that challenged the brutalizing norms of American society. The chapter centers on the life and career of Sonny Carson. In the course of the school conflict, Carson emerged as one of the best known black political figures in New York. His ascendancy marked the displacement

of faith in education and community organizing by the conviction that public schooling served to reproduce white supremacy and that black humanity required the development of an oppositional and insurgent racial identity. Still, no less than the integrationist civil rights movement, the campaign for black self-determination drew on
deeply and long held values. This chapter examines the eclipse of integrationism by
appeals to racial identity, and the dilemmas black militants faced in their alienation
from liberal visions of participation in American life.

The commitment to fostering a black identity that did not depend on assimilation
into white American culture infused black nationalism with pedagogical concerns.
Chapter Nine focuses on four black New York educators whose efforts won them recognition from African Americans across the United States. They challenged both the
view of black youth as a set of deficits and the facile pluralism that ignored the profound scars of racial oppression. They debated the degree to which a new identity
could be reconciled with participation in American society. New York's black educators not only confronted enduring dilemmas in the education of African American
youth, their efforts to balance engagement and autonomy offer insights into the situation of all children in an increasingly diverse society.[58]

In recent times, the efforts of educational researchers and policymakers have been en-
riched by an acknowledgment of the expressed concerns of parents and teachers. Still,
as Andy Hargreaves cautions, to speak of a singular teacher's voice neglects the place
of power dynamics, social context, and contested political ideas in teachers' thinking.[59] The divergent paths taken by teachers and community activists suggests the
need to speak not of teacher, parent, or community voice, but of voices, and to situate
those voices in the social and political contexts that shape and circumscribe them.

Both teachers and parents have often been portrayed in one-dimensional accounts
of celebration or blame. Amid all the ambiguities of social life, the ideologies in which
white teacher unionists and black activists grounded their opposing activities both
challenged and reflected racial and economic inequalities.[60] Full consideration of the
visions that guided teachers and activists invites the possibility of reflecting more ex-
pansively and realistically about the meanings of schooling.

The daughter of a rabbi, teacher Liz Fusco had grown up with the Biblical edict,
"Justice, justice shalt thou pursue." In its repeated call to pursue justice, the Biblical
verse highlights not only the centrality of justice to social life but also the multiple,
sometimes conflicting visions animating those who would pursue it. A veteran civil
rights activist before she came to New York, in 1968 Fusco pursued justice by breaking
with the vast majority of white teachers and supporting community control. Other
black and white New Yorkers, many of them as committed as Fusco to the pursuit of
justice, followed very different paths.[61]

How should we respond to the enduring presence of racial and economic inequality in American schools and society? An examination of activists' varied visions illuminates many of the obstacles and conflicts facing us today, but it offers no ready-made solution, no one sure path. Instead, this book is intended to foster discussion among educators committed to promoting social justice and activists seeking to transform divided urban school systems into models of democratic life.

Chapter 2

Race, Class, and the Triumph of Teacher Unionism

How does a radical—a mild radical, it is true, but still someone who felt closer to radical than to liberal writers and politicians in the late 1950s—end up by early 1970 a conservative, a mild conservative, but still closer to those who now call themselves conservative than to those who call themselves liberals?
— NATHAN GLAZER, "ON BEING DERADICALIZED"[1]

According to United Federation of Teachers President Albert Shanker, in the early days of the 1968 teachers' strike, he was greeted by the outstretched hands of black and Puerto Rican New Yorkers. "They used to reach out and say, 'Good luck, Al' or something like that." But as the strike dragged into October and November, Shanker recalled, there was "a polarization of racial feelings." The union leader absolved white teachers of inciting racial hostilities, and he was hopeful that once the strike was over, the UFT could "pick up the pieces" of the old labor-civil rights alliance. Invocations of a happier time when blacks and whites were united under labor's banner recur frequently in UFT accounts of the teacher strikes, but in the course of the school crisis, old ideals gained new meanings.[2]

The UFT justified its opposition to community control by insisting that poor black and white students and citizens were more like one another than they were like affluent members of their races. Urging New Yorkers to reject political and educational programs that added to racial differences, the UFT called for the enforcement of race-blind standards of equal treatment and for programs to help minority students enter the academic and social mainstream. Still, the UFT's advocacy of race-blind policies placed the union in direct opposition to black activists challenging a school system in which formal neutrality abetted racial inequality. Arguably, no change in the way Americans have discussed race in the decades since the school conflict has been more consequential than this transformation of race-blindness from a means of protesting white supremacy into a vehicle through which whites could oppose black demands. In their battle against community control, New York's white teacher unionists played a central role in this transformation.

The struggle over community control also revealed the competing pulls of trade unionism and professionalism in teacher's work. At the same time as UFT leaders portrayed teachers as aggrieved workers and called for solidarity with them, they asserted that as professionals, teachers merited freedom from outside interference. Like race-blind standards of equal treatment, invocations of professionalism protected teachers in their conflict with black activists. This chapter examines the UFT's case against community control and the enduring dilemmas of American schools and society that shaped it.

Civil Rights Versus Community Control

According to the UFT, community control threatened black children as much as it did white teachers. Curricular abuses, the UFT argued, would inevitably follow demands for community control. Unlike the pluralist compromises required in large, heterogeneous cities, small, homogenous districts, charged union leader Sandra Feldman, "almost always involved parochialism and frequent bigotry."[3] Moreover, the danger was not limited to classroom matters. "To the people of the community, the actual community," UFT supporter Maurice Goldbloom explained, community control "offers only the simulacrum of power—for they have no command over the economic resources that real power requires." Writer and activist Michael Harrington elaborated, "The only practical strategy for destroying both [poverty and racism] requires that the Negro seek access to the very mainstream of that very white society which has so outrageously abused him."[4]

Before the late 1960s, UFT leaders argued, the civil rights movement had been part of a liberal coalition that sought to prod the federal government into action and to integrate American society. Community control, UFT President Al Shanker contrasted, "represented a kind of backward step. It represented . . . people in the community saying, 'We've given up on integration, so we want to take hold of our own schools.'"[5] Community control enjoyed white support, according to Sandra Feldman, because "many liberals, weary and disoriented, are willing to settle for 'separate but equal' and grasp thankfully at the opportunity to cloak this retrogression in the militant-sounding rhetoric of Black Power."[6]

UFT leaders mounted a massive campaign to convince New Yorkers that while the union remained true to liberal ideals, black activists "polarized . . . the struggle for community control . . . into a black-white racial conflict."[7] Even as Shanker urged that the school conflict not be made into "a racial conflict,"[8] however, he warned that community control would mean "mob rule."[9] "We are faced with racial cleavage," Shanker told the UFT Delegate Assembly after the Ocean Hill-Brownsville governing board ignored the rankings from civil service exams and appointed a number of non-white school administrators. "Over 1,000 teachers are facing bitterness and hatred. We are not going to let those teachers down."[10]

In its campaign, the UFT appealed both to working-class interracial solidarity and to teachers' status as professionals. When the Ocean Hill-Brownsville Governing Board attempted to remove nineteen white teachers and supervisors from the district's schools in May 1968, Shanker noted the teachers had been working for up to ten years without a blemish on their records. "If a teacher is not good," he explained in a September 6, 1968 letter to parents, "he should be dismissed, but he must have a fair trial. Teachers, like any other jobholder, must be assured of job security and union rights."[11] Speaking in support of striking teachers, one-time civil rights leader Bayard Rustin erased black activists in order to cast teachers as an exploited proletariat victimized by an unrepentant bourgeoisie. "The mayor and the Board of Education are not part of the workers' concept," Rustin argued. "They are the ultimate enemy."[12]

At the same time as it argued for workers' rights, the UFT invoked notions of a race-blind standard of merit and teacher professionalism in its opposition to community control. Just as all people share a physiology that allows any competent doctor to minister to any patient, any competent teacher could educate any child. As long as teachers continued to be hired on the basis of their merit, UFT leaders argued, students of all backgrounds could be educated.

Social Democracy, Teacher Unionism, and Civil Rights

In the course of the school conflict, union leaders frequently recalled their participation in the civil rights movement, and they claimed that the same ideals which had, in earlier years, animated their support for legitimate black demands now motivated their opposition to community control. The way UFT leaders understood and fought for civil rights was the product of countless, decades-old debates within teachers' unions and the broader American left about the relationship of labor to issues of racial justice.[13]

Although the United Federation of Teachers was only eight years old at the time of the 1968 school crisis, its roots went back much further. The UFT was the direct descendent of the Teachers Guild, a union formed by social democrats who split from the more radical New York Teachers Union during the politically charged years of the Depression.[14] Not only did the UFT largely replicate the organizational structure of the Guild and receive its predecessor's charter as the New York local of the American Federation of Teachers; the new union occupied the Guild's offices, "inheriting," in the words of the UFT's first president, "its clerical staff and all the rest of the machinery of a going concern."[15]

Veterans of the Guild and other social democratic organizations dominated the UFT leadership. UFT founding president Charles Cogen had been the Guild's leader. David Selden, George Altomare and Albert Shanker had been Guild organizers before taking up similar positions in the new union. UFT Ocean Hill-Brownsville negotiator and future UFT and AFT President Sandra Feldman, future UFT Treasurer Jeannette DiLorenzo, AFT Vice-President Richard Parrish, staffer Rochelle Horowitz, and Shanker assistant Yetta Barsh were among the many UFT leaders who were deeply committed social democrats.[16]

Through electoral campaigns and, especially, labor organization, social democrats sought to extend America's political democracy to economic life. A nexus of beliefs defined social democracy—the belief that under the leadership of organized labor America could evolve gradually toward socialism without a fundamental re-ordering of its political structure; the belief that if distinctions of class could wither, the more epiphenomenal division of race would disappear even more easily; the belief that America possessed a universally valid culture of equal opportunity into which all should assimilate.

Ironically, social democrats were at their most passionate, not in fighting the bourgeoisie, but rather in battles with Communists, whose race-conscious politics and militant commitment to mass demonstrations challenged the socialist analysis of American society and the place socialist teacher unionists envisioned for themselves within it. Retired principal and Teachers Guild leader Abraham Lefkowitz epitomized the socialist stance. Lobbying the Joint Committee of Teacher Organizations to expel the Communist-led Teachers Union, Lefkowitz stressed the Communists' "unprofessional conduct, the undignified and rude mass delegations of the Union and their unwarranted coercion of members of the Legislature by mass picketing at hotels and at homes."[17] Through such efforts, Guild activists articulated both teachers' aspirations to professionalism and their resentment at its absence.[18]

For all their differences, however, the Guild and the Teachers Union spoke the same language of Marxian class relations. Their disagreements, in David Hollinger's apt phrase, were "carried out within the terms of the cosmopolitan ideal." Moreover, if, as Lionel Trilling has argued, the interaction of socialists and Communists "created the American intellectual class as we know it," in few milieux was that intellectual activity as intense as among New York's teacher unionists.[19] No less than their Communist adversaries, social democratic teacher unionists acquired an ideological coherence, a polemical skill and a political style that would rarely leave them. Like the

Communists, the social democratic teacher-unionists exerted an influence in New York and its schools far out of proportion to their numbers.[20]

In the 1940s and 1950s, social democrats and their allies, together with McCarthy-era government repression and the Communists' own failures, broke the Communist leadership of teacher unionism in New York.[21] The Teachers Guild came into its own as the focal point of teacher organizing. Like the Communist movement of earlier years, social democracy offered teacher unionists an opportunity to reach beyond occupational concerns to address broad issues of public life. Jeannette DiLorenzo was among the future UFT leaders who grew up in a home where "being part of an international movement" was "the religion" and the social democratic *Jewish Daily Forward* was "the Bible." DiLorenzo studied socialism and Marxism at the Rand School and honed organizational and leadership skills in the Young People's Socialist League (YPSL). Marches and pickets were weekly events. "I never stopped to analyze whether it was good people I was working for," DiLorenzo would remember. "It was the idea; it was working for a better world." Convinced that education was part of the "class struggle" and attracted to the Teachers Guild "because we were anti-Communist," DiLorenzo and her husband left another city agency and went to work for the Board of Education. The Guild, she found, "was a social movement as well as a trade union."[22]

Al Shanker also grew up in a left-wing home, where his mother, who was active in the social democratic garment workers unions, inculcated a commitment to unionism. In the late 1940s, Shanker attended the University of Illinois. There, he joined the YPSL chapter, campaigned for Norman Thomas, and chaired the campus Socialist Study Club. Shanker returned to New York to study philosophy at Columbia University, but he abandoned graduate school to become a teacher. Between classes, Shanker would pass copies of such anti-Communist standards as *The God That Failed* and *Darkness at Noon* to fellow teacher and Guild activist George Altomare. The future UFT president, as Altomare recalls, was "someone where ideology was important in the formal sense."[23]

The entrance of younger activists such as DiLorenzo, Selden, Altomare, and Shanker injected new militancy into the Teachers Guild, and the union began to organize in earnest.[24] In the eyes of UFT founder George Altomare, teachers had the same complaints as other workers. When he and Al Shanker began teaching in 1952,

even though [the school] wasn't a factory, it was run like a factory. [The assistant principal's] office was on the fifth floor; he would actually use binoculars to see that you were doing your yard duty outside. Or to look in your room. A real tyrant. . . . And you're exploited. You're underpaid, no benefits whatsoever, no job security . . . no sick pay. You came in when you were sick; you couldn't afford not to. There was nothing and no job security at all.[25]

Guild organizer and future AFT president Dave Selden became committed to social-ism and the labor movement in Depression-era Detroit. "The goals of the embattled teachers," Selden concluded, "were the usual worker goals—higher wages, better ben-efits and improved working conditions."[26] When the Guild became the UFT, the Guild veterans who occupied leadership positions in the new union maintained their militant blue-collar rhetoric. Teachers, AFT President Carl Megel warned, dare not have an inflated sense of their status: "A doctor or a lawyer is a businessman. . . . A teacher is a worker. You are a day laborer."[27]

When UFT supporter and Brotherhood of Electrical Workers President James B. Carey addressed 10,000 delegates at National Education Association's 1962 conven-tion, he condemned NEA "professionalism," telling the delegates, "One of the prime troubles—if not the chief curse—of the teaching *industry* is precisely that word *profes-sion*." The NEA's professionalism, he argued, "implies that your *craft* is somewhat above this world of ours; it implies a detachment, a remoteness from the daily battle of the streets, in the neighborhood, and in the cities." Without unions, he warned, teachers would lack decent wages and thus the ability to "afford integrity and hon-esty" in their work.[28] Years after the 1968 school conflict, UFT leader Jeanette DiLo-renzo would echo, "The highest professionalism is to realize that [teachers] were work-ers like everyone else. They work with their minds and they work with their hands as well. And the elitism of saying they were different from other workers had put them behind other workers."[29]

The image of themselves as militant workers held special promise for male teach-ers, and the UFT was created with them in mind. Despite decades of active participa-tion by women in New York's teachers unions,[30] UFT organizers paid little attention to women teachers. UFT founder David Selden saw in the angry young men in the junior high schools a foundation for the UFT. He was completely surprised—and un-affected—when thousands of female elementary school teachers participated in early UFT actions.[31]

"High school teachers are assembly line workers; they're piece workers," UFT founder George Altomare maintained. "You have five classes, three of the same thing . . . so it's tough, it's a grind. . . . Also, you get someone for forty minutes. You don't know the kids [well enough] to get any job satisfaction." Moreover, whereas elemen-tary school teachers go to college wanting to become educators, "high school English teachers want to be great writers; biology teachers want to be doctors; social studies teachers lawyers, the gym teachers superstars. . . . Your friends are in the professions." Thus, by interest and job conditions, secondary school teachers were alienated and ripe for organizing.[32]

Teacher unionists' gendered blue-collar rhetoric legitimized adversarial relation-ships with students. According to labor historian and UFT sympathizer Thomas Brooks, until teachers unionized, "tough kids believed 'teach' a 'softy.'" Then, in 1962 the UFT went out on strike. One teacher explained, "The kids saw teachers on television, fighting. We were tough like truck drivers and Jimmy Hoffa."[33] In a portrait of the strike's aftermath at a ghetto junior high school, the UFT's *United Teacher* claimed that when the teachers returned to their classrooms, students "set a record of perfect conduct." These changes occurred, according to the UFT, because of "the realization that teachers are not mice but people with gumption, who will carry signs and insist upon their rights."[34] By such logic, the inflexibility of the UFT in its confrontation with community control was a positive rather than negative attribute.

Ironically, the gendered language of blue-collar toughness did not increase tensions between teachers and their bosses in school administration. Speaking to the 1963 AFT annual convention, New York school superintendent Calvin Gross argued, "Up until now teachers have always been too complaisant, too docile, too willing to let themselves be put upon. I personally welcome the new show of vigor and muscle which has now become apparent in many parts of our profession."[35]

Workers Become Professionals

The UFT's call for a labor-civil rights coalition relied on teachers' blue-collar status. When AFL-CIO leaders endorsed the UFT's 1968 fight against community control, however, it stressed the union's importance "not only for the future of teacher unionism but for the growth and expansion of white collar and public service employee unions as well."[36] In their very endorsement of the UFT, labor leaders acknowledged changes in the American economy that undermined organized labor and its potential role in the struggle for racial justice.

After World War II, automation, together with McCarthy-era repression and pro-management changes in labor law, led both to a decline in the number of blue-collar workers and to a decline in the rate of union affiliation among those blue-collar workers who were able to keep their jobs.[37] While the number of private-sector blue-collar jobs was declining, the number of government jobs mushroomed. New York epitomized national trends. The number of manufacturing jobs declined from 1,039,000 in 1950 to 626,000 in 1969.[38] Government jobs, on the other hand, expanded from 374,400 in 1950 to 526,000 in 1968, with municipal employees, including teachers, accounting for almost the entire increase.[39]

Union membership, which had peaked at 17.5 million, or nearly 25% of workers, in 1956, declined to 17.1 million by 1962. Half a million members were lost in the metal, machinery and transportation-equipment industries alone. Furthermore, total U.S. union membership declined even though white-collar membership rose slightly. Although the vast majority of white-collar workers remained unorganized and they made up only a small percentage of total union membership, white-collar workers had become the most dynamic part of the workforce.[40]

By the 1950s, labor leaders were keenly aware of changes in the labor force, changes that made organizing groups such as teachers crucial to the future of the labor movement. In 1958 the AFL-CIO's James Goodsell argued that the issue of how to organize white-collar workers was "a life-or-death question for the American Labor Movement." Should the Federation fail to win such workers, it would represent a "dwindling minority" of American workers.[41]

By turning to white-collar workers, and especially to those in the public sector, the unions began to offset declines in blue-collar membership. Between 1962 and 1964, the unions regained about half of the 1.23 million members they had lost in the preceding five years. The American Federation of State, County and Municipal Employees for instance grew from 183,000 in 1960 to 350,000 in 1967, at which time it was expanding by 1,000 members a week.[42]

In its campaign to organize public servants, labor considered no group more crucial than New York's teachers. Unions donated tens of thousands of dollars to the UFT and lent field workers to aid the fledgling local's early campaigns.[43] Their contributions paid off. Noting that white-collar employees had come to outnumber blue-collar workers, UFT President Charles Cogen acclaimed the 1961 election in which the UFT won the right to represent New York's 43,000 teachers as American labor's biggest collective bargaining victory since the UAW organized Ford's River Rouge Plant in 1941. "How long will the file clerk go on thinking a union is below her dignity," *Business Week* asked, "when the teacher next door belongs?"[44]

At the same time as he compared teachers to industrial workers, UFT organizer, and later AFT president David Selden recognized differences between them. "A machine operator," Selden noted, "is paid . . . to operate his machine and so long as he is not 'sweated' and operates his machine under satisfactory working conditions, his only legitimate concern is with his wages and other benefits. . . . But a teacher is not merely a production worker." Like other professionals, teachers "are self-directed and use their judgment in their work. . . . Part of the compensation of a professional is the satisfaction he derives from successful use of his skill." By this definition, Selden argued, teachers could negotiate over class-size not because large classes "sweated" teachers but because teachers rightly had a say in pedagogical issues.[45]

Furthermore, notions of professionalism encompass the organization of the workplace as well as the scope of teachers' legitimate interests. Staff relations in the schools, like teachers' aspirations to self-directed activity, undermined UFT invocations of industrial unionism. In 1968, UFT claims that its strike was a conventional labor-management dispute were complicated by the considerable support that the union received from supervisors and administrators. Indeed, the Council of Supervisory Associations, which represented school principals, joined the UFT in striking and worked closely with the teachers union in fighting community control.[46] The union even received support from the central administration and school board.[47]

At the prestigious Bronx High School of Science, Principal Alexander Taffel locked up the building to prevent teachers from crossing the UFT picket line. Meanwhile, he chatted pleasantly with picketing teachers. "My mother was an organizer for the International Ladies' Garment Workers Union," Taffel told his staff. "As I stood outside the school . . . I have found myself thinking of her, and how it would have warmed her heart to see me there, as part of the labor movement."[48]

Forgetting that teacher strikes were themselves illegal, respected Brooklyn principal Abe Lass challenged the efforts of parents and teachers who tried to cross UFT picket lines. "By law, only the principal" could open schools, Lass argued, and "if anyone else would open the school, it would be over my dead body." While picketing with teachers, Lass "had time to think of where the school system was going. . . . When you put the responsibility for running a school system in the hands of people who are not teachers or administrators, I don't see anything good or promising on the horizon. . . . Right after the strike they started busing kids. In '71, we got about a hundred or so from Ocean Hill-Brownsville, where the strike had started. From there it's all down hill."[49]

Management support of striking teachers reflected the peculiarities of school organization. Unlike factory managers, virtually all school principals work as teachers before becoming supervisors, and, unlike most factory workers, ambitious teachers can reasonably aspire to advance their careers within the school system. For instance, Fred Nauman, one of the teachers dismissed by the Ocean Hill-Brownsville governing board, had been Acting Science Department Chairman at J.H.S. 271 as well as the UFT chapter leader, and he had organized the school's orientation program for new teachers.[50]

At the same time as it endorsed teacher unionism, the UFT advocated measures to increase teacher professionalism. In November 1967, the union proposed that supervisors be elected by tenured teachers and that teachers select textbooks. The next spring, the union's Executive Board moved to organize assistant principals as part of the union.[51] Even before the end of the 1968 strike, UFT President Shanker urged Chapter Chairmen to form political action committees because "more can be done through political action with less wear and tear than strikes."[52]

The combination of unionism and professionalism was a two-edged sword for progressive teachers. On the one hand, it encouraged teachers to concern themselves with questions of educational quality as well as with working conditions. On the other hand, it discouraged teachers from identifying with the poor minority children in their classrooms. As UFT leader Sandra Feldman noted, New York's teacher unionists

in general support civil rights and equal educational opportunity, but their commitment to a fight for improved schools was not primarily a product of social conscience. It was largely, and understandably, self-interest . . . a struggle to create a respected profession from a beleaguered, downgraded occupation.[53]

Finally, teachers' self-directed activity involves the direction of other persons. Thus professionalism involves a superordinated social relationship as well as a set of working conditions. Invocations of professionalism inevitably clashed with the rhetoric of working people's solidarity. At precisely the moment when black parents were challenging school officials' failure to combat racial inequality, the UFT argued that teacher professionalism precluded parents from exercising significant authority in the schools. Rather, the union envisioned parents acting in their role as guardians of individual students. For instance, in order to help parents more fully understand and support "what it is teachers are attempting to develop," the UFT worked to educate ghetto parents about "the kinds of things to look for in report cards."[54]

Teachers and not parents, the UFT's Sandra Feldman emphasized, "must have the power to construct and organize [students'] course of study and to determine methodology."[55] "It has always been the intent of the UFT," union president Al Shanker explained, "that community participation does not mean that those decisions under professional control should be surrendered."[56] Union teachers, Shanker stated bluntly, would not "teach in any school or district where professional decisions are made by laymen."[57]

For years before the 1968 school conflict, school authorities had unilaterally transferred teachers accused of wrongdoing. Although teacher unionists would have preferred due process in such cases, involuntary disciplinary transfers had never been a major focus of union activity. The UFT's opposition to parent and community participation in educational matters was the basis for its militant response when the Ocean-Hill Brownsville Governing Board ordered the nineteen teachers and administrators out of the district.

In 1967, the Council of Supervisory Associations sued to block the appointment of five Ocean Hill-Brownsville principals. All had New York State certification but were not at the top of the New York City eligibility list. Although the petty and racist criteria used by New York's Board of Examiners in ranking candidates had long been a bone of contention with teachers, the UFT filed an *amicus* brief in support of the suit. Like its commitment to due process, the union's new interest in "merit" aligned teachers with an imperfect system instead of an imperfect community.[58]

While walking the picket line during the 1968 strike, one white teacher articulated the overlapping visions of race and class that had come to animate and delimit teacher unionism. The teacher explained, "We don't deny their equality, but they shouldn't get it by pulling down others who have just come up. It's wrong and reactionary for them to pit their strength against a group that struggled for years to make teaching a profession."[59] For all the rhetorical use the UFT made of its labor union roots, the 1968 fight against community control confirmed its commitment to professional privilege.

❊ ❊ ❊

Teacher Unionism and Civil Rights

The social democratic response to American racism received its most famous expression over a half century before the New York school crisis. Socialist leader Eugene Debs defended "the Negro's right to work, live and develop his manhood, educate his children, and fulfill his destiny" equally with whites. Still, he claimed, "The Socialist Party is the Party of the whole working class, regardless of color," and therefore it had "nothing special to offer the Negro."[60]

As the civil rights movement challenged the southern caste system in the 1950s, social democratic teacher unionists in the Teachers Guild and the national union with which its was affiliated lived up to their professed commitment to judge all workers equally, irrespective of race. As early as 1951, the American Federation of Teachers voted to charter no segregated locals, and by 1956 the union ordered southern affiliates to desegregate or be expelled. A number of southern locals, including the 1855-member Atlanta Teachers Association, disaffiliated. All told the AFT lost about 14% of its members. Among those leading the AFT desegregation effort was black New York teacher and future UFT officer Richard Parrish. A few years later, the UFT opposed holding the American Federation of Teachers' 1963 convention in Miami because the city was segregated. The New York local actively supported the Freedom Rides, the 1963 March on Washington and the 1964 Mississippi Freedom Summer. The AFT's efforts contrasted with those of the larger National Education Association, which did not fully desegregate until the end of the 1960s.[61]

Teacher unionists' commitment to eliminating racial categorization paralleled the dominant American liberal view in the years after 1940. Gunnar Myrdal's An American Dilemma was the best known articulation of the liberal case against racism. Myrdal and other liberals argued that racial prejudice was an aberration from the American commitment to democracy and equal opportunity and that whites could abandon racism without having to fundamentally refashion their values or lives. The view that mainstream America could fully accommodate black aspirations assumed that anything distinctive in black life was a dysfunctional manifestation of racism. Blacks, in Myrdal's words, were "exaggerated Americans" whose culture was "a distorted development, or a pathological condition, of the general American culture." Assimilation was, therefore, a crucial element of racial justice. A civil rights platform that mirrored this liberal anti-racist vision won the AFT considerable support among teachers in northern cities.[62]

As long as the civil rights movement focused on the Southern system of legally enforced racial segregation, the liberal argument for integration and assimilation enjoyed considerable plausibility. Then, in northern school systems such as New York's the assimilationist liberal creed was put to the test. Although the UFT continued to support the elimination of Jim Crow in the South, it resisted proposals to promote racial equality in New York's schools. Among the UFT's accomplishments, the union boasted to teachers, was its having "killed the Superintendent's plan to force teachers to transfer to difficult schools."[63] When civil rights activists launched a massive school boycott to win integration in 1964, an effort which would having required taking students' race into account when assigning them to schools, the union refused to endorse the protest.[64]

Called to account by black activists, the self-described socialists of the UFT gradually slid from the notion that superficial racial divisions masked more fundamental ones of class to the notion that inequality would wither without any intervention from activists. Moreover, even as they opposed measures to integrate the schools, UFT leaders and their allies persisted in demanding programs to foster black assimilation. The union's most important proposal to address racial inequality was its campaign for the More Effective Schools program, which provided added services to ghetto schools. Copied in districts from Baltimore to San Francisco, MES was based on the belief that in order to succeed in school and life, ghetto students needed to replace what social democrat Michael Harrington called the "simpler joys of 'acting out,' of immediate gratification and violent expression" with the "work ethic" of "discipline . . . long-range calculation, saving and investment."[65] Like the race-blind merit system in teacher hiring, MES suggested that the social order was basically fair and that with proper mentoring, blacks could gain full participation in it. "The single-mindedness with which the UFT supported MES," observes historian Jerald Podair, "testifies to the hold of the culture of poverty idea on its members."[66]

If the elimination of cultural deficits would solve the problems of black students, the course of history rather than the race-conscious hiring policies of community control would integrate school staffs. According to UFT President Al Shanker, blacks would replace Jews as New York's teachers through a natural evolution that required no special state intervention other than the prohibition of discrimination:

> [It] has almost always been that the teachers in urban school systems represented predominantly the immigrants of the previous generation who were teaching the children of the newer immigrants. So, when the Irish came into the system, they were taught by WASP's; and the Irish then taught the Jews; and the Jews, the Italians; and I suppose the next group of black and Puerto Rican teachers and administrators will be teaching the newly affluent grape-pickers, represented by Cesar Chavez, moving up from the lowest to the next rung.[67]

The UFT's claim that blacks would follow earlier immigrants into the mainstream of American society ignored the actual, varied paths by which blacks came to New York and exaggerated the cultural shock of black migrants arriving in the city. It discounted both the decline of the urban economy that had enabled European immigrants to enter the workforce and the durability of racial subordination. According to a 1963–64 survey, among black New Yorkers whose parents and grandparents were born in the United States, roughly the same number had grown up in New York City as had grown up in the farms of the south. In addition, almost a third of black New Yorkers were Caribbean immigrants or of mixed origins. Whatever the shock of arriving in New York, these blacks generally fared better than native African Americans in educational and occupational attainment. In sum, "peasant" origins do not account for the overall position of blacks in New York or for variation among them. New York produced its own racial inequality.[68]

In their struggle against black activists, UFT leaders equated the ideal of a race-blind society with the claim that such a society already existed. The goal of education, Shanker declared, is to teach children how to "make it within our society."[69] Black activism, in this account, was dismissed as irrational expressions of frustration that ignored the inevitable movement of American society toward racial equality.[70] When New York's Jewish Museum mounted an exhibition on black-Jewish relations in 1993, UFT leader Jeannette DiLorenzo objected to the portrayal of the 1968 crisis as a racial conflict. It was, she explained, a matter of contractual rights and due process, pure and simple.[71]

❂ ❂ ❂

Teacher Unions and Teachers' Work

Although UFT leaders often claimed that teachers shared the blue-collar identities of their disenfranchised students, the nature of schoolwork itself, together with the evolving demographics of urban life, separated educators from their students. As much as teachers are committed to the growth of their students, social control, manifest in such activities as grading and monitoring attendance, is a fundamental part of teachers' work. Moreover, at the time of the school conflict, the same demographic and economic changes that catalyzed teacher organizing caused deteriorating conditions in New York and its schools, thus adding to the oppressiveness of teachers' work.

Perhaps the most vivid account of teaching in the years leading up to the school crisis is Bel Kaufman's celebrated 1964 comic novel, *Up the Down Staircase*. Kaufman based the novel on her fifteen years' experience as a New York City high school teacher. Beneath the comedy, she paints a grim picture: "cracked plaster, broken windows, splintered doors and carved up desks, gloomy corridors, metal stairways [and] gloomy cafeteria" made the very buildings "hostile" to teachers' efforts. Even the prerequisites of instruction were all too often missing: "blackboards but no chalk, students but no seats, teachers but no time to teach." Instead of fostering joyful moments of discovery, the school system promoted "all that is petty, regimented and rote . . . and degrading to the human spirit." Although teachers fought "the unequal battle against all that stands in the way of teaching," victories were "few" and had to be weighed against "the drudgery and the waste." Unable to challenge the school system, most teachers "have given up or take out their frustrations on the kids."[72]

Kaufman's frustrations were not an eternal characteristic of urban schools. Rather, school conditions mirrored wider changes in New York life after World War II. The post-war years witnessed a dramatic growth in the city's minority population at the same time as the decline of New York's industrial economy deprived new residents of jobs. These trends, combined with the growing availability of suburban housing for whites, created a wide physical, cultural and political gulf between the teachers, most of whom had grown up in New York, and their students, who lived in the city's transformed neighborhoods.

The Bronx elementary school at which Robert Lichtenfield taught exemplified the changes. In the early 1960s the school had a student body of some 1200 middle-class white students. Then, "virtually the entire neighborhood" moved out. Within a few years, the school was transformed into one with 1700 students, 85% of whom were Hispanic, 10% of whom were black, and few of whom were middle-class. According to Lichtenfield, who served as the school's UFT Chapter Chairman, teachers were ill-prepared for the changes.[73]

Oppressive conditions and unfamiliar students produced a sense of confusion and alienation among New York's teachers. "I feel the desperation and the hopelessness of the situation," a teacher lamented.

> I'm not reaching anybody. I sweat blood and try to teach and get no place. I do a day's work and I don't feel the children are profiting. They don't show that they have learned anything. They don't change their behavior. Sometimes I wonder why I stay on the job.[74]

At the same time as they were feeling hopelessness, teachers brought to their work racial attitudes which they shared with other white New Yorkers. According to Robert Lichtenfield, when one black fifth grader came to his school, rumors began "flying among the kids and the teachers about having a student like that in the school, coming in with a weapon perhaps." Brownsville teacher Richard Piro remembered "few, if any" teachers who were "totally free of inherited prejudices, including one which said that black children couldn't learn." Teacher activist and future principal Deborah Meier argued that the majority of teachers brought prejudices against poor minority children to their work and that "rather than undermining these prejudices," the teaching experience "arouses them."[75]

Teachers synthesized out of this combination of frustration and prejudice an explanation for their troubles. In the words of one teacher,

I've worked with other children, you know, the middle-income children, and they learned. Then it must be something wrong with these children. It can't be me. . . . So you think, "Well, it's the home . . . it must be the home. . . . We can't do anything about the home, so it's not our fault."[76]

Robert Lichtenfield, whose Bronx school won the UFT's Eli Trachtenberg Award as an outstanding chapter, remembered how these frustrations and insecurities led to the 1968 conflict:

The population changed and the teaching strategies didn't change. . . . You're dealing with a lot of teachers who had no contact with minority kids or groups or parents suddenly in a sense being attacked as they saw it by a minority community. And what do you do when you're attacked? You sort of rally the troops; you circle the wagons.[77]

Teachers rationalized the low expectations they had for themselves and their schools. According to the UFT's Sandra Feldman, rather than welcoming community efforts, teachers at Ocean Hill-Brownsville's J.H.S. 271 "immediately felt defensive because this community group was agitating about the school." When Feldman visited the school, students appeared to her to be out of control, and the building "needed a lot in the way of repairs and maintenance and cleaning and supplies." Things, however, seemed different to local UFT leader Fred Nauman, who worked every day in J.H.S. 271. To Nauman, the school

was not a prestigious school. It was a ghetto school. But as a ghetto school, it was probably one of the best—at least that's how most of us felt about it. It was a school that had its share of successes, and I know a good many of us felt good about going to work every day.[78]

Teacher Richard Piro was mugged on his way home from work on the first day of school in September 1968. Blacks who respected him as a conscientious teacher looked on while he was stabbed repeatedly at a subway station near Junior High School 275, where he taught in Brownsville. Piro associated the transfer of the nineteen demonstration district teachers with the mugger: "The face of . . . black demonstration-school project administrator [Rhody] McCoy . . . became the face of my mugger and I struck gladly."[79]

Conclusion

The UFT argued that community control would fail to improve the education of African Americans because poverty, and not racial identity, created the ghetto. The argument that a race-blind politics could benefit blacks depended on the possibility of meaningful proletarian unity. By the mid-1960s, however, economic and social changes had undermined the potential of social democracy to sustain the struggle for progressive social change. Automation and plant flight made evocations of industrial unionism increasingly anachronistic, while suburbanization and the steady growth of urban segregation made visions of integration and common schooling increasingly implausible.

In an earlier time, racial politics was shaped by the battle against Jim Crow forms of legally enforced segregation and the struggles of progressive labor activists to advance the interests of the entire working class. Then, the UFT's rhetoric of equal opportunity, due process, industrial unionism and professionalism might have enabled members to transcend narrower views and individual bigotry.

In 1968, however, the world had turned upside-down. In the face of the profoundly troubling and ever more visible tragedy of student failure, the invocation of interracial solidarity and equal opportunity justified the seemingly uniform standards and treatment of the bureaucratized school system. It thus asserted teachers' professionalism even as it absolved them of responsibility for their ineffectiveness.

In the course of the school conflict, the UFT's anachronistic appeal to industrial unionism did not move teachers to more fully embrace the concept of racial equality. Rather, it further legitimized their racial privilege in the contested world of the schools. Despite the UFT's unswerving allegiance to principle, union founder Dave Selden called the 1968 conflict "a watershed" in the history of the union and the career of Al Shanker. Never again, Selden argues, would Shanker embrace progressivism.[80]

In spite of UFT protestations that it was the steadfast voice of economic and racial justice, in 1968 few people were so vilified by black New Yorkers as UFT President Al Shanker. He expressed perfectly the logic and tone with which liberal race-blind politics was transformed from a way of challenging racial inequality into a way of justifying it. In a school system where some ninety percent of teachers and virtually all principals were white—where whites held virtually all positions of power—Shanker argued eloquently that whites were the victims of racial discrimination.

In 1967, the UFT had gone out on a strike that was in many ways a dress rehearsal for the 1968 conflict. In contract negotiations before the strike, President Shanker recounted the kind of math problem he had assigned as a ghetto junior high school teacher many years earlier. "If," he would ask his students, "it takes four ounces of poison to kill a person, how many ounces would it take to kill your mother, your father, your sister and your brother?" Such problems, Shanker told his Board of Education negotiating adversary, were "the only way I could get them to learn. . . . They loved it."[81]

Shanker recalled the math problem during labor negotiations in which union demands included greater professional authority for teachers to remove "disruptive students" from their classrooms. A number of black and civil rights organizations had countered that black children confronted by a racist school system needed more due process and not less.[82] Shanker's recalled math problem, suggesting the criminality of black children, only confirmed their fears that increased teacher discretion would be used arbitrarily and discriminatorily against black students.[83]

The response to Shanker's math joke in the late 1960s contrasted diametrically with the response to Gunnar Myrdal's *American Dilemma* some twenty years earlier. When Myrdal asserted that the African American family and culture were pathological, black reviewers almost uniformly applauded his work and its assimilationist vision. They could do this because they were convinced of the possibility and desirability of integration. By the late 1960s, when teachers and other white Americans had turned back the movement for racial equality, black activists and intellectuals repudiated hypotheses of black pathology. In clinging to an assimilationist politics, Shanker exemplified how what had been seen as a progressive racial politics had come to serve the interests of white supremacy and black racial subordination.

In the early 1960s, the progressive unionism of the fledgling UFT mirrored a widespread, even if incomplete, commitment to liberalism in American politics. By the late 1960s, however, the national mood began to shift. At the same time as teachers' unions became increasingly secure fixtures in urban school hierarchies, the resurgent American right exposed broad disenchantment with liberalism. Within the UFT, the rhetoric of an increasingly conservative professionalism was wedded to the enforcement of contractual regulations that made teacher accountability extremely difficult. Together, these developments protected teachers' jobs but discouraged efforts to promote racial justice in the schools or to add fulfillment to teachers' daily classroom work.[84] By 1982, Al Shanker would muse, "Somewhere around 1960 . . . something in our attitudes toward teachers and schools changed." He lamented that educational standards had declined and the schools had ceased to teach values. Invocations of merit, teachers' authority, and universal principles were fully stripped of any commitment to proletarian solidarity or to racial justice.[85]

Chapter 3

The Ambiguities of Identity: Whiteness, Ethnicity, and the Racial Politics of Schooling

Thou art the man.
—II SAMUEL 12: 7[1]

On October 15, 1968, New York Mayor John Lindsay went to Brooklyn's Midwood neighborhood, seeking to ease the tensions between Jewish teachers and black activists battling over community control of the city's schools. The mayor spoke at the East Midwood Jewish Center, in a middle-class, liberal Jewish neighborhood that was home to many civil servants. Although Lindsay had previously relied on such charismatic appearances to cool the urban crises that swept New York, in Midwood his charisma failed. When the mayor reminded his audience that both sides in the school dispute were guilty of "acts of vigilantism," the crowd, which included many teachers, heckled and jeered. "Is this the exemplification of the Jewish faith?" Rabbi Harry Halpern admonished. To his surprise, the answer shouted back was "Yes! Yes!" Forbearance was out; toughness was in. By means of the school conflict, a community was redefining itself.[2]

Explaining their new attitude, Jews charged that demands for community control were a smokescreen for anti-Semitism. "If community control becomes a fact," United Federation of Teachers president Al Shanker warned the union's Delegate Assembly, "they will paint swastikas on your schools."[3] Two-thirds of New York's Jews believed that the anti-Semitism propelled demands for community control, and they listed Al Shanker among the leaders they admired most. By a 59% to 23% margin, Jews held that unless anti-Jewish black militants were put "in their place," there would be "a lot more" anti-Semitism.[4]

Opposition to anti-Semitism was fully in keeping with the UFT's assimilationist liberal ideology. Still, in the course of the school crisis, New York's teachers embodied a second shift in America's political culture, one almost as consequential as the UFT-led appropriation of liberal rhetoric to fight against black activism. Even as the vast majority of teachers, most of whom where Jewish,[5] belonged to the UFT, with its ideology of universal rights, they also joined the right-wing Jewish Teachers Association, with its appeals to distinctive Jewish interests and identity. JTA membership swelled from 10,000 in 1962 to 28,000 in January 1969. In the 1969–70 school year it peaked at over 30,000 members.[6] New York's Jewish teachers thus heralded the celebration of ethnic identity, which would become a major element of Americans' response to issues of race in the decades that followed the school conflict.

Ironically, in the decades before the school conflict, when the assimilationist liberal ideology invoked by teacher unionists had been a crucial component of Jewish identity, advocacy of black equality played an important role in Jewish efforts to define their place in America. Indeed, Jews saw themselves and were seen by other Americans as the quintessential embodiments of the America's liberal Creed.[7]

Then, the relationship between the universalistic ideal of liberalism and the assertion of a distinctive, ethnic identity was reshaped amid the racial politics of schooling. The transformation of Jewish identity epitomized a broader rebirth of white ethnicity in American schools and society. This chapter explores the ways charges of black anti-Semitism propelled and reflected changes in Jewish identity, a process in which New York's Jewish teachers took the lead but whose impact extended to wider debates about the nature of multiculturalism, ethnicity, whiteness and racial justice.[8]

Anti-Semitism Among Blacks or Black Anti-Semitism

That there were occasions on which black teachers and other black proponents of community control expressed anti-Semitism is indisputable. In a 1967 African-American Teachers Association newsletter article attacking the UFT, John Hatchett labeled the opposition of "Anti-black Jews and the black Anglo-Saxon" to community control "A Study in Educational Perfidy." Hatchett began,

> We are witnessing today in New York City a phenomenon that spells death for the minds and souls of our black children. It is the systematic coming of age of the Jews who dominate

and control the educational bureaucracy of the New York Public School system and their power-starved imitators, the black Anglo-Saxon. . . . This coalition or collusion . . . is one of the fundamental reasons why our black children are being educationally castrated.[9]

When Hatchett ignored a February 1968 Board of Education directive that prohibited taking students to a Malcolm X memorial assembly, he was fired. Any relief Jewish teachers might have felt, however, disappeared a few months later when New York University appointed the 37-year-old ex-teacher to be director of its new Afro-American Student Center, established by the university following the assassination of Martin Luther King, Jr. NYU officials claimed not to have known about the "Perfidy" article, and Hatchett had impressive qualifications for the NYU job. Graduated from Wayne State University, he had a theology degree from Boston University and was working on his Ph.D. at Columbia. In addition, Hatchett had taught at a number of black colleges in the South.[10]

Hatchett's very academic qualifications signaled to Jewish teachers that his was not the uneducated anti-Semitism that sprang from ignorance and Christian folk tradition. Although Brooklyn junior high school principal Leo Blond traced the word perfidy to the Catholic Good Friday prayer, "Pro Perfidis Judaeis," he attributed Hatchett's use of the term to theological training rather than a religious upbringing. The sophisticated product of an ideological mind, such bigotry could not be eliminated by education or participation in modern life; only a forceful political response would do.[11]

In September 1968, as UFT teachers struck against community control, American Jewish Congress official David Haber urged NYU to rescind Hatchett's appointment on the grounds that his attributing the faults of the school system to a racist "Jewish conspiracy" was itself "racist." University officials replied that Hatchett had been selected by black students and approved by black faculty; to remove him invited campus disruption. Furthermore, United Nations ambassador Arthur Goldberg interviewed Hatchett and attested to his openness to intergroup dialogue. The New York Civil Liberties Union also opposed attempts to fire Hatchett, arguing that a person should be judged on the basis of professional performance and not private thought.[12] Only after Hatchett told several hundred NYU students that Albert Shanker, Hubert Humphrey and Richard Nixon "all have something in common—they are racist bastards," did NYU terminate him. Given that the university acted only when Hatchett included white Christian leaders among those he denounced, NYU's actions did little to relieve Jewish concerns.[13]

Even more than the incidents involving John Hatchett, a series of anti-Semitic fliers that inundated the city during the teacher strikes convinced Jewish New York[14] that black Jew-hating had reached crisis levels. Taxi drivers gave copies of the fliers to their riders; merchants stacked them on counters for their customers. Distributed by the hundreds of thousands, the fliers incited terror and panic among Jews.[15]

The most talked-about flier was the "Tentative Plan" of the "Parents Community Council, J.H.S. 271, Ocean Hill-Brownsville." After demanding black control of schools in black neighborhoods, the leaflet addressed the teaching of African American history and culture:

> It Is Impossible For The Middle East Murderers of Colored People to Possibly Bring To This Important Task The Insight, The Concern, The Exposing Of The Truth That is a *Must* If Years Of Brainwashing And Self-Hatred That Has Been Taught To Our Black Children By Those Bloodsucking Exploiters and Murderers Is To Be OverCome. The Idea Behind This Program Is Beautiful, But When The Money Changers Heard About It, They Took Over, As Is Their Custom in the Black Community. . . . We Know From His Tricky, Deceitful Maneuvers That . . . The So-Called Liberal Jewish Friend . . . is Really Our Enemy and He is Responsible For The Serious Educational Retardation of Our Black Children.[16]

Incidents of anti-Semitism seemed only to escalate in the course of the school conflict. Thirty teachers at one school reported that anonymous death threats, with words cut out of newspapers, had been mailed to their homes. Many of the letters contained crudely drawn swastikas.[17]

In Jewish minds, anti-Semitism climaxed on December 26, 1968, when black teacher Leslie Campbell read an anti-Semitic poem on a black nationalist radio program. "To Albert Shanker: Anti-Semitism" began,

> Hey Jew boy with that
> yarmulke on your head
> You pale-faced Jew boy
> I wish you was dead

Other verses included

> I got a scope on you, Yeah,
> Jew boy, you gonna die.
> . . .
> Jew boy, you took my religion
> and adapted it for you
> But you know black people were
> the original Hebrews
> . . .
> . . . you came to America
> land of the free
> Took over the school's system to
> perpetuate White supremacy[18]

The UFT demanded that WBAI's license be revoked and that Campbell, who was already notorious among white teacher unionists,[19] be suspended from teaching. The Anti-Defamation League, the Workmen's Circle, the New York Board of Rabbis, and the Jewish Teachers Association joined in the union's protest.[20]

Although there can be no doubt that certain blacks committed anti-Semitic acts, proponents of community control argued that such acts were marginal to black educational activism. John Hatchett, they noted, was a substitute teacher, not a powerful player in school politics. Similarly, no black nationalist organization had the capacity to blanket New York with hate-mongering fliers. Rather, Jewish muckraker I. F. Stone charged, the UFT itself was

> exaggerating, amplifying and circulating any bit of anti-Semitic drivel it can pick up from any far-out black extremist, however unrepresentative, and using this to drive the Jewish community of New York into a panic.[21]

Three hundred and seventy nine of Ocean Hill-Brownsville's 541 teachers also protested the union's distribution of several hundred thousand copies of the "Parents Community Council" leaflet. In an open letter to the *New York Times*, the teachers noted that the flier

> is actually a composite reprint of two separate leaflets. One . . . is anti-U.F.T. and urges the exclusion of whites from teaching black or Puerto Rican children. The other section, with its anti-Semitic references, is reproduced from a different, anonymous leaflet.

Whereas the UFT created the impression that community control leaders endorsed violent assaults on Jews, the Ocean Hill teachers argued that "by their words and actions" black officials had shown that they would "not tolerate any form of anti-Semitism." They noted that 70% of the teachers hired by their district were white and half of these Jewish.[22]

The authenticity of other leaflets was dubious as well. Keith Baird, an African-American teacher and a sociolinguist, had run against Shanker for UFT President in 1967. In a debate with Shanker, Baird did a "textual criticism" of an anti-Semitic pamphlet that purported to come from the African American community. "The locutions," Baird argued, "were not African American but in fact they were what a White European American person would think an African American person would say."[23]

Even Leslie Campbell's reading of "To Albert Shanker: Anti-Semitism" contained more ambiguity than the UFT admitted. The poem was not written by Campbell, but by one of his fifteen-year-old students. Campbell had shown the poem to

Julius Lester, who asked him to read it on his program on WBAI, an obscure radical radio station. Although Campbell did assert that the poem "tells it exactly the way it is" and had "a tremendous sense of truth," he acknowledged that the poem was anti-Semitic and stressed that he read it in order to expose the pain and anger generated by the school conflict.[24]

Ample data supported the view that anti-Semitism was marginal to black politics. In 1967, major studies by the American Jewish Committee and the Anti-Defamation League concluded that blacks were less anti-Semitic than non-Jewish whites. Moreover, the ADL affirmed that although anti-Semitism among blacks generally reflected a wider anti-white bias, the more militant the black person was, the less anti-Semitic he or she was likely to be. A 1968 survey found that the school conflict produced no substantial change. Whereas less than one white Christian in four believed that Jews continued to experience discrimination in New York, slight majorities of blacks and Jews recognized ongoing injustices. Even in the wake of the school conflict, 70% of black New Yorkers, as compared to 41% of non-Jewish whites, believed that blacks and Jews were kept down by the same people. By an eleven-to-one ratio, blacks agreed that the real bigots liked nothing better than to see blacks and Jews at each other's throats.[25]

Even in matters where blacks appeared to harbor more anti-Semitic biases than white Christians, those stereotypes had little impact. The 1967 and 1968 surveys both found that blacks were far more likely than white Christians to attribute shady business practices to Jews.[26] Not surprisingly, blacks cast attacks on Jewish teachers in this traditional anti-Semitic language of Jewish greed. Thus, the African-American Teachers Association, in the November 1968 issue of its newsletter, editorialized that "the Jew, our great liberal friend of yesterday . . . is now our exploiter!"[27] Still, over two-thirds of blacks made no distinction between Jewish merchants or landlords and other whites. The minority of blacks who expressed a preference were as likely to prefer Jews as to prefer non-Jewish whites as landlords, store managers or employers. Although 13% of blacks considered Jews worse than other white educators, 11% preferred Jews, and 76% expressed no preference.[28] For all its rhetorical flourish, the expression of anti-Semitism remained marginal to black concerns in 1968. What changed crucially was not the level of anti-Semitism among African Americans but rather the Jewish response.

✪ ✪ ✪

Assimilation, Jewish Liberalism and Racial Justice

Before 1968, Jewish organizations downplayed instances of prejudice by blacks. On the eve of the New York school conflict, the Jewish Community Relations Council warned Jews not to mistake "legitimate" black protest for anti-Semitism,[29] and even at the start of the UFT strikes against community control, Anti-Defamation League chairman Dore Schary cautioned Jews "not to exaggerate fears of Negro anti-Semitism," which "presents none of the dangers of fascism."[30]

Schary's warning reflected the long-held position of Jewish organizations that Jews and blacks shared common foes and common goals. It was a stance grounded in the main currents of twentieth century American liberalism. American liberals sought to free individuals from poverty, from limits on their free expression, and from artificial social distinctions such as those based on race or religion. They saw prejudice as an aberration from the American commitment to democracy and equal opportunity. This belief that democratic aspirations of individual autonomy and equal treatment constituted the American Creed shaped liberals' understanding of race. Rather than celebrating diversity, liberals—black as well as white—focused on removing the obstacles to individuals' entry into the political and cultural mainstream.[31]

The traditional liberal insistence that persons be viewed as individuals held special promise for Jews, and Jews, from their particular situation, became preeminent voices of American liberalism. Thousands of Jews helped organize and finance the civil rights movement.[32] These Jewish advocates of black rights, as Arthur Hertzberg argues, were "passionately convinced idealists—but their efforts for black revolution served Jews in a very deep way." Advocating racial equality allowed American Jews to challenge their own marginalization while avoiding the need to confront anti-Semitic stereotypes.[33] Moreover, activism at "the very cutting edge of social change" placed American Jews "at the center of American life."[34] Even as liberal Jews battled to transform the American mainstream, they entered it.

The notion that Jews could command the political status of unhyphenated Americans propelled a strongly assimilationist thread in Jewish-American thought and shaped what the National Jewish Community Relations Advisory Council termed the Jewish community's "love affair with the public schools."[35] Jews "become teachers," writer Roger Kahn declared in 1968, "quite as naturally as Irishmen become corner cops." Occupying an esteemed position in the self-image of American Jews, teachers had long played a significant role in Jewish-American political culture.[36]

In the decades before the 1968 school conflict, the belief that a deeper appreciation of America's core values would lead Americans to live up to them placed education at the center of the liberal Jewish activism. Hoping to inoculate American Christians against anti-Semitism by encouraging tolerance, open-mindedness, and respect for the individual, the American Jewish Committee funded the work of pioneer "intercultural" educator Rachel Davis DuBois in the 1930s. Still, during the years of the Great Depression, many Christian teachers, inspired by such right-wing demagogues as Father Coughlin, openly expressed their anti-Semitism, and public school officials discriminated against Jews. Amid growing anti-Semitism in Europe and America, the AJC feared that calling attention to particular cultures would heighten rather than lessen discord. When DuBois insisted on characterizing Revolutionary War hero Haym Solomon as Jewish rather than as Polish, the AJC cut off its support.[37]

Even radical Jews shared the commitment to assimilation through schooling, and high school teachers occupied a central place in the nurturing of Jewish radicalism. Boys High School teacher Bertram Wolfe was among the founders of the American Communist Party. Still, Wolfe's youthful radicalism did not preclude his working to replace his "Brooklyn accent" with "what I took to be the cultured speech of my teachers and educated Americans generally."[38] "Even those radical teachers who proposed to criticize" America's crass commercialism, Irving Howe remembers, "did so in the name of a superior version of the commonly accepted culture." Capturing this immigrant Jewish synthesis of radicalism and assimilation, Howe observed that "my entry into the little world of socialism must have struck my parents as part of the estrangement that had to be accepted whenever a boy or girl went out into 'the real world,' the world of gentiles."[39]

Many black educators and activists shared the assimilationist aspirations of American Jews. "If a modern Pied Piper of Hamlin should appear in the town of Tuskegee and induce a wholesale desertion of the village," Tuskegee Institute educator J. Max Bond claimed, "that which would remain—houses, stores, schools, and churches— would give little indication of the race of the former inhabitants." The Director of Tuskegee's School of Education, Bond dismissed any distinct Negro cultural manifestations as "deviations."[40]

Assimilationist liberal ideals shaped efforts to understand and address anti-Semitism among blacks. African Americans, like most white Americans, "hated Jews," writer Richard Wright noted, "because we had been taught at home and in Sunday school that Jews were 'Christ killers.'"[41] Then, when blacks migrated to northern cities, racial discrimination and inter-ethnic tensions added a distinctive black element to Christian folk anti-Semitism. The notorious Bronx "slave market" of black women seeking low-wage domestic work in Jewish homes and the refusal of Blumstein's and other 125th Street stores to hire blacks, for instance, fueled resentments.[42]

Still, in the 1930s and 1940s, similar conditions in working-class neighborhoods, shared assimilationist aspirations, and militant intergroup organizing for social justice encouraged black and Jewish activists to minimize the significance of anti-Jewish expressions. Writer Roi Ottley termed Depression-era anti-Semitism among blacks "essentially an *anti-white* manifestation."[43] Similarly, veteran black activist Chandler Owen argued that "his former slavery is too fresh in the Negro's mind to permit him to indulge in the fascist hooliganism of the Ku Klux Klan, the Silver Shirts, the German-American Bund, the Christian Front and other vicious organizations."[44]

For Jews too, the elimination of obstacles to individual opportunity seemed the most potent antidote to anti-Semitism, whether due to traditional Christian prejudice or modern urban discrimination. Moreover, the growing threat of fascism left

Jews with more serious concerns. "Jews and Negroes today find themselves thrown to-gether as a consequence of direct peril from the fascists, native as well as foreign," Louis Harap claimed. The "essential similarity of their status as oppressed minority groups" made their fates "inextricably intertwined."[45]

In the years following World War II, Jewish organizations continued to devote sub-stantial energy to programs that helped public schools fight bigotry. The American Jewish Committee funded research on the psychology of prejudice, including Kenneth Clark's famed doll experiments, which the Supreme Court cited in its 1954 Brown de-cision banning segregation. The Anti-Defamation League's staff devoted more than half of its time to educational work, concentrating on the development and distribu-tion of curricula that challenged bias in group dynamics and individual attitudes.[46]

It was the kind of lesson future writer Barbara Grizzuti Harrison received in 1948 on her first day at Brooklyn's New Utrecht High School. English teacher David Zeiger announced that only students with blue eyes had to do homework. The students pro-tested, as Zeiger knew they would. The teacher then spent the rest of the period

> telling freshman English students in Bensonhurst—many of whom had never seen a Negro—why it was wrong to judge people by the color of their eyes or their skin. . . . It wasn't race relations I learned from David Zeiger (or "tolerance" which was the word we used back then) as much as the idea, new to me and radical, that lives could and should exemplify fairness, that justice wasn't exercised only by God but by human beings.[47]

Jews also participated in political actions to promote equal opportunity in schools. In 1955, the American Jewish Congress joined protests against the student school as-signment plan for Brooklyn's newly built JHS 258, a plan which created a segregated school only months after the New York Board of Education had pledged its commit-ment to integration.[48] Three years later, New York City judge and American Jewish Congress vice president Justine Wise Polier ruled the Board of Education could not punish black parents who refused to send their children to segregated schools. *Amster-dam News* columnist James Hicks called the ruling, which provided legal justification for the school boycotts of the 1960s "the most important decision ever handed down by the courts on the New York City school system." Thurgood Marshall affirmed that if the landmark decision were appealed, the NAACP would take the case all the way to the Supreme Court.[49]

The United States, American Jewish Congress leader Shad Polier claimed in a testament to liberal faith, "is rich enough and skilled enough to provide quality edu-cation for all children without penalizing any of them." Jews had no fear of equal schooling for blacks, Polier explained, because "we believe that there is room in America to provide a full economic life for everyone." American Jewish opposition to racism drew on this liberal conviction that in America's abundant society all could be free and prosper.[50]

Even as Jews continued to affirm a commitment to liberalism, however, changes in urban life and in Jews' place in American society were beginning to transform that commitment. When the United States Supreme Court's 1954 *Brown* decision outlawed school segregation, the newsletter of New York's Jewish Teachers Association responded with a cartoon entitled "One Down and Two to Go." The cartoon called for the court to finish its work by banning discrimination against Jews seeking medical school admissions and jobs in large corporations. Beyond the ethnic self-interest visible in the JTA's stance on school segregation, the disproportion of the equated wrongs suggests the distance separating the position of blacks and Jews in America.[51]

In the decades following World War II, moreover, the immigrant Jewish ghetto dispersed and radical interracial organizing faltered amid government repression.[52] As American Jews increasingly entered middle class jobs and suburbs, the distance that separated them from African Americans steadily widened. Black activists charged that relations with Jews were characterized by an increasingly profound asymmetry. In writer Claude Brown's eyes, "Goldberg" never understood the assertiveness of angry blacks consigned to northern ghettos:

> We were supposed to work for them; we were good enough . . . to clean their houses. They were supposed to sympathize with us. . . . I had the feeling that he never saw us .[53]

Changing circumstances, as Bernard Rosenberg and Irving Howe suggest, were the material basis for Jews' estrangement from the black freedom struggle and their disenchantment with liberalism:

> a body of sentiment has been growing among many American Jews, especially those living in large cities . . . that if . . . there is indeed a threat to Jewish well-being, it comes mainly from below . . . from urban blacks in the schools, a few industries, and some unions who are pressing to undo Jewish positions and accomplishments.[54]

McCarthy-era attacks on interracial working-class solidarity reinforced the impression that blacks and Jews possessed distinct and antagonistic identities. Charging that the International Ladies' Garment Workers Union, the flagship of the Jewish labor movement, discriminated against non-white members, Harlem intellectual Richard B. Moore insisted that the union's Jewish-American leaders had

> more in common with Jewish-American employers in the industry than with the Puerto Rican and Afro-American workers. This is due to similarity of income status, cultural conditioning, and psychological identification.[55]

The Irony of Ethnic Identity

Following World War II, the assertion of Jewish identity, what Irving Howe called "the reconquest of Jewishness,"[56] became an increasingly important project in Jewish American life. Rather than constituting the rediscovery of traditional Jewish values, however, the Jewishness of 1950s and 1960s was, in the words of Alfred Kazin,

> a sentimental tradition that developed as an American Jewish product. . . . It grew up among a great many radical Jews. . . . When the radical component went, which it often did . . . Jews who wanted to keep their "heritage" or their "identity" . . . adopted something called "Jewishness."[57]

Despite its secular roots, Jewishness expressed itself in religious terms. Whereas in the 1930s, less than one quarter of American Jews were members of synagogues; after World War II, nearly 60% of American Jews joined. Before the war, there were fewer than 20 Jewish day schools in the entire United States; by 1963, there were 132 in greater New York alone, and by the mid-1970s, almost all Orthodox children attended parochial schools. Still, the Judaism constructed in America's cities and suburbs did not recover ancestral faith. Although synagogue membership rose weekly attendance declined. Rather, Jews "largely ignorant of Jewish religious tradition"[58] invented a practice that served their current American needs. Mimicking churches and Christian schools, synagogues and Jewish parochial schools, as Arthur Hertzberg suggests, offered Jews a way to be respectable Americans.[59] The gender division of Jewish religious labor began to mirror Protestant American practices, and as women gained a greater role in religious observances, men were freed to pursue economic opportunities in the wider society. Little wonder that whereas intermarriage of Jews and Christians was rare before World War II, it became increasing common in the post war years, and Christian spouses saw increasingly little problem with converting to Judaism.[60]

As Judaism converged with Protestantism in the 1950s, the Anti-Defamation League softened the longstanding liberal Jewish commitment to the separation of church and state, and began to support joint "Christmas-Chanukah" and "Passover-Easter" programs in the public schools. Like the invocation of a "Judeo-Christian tradition" more broadly, public school Judeo-Christian holiday programs suggested that Jewish holidays were duplicates of Christian ones. The incorporation of Jewish observations within the larger Christian framework thus trivialized differences even as it publicized them.[61]

The Post-war articulation of Jewish identity also mirrored the practice of other Americans in serving as a vehicle for the assertion of masculinity. Once again, references to blacks were central in this transformative process. For teachers like Bernard Rogovin who experienced "castration" when they were ignored by their ghetto students, militant opposition to black activists was an opportunity to demonstrate that they had what Al Shanker labeled the "guts to stand up to vigilantes."[62] Consciously mimicking black militants with its calls for Jewish Power and armed self-defense, the Jewish Defense League was formed to fight black activists. The group's goal, according to JDL general counsel Bert Zweibron, was "to change the image of the Jew as the eternal patsy."[63] The JDL slogan, "Never Again!" electrified New York Jews by articulating what conservative writer Lucy Dawidowicz called "the new mood of Jewish assertiveness."[64] Triumphant nationalism replaced fragile cosmopolitanism as the most probable path to Jewish security. Nathan Glazer and Daniel Patrick Moynihan, in an early attempt to associate toughness and the repudiation of Jewish liberalism, claimed that "Jewish liberalism" reflected "many decent impulses . . . but also, simply, an excessive timidity or fright."[65]

The Jewish assertion of ethnic identity not only marked the diminution of differences between Jews and white Christians, it also epitomized an important change in the wider white political culture. In the post–World War II years, white ethnicity had increasingly little impact on educational achievement or socio-economic status. Ethnic foods were shared increasingly by Americans of various backgrounds, and intermarriage grew more common. And yet, as Richard Alba argues, ethnic identity took on tremendous symbolic importance not only for Jews but for many white Americans.[66]

When teacher Richard Piro organized a school production of *Fiddler on the Roof* at the time of the 1968 school conflict, a colleague protested, "How could you even think of placing our sacred Jewish traditions, our precious and wonderful and special heritage, into the hands of *those* kids?"[67] There was, however, nothing sacred about the Broadway musical. The Jewishness extolled in *Fiddler* was a parodical, generic "tradition," a sentimentalized revision of Shalom Aleichem, devoid, as Arthur Hertzberg notes, of class conflict and religious duty.[68]

Despite the popular Jewish notion that the legacy of Moses and the Hebrew prophets fostered Jewish liberalism,[69] non-affiliated Jews were most likely to see blacks as victims of discrimination in New York and their demands as justified; Orthodox and Conservative Jews the least likely. Whereas non-affiliated Jews supported the UFT in its battle against community control by a relatively narrow three-to-two margin, only one percent of Orthodox and Conservative Jews supported community control. Although a third of non-affiliated Jews felt that white teachers discriminated against black children, only one Orthodox Jew in fifty agreed.[70]

"The so-called white ethnic experience," Alba notes, "emerged into prominence during a period when the civil rights movement was most active and racial minorities were challenging in basic respects the fairness of the American system."[71] Jewishness, like other white ethnic identities, demonstrated that ethnic and cultural differences did not limit an individual's success in American society.[72] The invocation of ethnicity thus suggested that minority individuals and groups who were willing to work hard needed no special treatment in schools or economic life. Blacks turned to anti-Semitism, according to B'nai B'rith leader Rabbi Jay Kaufman, because they were unable to achieve the gains that Jews attained through "training, labor, proficiency and seniority." Despite a decade and a half of commission reports and protests documenting the impact of segregated and unequal educational opportunities, only one quarter of Jews believed that blacks experienced discrimination in New York's public schools.[73] Ironically then, distinctive white ethnicities became mechanisms through which to assimilate into and legitimize a shared white status; the highlighting of Jewishness through charges of black anti-Semitism did much to establish Jews as white people even as it undermined the claims of an earlier assimilationist liberal Jewish American identity.

Anti-Semitism and Ethnic Identity

In earlier years, Jewish commentators might have dismissed the anti-Semitic statements that occurred during the 1968 school conflict as the detritus of social tensions, neither new nor crucial to intergroup relations. In 1968, however, a different attitude prevailed. Although Leslie Campbell read "To Albert Shanker" after UFT strikes had ended in the defeat of community control, teachers would remember the incident as a pivotal moment, sustaining them in their fight. In vivid, if imagined, detail, Richard Piro placed the reading in early September at the start of the teacher strikes. "Someone threw a copy of the [*New York*] *Times* on my table [in the faculty room] growling, 'See? Do you still have any doubt where we stand with the niggers?'"[74]

Black acts of anti-Semitism did not cause Jews to rethink their commitment to racial equality, so much as allegations of black anti-Semitism served to delegitimize Jewish support for black activism. The role of prejudice in Jews' changing stance was exposed by the act of vandals who set fire to a Brooklyn synagogue in the winter of 1968. Rumors spread that the arsonists were black, and even when the culprits, all white and some of them Jewish, were arrested, one fourth of Jews continued to believe that the crimes were part of a rising tide of black anti-Semitism. Only 12% of Jews identified the vandals as white.[75]

Misled by the UFT's inflammatory actions and by their own prejudices, Jews underestimated black opposition to discrimination against Jews. Although 70% of blacks agreed that "the same people who keep Jews down also keep blacks down," only 39% of Jews expected a majority of blacks to concur. Whereas blacks agreed that Jewish organizations could contribute to improved inter-group relations, Jews tended to reject the idea that black leaders could help address the problem.[76]

Pressured by their members, influential Jewish organizations joined the UFT in pressing attacks on "black anti-Semitism."[77] On January 23, 1969, the Anti-Defamation League reversed itself, claiming that "the use of anti-Semitism—raw, undisguised—... by black extremists ... has gone unchecked by public authorities for two and a half years."[78]

B'nai B'rith also supported the UFT's charges that black anti-Semitism was at the heart of the school conflict. The 500,000-member organization concluded that black militants were "destroying our City and leading our democratic society toward anarchy."[79] Reiterating the organization's hyperbolic fears, B'nai B'rith Vice-President Rabbi Jay Kaufman believed that "no factor" was as likely to "destroy the stability of American society as the unique brand of anti-Semitism racing through parts of the Negro community." According to Kaufman, anti-Semitism was a disease of black America and not just of some black Americans: "striking out at only the most raucous, visible spokesmen leaves the underground, less visible infection to spread undeterred."[80]

Not surprisingly, the Jewish Teachers Association was among black activists' most militant foes. In the eyes of JTA president Herman Mantell, the anti-Semitism of black militants and their well-heeled white allies demonstrated that it was time to stop worrying about what was fair for everybody else and start worrying about what was good for Jews. "I, and those to whom I have spoken," he warned a major funder of community control, "are beginning to have doubts about the anti-Semitic influence in the Ford Foundation and/or some of its officers and/or directors."[81]

The JTA's repudiation of liberalism is suggested by its support of the ultra-right wing Jewish Defense League. Founded in May 1968, the JDL violently opposed black activists and "the inexplicable, masochistic drive that sends liberal Jews sprawling at the feet of black intellectuals to be berated, insulted, and spat upon."[82] The group's first action attacked John Hatchett's appointment by NYU. In January 1969, the JDL staged protests at the African-American Teachers Association office in Bedford-Stuyvesant and at J.H.S. 271 in Ocean Hill, and it broke up a community meeting being held at a public school in the Rochdale Village cooperative housing project, where black teacher Les Campbell had been invited to speak.[83]

Shortly after the UFT's 1968 strikes, JTA Pres. Herman Mantell commended the Jewish Defense League for its "wonderful job in cooperating with us and in fighting anti-Semitism." The two groups, in Mantell's eyes, shared a commitment to protecting "civil, human and Jewish rights."[84] A few months later, at a time when virtually no Jewish organization publicly endorsed the JDL, Mantell praised JDL members who gave "their time, energy, safety and even their lives to defend Jewish Civil Rights."[85] In return, the JDL honored Mantell as its first "Jewish Man of the Year."[86]

Although the JTA's response to the liberal social reform of the post–World War II period had been only lukewarm, Michael Leinwand, who became the organization's president in 1971, relied on a myth of uncompromising Jewish liberalism to justify the JTA's conservative politics. The Jewish teacher, Leinwand claimed,

by training, by inclination, by heritage, has consistently been in the forefront of liberal cause struggles. He has defended integration of the schools, fought for teacher unionism, marched in Selma, Alabama and devoted much of his life toward serving the goals of equal education and opportunity for all.[87]

Jewish liberalism, in this mythic account, simultaneously drew from a unique and altruistic Jewish commitment to the prophetic ideal of Justice and exemplified America's liberal ideal of judging each individual by the content of his character. Until blacks demanded community control, according to this account, Jewish support for black rights had produced a Golden Age of interracial harmony and progressive social reform.

The Jew, according to Leinwand, did not freely abandon his liberal ideals. Rather,

> these priorities have been forcibly changed. . . . Those whom he supported in the past have abandoned him and actively seek to dispense teaching and administrative positions on the basis of political opportunism and ethnic quotas. It has therefore become the obligation of the Jewish teacher to forge a strong alliance to preserve his livelihood and his right to practice his profession.[88]

If nationalist demands for community control represented a repudiation of the American ideal by its black beneficiaries, then who could blame Jews for also repudiating liberalism?

When the Jewish Teachers Association invited JDL head Meir Kahane to address its 1972 annual luncheon, the UFT withdrew its support of the affair, and union president Al Shanker canceled his appearance. Still, 1200 teachers attended the luncheon, and the JTA received wide support from its members for Kahane's presence. The overlapping constituencies of the two organizations mirror the ambiguous commitments of New York's Jewish teachers and of American Jews more broadly.[89]

Conclusion

Jewish political life changed in the course of the school crisis. The campaign against black anti-Semitism reflected and furthered both the public visibility of Jews' Jewishness, and Jews' increasingly secure incorporation into white America. At the same time, the myth of black anti-Semitism—the unquestioning belief that incidents of anti-Semitism among blacks represented a unique and uniquely potent form of bigotry—justified Jews' declining commitment to assimilationist liberalism and their growing attentiveness to their particular self-interest.

When Charlie Isaacs, a young Jewish J.H.S. 271 teacher, addressed a meeting in the conservative Jewish community of Forest Hills, he told them that he had never experienced anti-Semitism in Ocean Hill-Brownsville. Instead of feeling relief, however, the audience "simply could not—or would not—believe that charges of anti-Semitism had no basis in fact. . . . One woman said: 'You only tell us what you've seen. Shouldn't you tell us about what you haven't seen?'"[90]

Preoccupation with anti-Semitism among blacks displaced other plausible objects of Jewish concern. Although 68% of New York Jews said that there was "a lot" of anti-Semitism among black militants, Jews were far less worried about more powerful white groups with well-known histories of anti-Semitism. Only 22% of Jews imagined "a lot" of anti-Semitism among White Anglo-Saxon Protestants, 18% among owners of large corporations, 14% among people of German descent, 7% among Catholics, and 3% among real estate agents.[91]

Jews sympathetic to black demands tried to refocus Jewish concerns. American Jewish Congress Community Interrelations Chairman Leonard Fein noted that the Anti-Defamation League's January 1969 report condemning black anti-Semitism failed to "distinguish gutter anti-Semitism . . . [from] the statements of public men," thereby placing marginal remarks at the center of the school crisis. Fein added that the ADL's list of 43 anti-Semitic statements included a number by whites, many by unnamed persons, and a number not clearly anti-Semitic. Henry Schwarzchild offered that in a city of over a million blacks and almost two million Jews, the ADL should have been surprised only at how few anti-Semitic utterances it found. The small number of examples in the report is all the more surprising because the UFT urged members to submit accounts of bigotry to the ADL for inclusion. By contrast, Schwarzchild added, the ADL might have found among the 120,000 New Yorkers who voted for white supremacist presidential candidate George Wallace not forty bigoted statements "but literally thousands."[92]

"There are some blacks who are anti-Semitic," Reform Jewish leader Albert Vorspan argued, "but there is no such thing as black anti-Semitism. Anti-Semitism does not inhere in blackness as it does, for instance, in Christianity."[93] If the militant African-American struggle to find authenticity in blackness succeeded, Leonard Fein argued, "it will succeed because America will have learned to live with difference. If, therefore, it succeeds, we ourselves will be among its unintended beneficiaries."[94]

Further evidence of the irrational nature of Jewish concerns, Vorspan argued, was the fact that black anti-Semitism "preoccupied" Jews across the United States who "tended not to have complaints about local interactions." During and after the school crisis, anti-Semitism was marginal to black politics, just as it had been before. Nevertheless, concerns about black-Jewish relations, as bibliographer Scott Cline notes, "mushroom[ed]" into "one of the most discussed issues . . . in the current literature on American Jewry."[95] "Why is it," as Vorspan asked, that "Jews, who were not panicked by Wallace, Rockwell, Gerald L. K. Smith, or the Ku Klux Klan, can be panicked by anti-Semitism coming from blacks?"[96]

Newly militant invocations of Jewish identity came not at a moment when Jews were marginal to American life, but rather at a moment when they embraced and, however provisionally, were embraced by whiteness.[97] Social and economic mobility, the post–World War II reconstruction of Jewishness, and American Jews' assimilation of white racist attitudes, all undermined Jews' liberalism. Invocations of victimization at the hands of black anti-Semitism legitimized racial privilege of Jews and other white Americans. Although this shift occasionally led to the repudiation of liberal candidates by Jewish voters,[98] it was more evident in the declining interest of Jewish organizations in civil rights in the years since the school conflict and their growing preoccupation with communal concerns such as Zionism and the plight of Soviet Jewry.[99] Although the years after the school crisis witnessed incidents of anti-Semitism from American presidents and their advisors,[100] black anti-Semitism has remained a preeminent scholarly and popular concern among Jews.[101]

American Jews are not monolithic in their political beliefs.[102] Interracial coalition politics, no less than invocations of Jewishness, offers a plausible response to anti-Semitism. Many Jewish workers, civil servants and professionals retained an attachment to progressive politics, and Jews remain unique among white Americans in the degree of their commitment to equality, the welfare state, to liberalism.[103] Precisely because political values continue to be unsettled and contested among Jews, charges of black anti-Semitism have continued to serve as a vehicle through which Jews consider their identity and their situation in white America.

The efforts of American Jews to carve a new identity during and after the school conflict reflected the fundamental dilemma poised by the competing pulls of commonality and difference, of *plurum* and *unum* in American life. How to reconcile the claims of particularistic identities with those of the larger culture and the claims of self-interest with the common good, remains a question not only for Jews but for all Americans.

Chapter 4

Teachers for Community Control: The Limits of Anti-Racism

The discussion of the wrongs of slavery has opened the way for the discussion of other rights, and the ultimate result will most certainly be the "breaking of every yoke," the letting of the oppressed of every grade and description go free.
— ANGELINA GRIMKE[1]

In June 1968, an advertisement in New York newspapers called upon the UFT leadership to end its opposition to community control and to "reverse its present collision course with the communities of New York City." Appearing soon after the Ocean Hill-Brownsville school board had removed the nineteen teachers and administrators, the advertisement was sponsored by five veteran teacher activists. They accused UFT President Albert Shanker of seizing on the dismissals "to frighten teachers with the specter of wholesale firings." Opposition to community control, the ad warned, would "inevitably lead to disaster for our union."[2]

As the school conflict escalated with the UFT strikes in the fall of 1968 and then after teachers returned to work, the *ad hoc* effort to run the advertisement evolved into the founding of Teachers for Community Control (TCC). TCC was the most important organization aimed at convincing teachers—some 90% of whom were white—that an alliance with black activists could defend both "the community['s] right to control the education of its children" and teachers' "full tenure rights and due process."[3]

Although teachers frequently call for increased parental involvement in education, they often feel ambivalence about parents' presence in schools, especially when the parents are poor or black or otherwise marginalized by American society.[4] In its effort to reconcile the interests of teachers and parents, TCC confronted enduring problems not only of urban schools but of American life. The dilemma that TCC faced—how to convince whites that they had an interest in black equality—has occupied a prominent place in American social science and social reform. Like the UFT leadership, TCC activists argued that teachers' place in the American social class structure was a primary determinant of teachers' work and that organized labor was a primary vehicle in defending the interests of teachers and other workers. Still, whereas the UFT discounted the significance of racial oppression, TCC argued that it was an enduring and distinct element of American life. The group sought to build an interracial coalition not by denying the power of racism but by confronting it. This chapter explores how TCC articulated the need for unity between white teacher unionists and the black community, the roots and trajectory of its campaign, and why it failed.

Organizing Teachers for Community Control

The June advertisement's five teacher-sponsors, Bob Couche, Ben Mazen, Carmen Miranda, Dave Weiner, and Clayton Flowers, represented diverse ethnic origins, ideological orientations, and organizational affiliations. Guidance counselor Bob Couche, for instance, was active in church and NAACP efforts in Queens' black community; Ben Mazen was a white former UFT officer and a dissident within the union.[5] Endorsed by nearly one thousand UFT members, the advertisement offered little hint at a coherent ideological and organizational basis on which to build effective teacher support for community control.[6]

Behind the scenes, however, the ad's organizers worked to build a unified organization, even as they reached out to the broad range of teachers sympathetic with community control. The idea to run the advertisement had originated in the living room of long-time teacher-activist Zippy Bauman. Early in the spring of 1968, even before the nineteen educators had been ordered out of Ocean Hill-Brownsville and talk of a strike had surfaced, veteran teacher activists gathered to discuss the UFT's growing hostility to community control. Bauman would recall,

> About a dozen of us . . . met . . . week after week after week. . . . . And we talked and talked and talked, and decided that this was a question of racism, that it would become clearer as time went on, and that we couldn't support this kind of action. So what were we going to do about it?[7]

With Bauman as Chairman, the group, naming itself the Ad Hoc Committee for Community Control, recruited the five sponsors for its advertisement and called an initial meeting to "get people together around the storm that was coming."[8] In order to solicit teacher endorsements for the advertisement, Bob Greenberg recalls, "we circulated among people we knew, and it just kept growing. . . . So we published the ad and we had a mailing list."[9]

As the school conflict heated up, the Ad Hoc Committee leafleted UFT members, urging them not to go out on strike over the Ocean Hill-Brownsville teachers' dismissals. According to the committee, UFT opposition to community control reflected the "social, economic and cultural distance" between an emerging black and Puerto Rican majority of pupils and a "Board of Education and professional staff still dominated by and reflect[ing] the interests and concerns of the white middle class." Despite having acknowledged racial and class conflict between teachers and students, organizers nevertheless sought to convince educators to ally themselves with the poor, minority communities whose children filled the schools and to confront their real antagonists, the Board of Education. A walkout, the committee charged, would "inevitably be interpreted as a strike against the black, Puerto Rican and even the white communities." [10]

The activists' efforts failed to sway teachers, who voted overwhelmingly to strike.[11] The UFT walkout inaugurated a period of frenetic activity. Zippy Bauman went

> to the office every day after school. . . . I had meetings sometimes three and four a day, some weeks over twenty meetings. I was interviewed at lunch time, and a reporter came at three o'clock, and then I dashed down to the office, and then I had a meeting at six and another meeting at nine, and I went out speaking at Co-op City and all over town.[12]

Activists addressed countless PTAs and community groups; they "went to every rally and every meeting and gave out leaflets by the thousands."[13]

The UFT picket lines provoked "very hot discussions" among teacher supporters of community control, forcing them to clarify their politics. Many young white teachers with few connections to the labor movement saw teacher unionism itself as an obstacle to social change. Convinced that the UFT was thoroughly racist and could never serve the educational needs of the black community, they had few qualms about crossing UFT picket lines.[14] By contrast, the veteran teachers who organized the Ad Hoc Committee attempted to balance their critique of racism and endorsement of community participation in school governance with a commitment to trade unionism and to teachers' rights.[15]

When the strike began, teacher Anne Filardo did not cross the picket line immediately: "I came down to the picket line every day. . . . I would talk with my colleagues [and] have lunch with them." Although Filardo convinced her coworkers to attend a meeting at which black parents could explain their viewpoint, "there was no way you were going to convince people. . . . The meeting . . . didn't change anybody's mind." About three weeks into the UFT strike, Anne Filardo and three other teachers crossed the picketline and opened their school. "Parents came with us, and I remember we gathered the children in the auditorium, and with tears streaming down my eyes, I was talking to the kids about why we were there and what we were going to do."[16]

At Wingate High School, Paul Becker's few black colleagues crossed the UFT picket line immediately. As the school conflict wore on, white teachers started to join them. By the second UFT strike about twenty-five or thirty of one hundred and fifty teachers entered the school. Becker, who was the Assistant Chairman of Wingate's UFT chapter, remembers,

> I was getting calls from some of my white colleagues on the left, saying. . .."How can you allow [black teachers] to face those whites alone?" I went down to the picket line . . . and what I saw sickened me. . . . [Teachers] yelling, "Hey . . . you're white! You don't belong in there with them." Vile racist slurs. [One white striker screamed at a black teacher], "We pick people like you out of the gutter, and this is the way you reward us.". . . The racist nature of this thing . . . was bringing out the worst in people. . . . I knew I had to go in.[17]

Once the strikes finally ended in November 1968, the Ad Hoc Committee's leaders felt that "our place was in the union to try and work with teachers to influence what went on."[18] "If we walked out," Bob Greenberg argued, "it would certainly be a racist and reactionary union, but if we went in there and fought," there was a chance the UFT might be turned in a different direction.[19] The committee dropped "Ad Hoc" from its name and called itself Teachers for Community Control.[20] TCC activists maintained a hectic pace of organizing. The agenda for the group's January 1969 meeting, for instance, included a list of forty-nine tasks to be done.[21]

Reestablishing a presence within the union was not easy. UFT leaders vigorously opposed the efforts of TCC activists, and whereas virtually all teachers received UFT publications, fewer than one in ten received the TCC newsletter.[22] In their own schools, TCC organizers faced difficulties as well. Before the strike, Anne Filardo had been a leader of her school's UFT chapter: "I was the legislative chair; I was a delegate to the Delegate Assembly; I was on the Sunshine Committee. . . . I was a very popular gal until the strike." Then, "the day the strike ended and people came back, they sent an emissary to me for the check book and the records of the Sunshine Committee, and the next day they called a union meeting." Much to Filardo's surprise, the administration had been invited to the meeting. A teacher moved that those who had crossed the picket line be expelled from the chapter. Filardo protested that during the UFT's 1967 strike, "there were people sitting in this room who crossed the picket line. . . . How come we didn't have a meeting like this?" The answer: "this time it's different; we're all together in this—the administration, the teachers."[23]

Racial polarization in the schools also hindered TCC activists' efforts. A Citizens Committee for Children survey of New York's schools found that the strike had left in its wake "an increasing estrangement between students and faculty, an estrangement which heightens racial tensions within the schools and encourages mutual distrust between student and teacher."[24] According to TCC's Nettie Becker, after the strike, "it was black against white" at school:

> The teachers were always protecting the white kids. . . . Black kids . . . looked at the teachers and said, "these are people who are against me.". . .There was no way you could . . . discuss the issue because there was such hate.[25]

Bob Greenberg recalled, "kids are turned off; parents are angry. . . . After the strike it was very tense. . . . There was no talking."[26]

In order to help establish TCC's place in the UFT, Paul Becker proposed that TCC broaden its interests to include issues of union democracy and educational policy and that the group adopt a new name in order to signal the enlarged scope of activity.[27] After months of discussion, TCC adopted the name Teachers Action Caucus (TAC), with three subheads—For Community Control, For Quality Education, and For Democratic Unionism. Aspiring to organize the bulk of teachers, TAC divested itself of its more provocative rhetoric.[28]

In December 1969, TAC issued a statement seeking to combine militant bread-and-butter unionism with demands for racial justice. TAC, it proclaimed,

> fought against the union's failure to implement the contract on working conditions, its tail dragging on grievances, its neglect of thousands of substitute teachers. At the same time we have fought against the basic reasons for the union's sell-out on these issues—its total war against the growing involvement of parents and communities in the schools, its alliance with the Council of Supervisory Associations for the preservation of the present educational bureaucracy, [and] its all-out fight against any attempt to come to grips with the [Vietnam] war issue as it affects education and trade unionism.[29]

Gradually, the commitment to union activity began to pay some dividends. As experienced activists, TAC organizers "always had a lot of information, so [many teachers] were willing to overlook the past."[30] High turnover at many schools also facilitated fence-mending.[31] Still, the reconciliation process was extremely slow, and TAC activists' effort to reshape union policy toward the black community met with little success.[32]

Long before the conflict over community control, TCC/TAC's founders had protested the inadequacy of school facilities in minority neighborhoods, the utilization of racist textbooks and curricula, reliance on racist IQ tests in student placement, and the re-fusal of New York's Board of Education to adopt a serious school integration plan. In the 1950s, for instance, Zippy Bauman and Paul Becker began producing widely distributed Negro History Week curriculum supplements.[33]

When black children were bused from Brownsville and East New York to her daughter's Midwood, Brooklyn elementary school in the mid-1960s, Anne Filardo was a leader of the white parents who supported integration. Filardo had lived and worked in Brownsville and East New York and, like a number of busing supporters, had gained organizing experience in Women Strike for Peace and the PTA. The women learned that the bused-in students ate lunch in the cafeteria while the white children, who brought their lunches, ate in the auditorium. Integrating the lunch-room, Filardo remembers,

> took a whole struggle. . . . The lunchroom was not large enough to accommodate all of the children. . . . The opposition . . . didn't understand why it was important to have the kids eat lunch together. . . . We set up a committee . . . and we finally came up with a plan.[34]

Next, the women challenged the school's practice of tracking the black students into the slowest classes. "Professional resistance" to busing, one-time school superintendent John Theobald acknowledged, "was subtle. . . . There was much talk . . . [of] the values of home lunches; there were constant attempts at segregated groupings in the receiving schools."[35]

Filardo recalls, "the teachers treated them like dogs." At the end of the day, the bused students had to be dismissed before the neighborhood children. Teachers would say, "Oh, the bus kids have to leave; we interrupt our lesson again." Filardo and other mothers organized workshops to get the teachers instead to say, "Oh, aren't we lucky we're going to have a little break." It was, she remembers,

> a million things all the time. Very low expectations, fear of the black kids. . . . Sixth grade graduation came; they were afraid to have a dance because the black kids might dance with the white kids. . . . And this is in a comparatively progressive white community.[36]

Teachers, TAC leaders noted, share the biases the wider society. At a social studies department meeting Paul Becker attended in the early 1960s, a teacher had written

> racist crap on the blackboard. A "joke". . . it went, "Wanted: White Women for Black Men, pulkeys preferred." A pulkey usually referred to a chicken thigh. The whole idea was, "we like white meat, we like white women". . .and everybody laughed. . . . And then the Chairman comes in, looks, laughs and starts the meeting.

Becker forced the department to erase the board before proceeding with the meeting, but racial insults were an ongoing part of the culture of teaching. In the teachers' room, Becker remembers, staff "loved to . . . make fun of the kids and mimic their accents."[37]

When Nettie Becker returned to teaching in 1967 after having taken off eight years to raise her children, the teachers she encountered at Springfield Gardens High School in Queens were "people who . . . ran away from the city. These were people who lived [in the suburbs and] who didn't want to work in the city schools. Their attitudes were very, very bad."[38]

Despite the existence of racist attitudes among their co-workers, TCC activists envisioned a crucial role for teachers as well as parents in school matters. "Racism," Paul Becker notes, "is a problem in American society, among all workers. [We] believe in working [with workers] and organizing unions among workers, but [we] have to combat it at the same time." Community control, according to Bob Greenberg, was "the pressure for [progressive reforms that] comes from people like us from within the system, and black and Hispanic parents."[39]

Like their commitment to anti-racist activism, TCC activists' identification with the labor movement long predated the school crisis. Zippy Bauman's political activism began in the 1920s, when she carried a collection can on the subway for striking Harlan County coal miners. Anne Filardo joined her first union, the Department Store Workers, in 1942, soon after graduating from college. Shortly thereafter, while working as a machinist at Ranger Aircraft in Queens—she was one of the first three women operating machines—she became a shop steward and was the only woman on the contract negotiating committee.[40]

Before the 1968 school conflict, Zippy Bauman, Paul Becker and a number of other TCC leaders had been active in the UFT, particularly at the chapter level.[41] As Bob Greenberg notes, TCC's leaders shared with their UFT counterparts "certain common views, which are very strong. One is the trade union vehicle. Second is the ability, through a trade union framework of life in the schools, to change anything and everything."[42] Like the UFT's leaders, many TCC activists traced their commitment to unionism to family roots in the labor movement. The fathers of Nettie Becker and Bob Greenberg, for instance, were members of the Furriers Union, long a stronghold of labor radicalism. Greenberg's father was blacklisted for his union activities.[43]

Moreover, family roots in the labor movement were not all that TCC activists shared with striking UFT leaders and teachers. Like most teachers, TCC's organizers had grown up in New York and had attended the city's schools and colleges. Bob Greenberg was born on Manhattan's Lower East Side and spent most of his life in Brooklyn. Paul Becker grew up in Bensonhurst; Ann Matlin and Nettie Becker grew up in the Bronx. TCC activists lived, shopped, taught and organized out of the limelight in New York's far-flung working- and middle-class neighborhoods. Their children and those of other teachers went to school and played together.[44]

Relatives active in the labor movement frequently failed to understand TCC activists' opposition to the UFT. Anne Filardo remembers, "I didn't tell my father and mother that I would cross that picket line for weeks." Zippy Bauman recalls, "My own brother and sister-in-law called me a scab; they wouldn't talk to me for a long, long time. My sister-in-law was a teacher and a union person, a member of Shanker's caucus, and our relationship has never been the same since." Bob Greenberg's father "could not understand" what his son had done. "He understood that sometimes unions don't make the right decisions, but essentially it was a strike. He couldn't conceive of the whole idea of crossing a picket line."[45]

Relatives were not the TCC's only critics. Many progressive activists and organizations sympathized with the UFT. *Jewish Currents*, a magazine long associated with the Communist Party,[46] found the strikes "unjustified" but noted, "We have among our readers veteran, devoted and conscientious progressives who have been on strike" as well as ones who have "been doing everything they can to open closed schools."[47] In Communist Party newspapers, a number of teachers took issue with the party's anti-UFT position. One reader, for instance, charged that community control went "counter to Marxist thinking, particularly with respect to a working-class outlook in general and trade unionism in particular."[48]

The effort to reconcile their support for black activism with their pro-labor beliefs shaped the way TAC activists interpreted the UFT's actions in the school conflict. Although Paul Becker "was very critical of the transfer of teachers" and acknowledged that "no union could tolerate" such actions, he charged that the transfers were not the cause of the strike. The school conflict, he argued, was

> the first time we have ever gone out on strike over teachers being arbitrarily transferred. We usually grieve it, protest it, we write an article in the newspaper. We do all kinds of things. Why suddenly when a black superintendent transfers . . . white teachers [do we need to strike]?

According to Paul Becker, "people who had never supported the union before were a thousand percent behind" the 1968 walkout. Then, when the strike ended, school administrators punished teachers who had crossed UFT picketlines and not those who honored them. For these converts to teacher militancy, 1968 was not a union issue but rather "the blacks versus the Jews."[49] "This is not a strike in the tradition of the labor movement," Zippy Bauman argued in the *New York Times* and the Communist *Daily World*. "This is not a strike directed against an employer for better working conditions or higher salaries. It's being directed against the children and their parents—against community control."[50] Bob Greenberg echoed, "the transfers were a cover for another agenda, the destruction of the experiments. It was pretending to be a regular strike, and it wasn't. . . . It was a racist strike. . . . It wasn't a strike; it was a reactionary political action."[51]

❂   ❂   ❂

The Roots of TCC

Although TCC emerged in response to the UFT's opposition to community control, the group reflected the legacy of the Teachers Union, a militant, Communist-led organization that had been the preeminent voice of New York's teacher unionists before the creation of the social democratic UFT. Communists argued that independent black organizing would not only help to secure political rights for African Americans, but would also lead to the democratization of American society as a whole. Autonomous activism by marginalized blacks, according to this dialectic, would establish the conditions necessary for their integration into a democratized American mainstream. In the 1930s and 1940s, TU activists united with black parents and activists in a militant campaign against racial inequality in New York's schools.

TCC's efforts to build teacher support for community control reflected notions of interracial solidarity that had been nurtured in the TU. Indeed, Zippy Bauman and Paul Becker, TCC's first two Chairmen, had been part of the TU leadership.[52] Although TCC attracted "a mixture of people, the Party was very strong in it," and, as Bob Greenberg notes, "the independents fit within that framework and that way of seeing things." Whether or not individual TCC activists were affiliated with the Communist Party, they embraced its argument that independent black activism need not threaten white teachers.[53]

For its members who went on to found TCC, the Teachers Union had been more than a mechanism for seeking redress of work-place grievances. In its heyday between the Depression and the McCarthy era, the TU, according to Cedric Belfrage, "was the educational field's chief nursery of heretics." Hundreds of its members, "clamoring simultaneously against Fascism and for bigger school budgets," joined the Communist Party.[54] For teachers who came of age in the 1930s and 1940s, the TU was part of a radical counter-culture that shaped participants' entire lives. Zippy Bauman helped organize music students to perform at rallies and mass meetings in solidarity with the Spanish republic.[55] Ann Matlin, like many TU members, remembers the civil war in Spain as "open[ing] my eyes to everything else going on in the world" and leading her to "become an activist in general." Like the Communist Party itself, the TU led efforts to win white Americans to black equality.[56]

The year 1935 was a turning point for teachers committed to opposing racism in the schools. A city investigation following the 1935 Harlem riot acknowledged that district's "old, poorly equipped and overcrowded" schools were a major source of black discontent. Although blacks constituted only a small percentage of New York's students, school discrimination and segregation, like housing segregation and job discrimination, were already entrenched in the city. "Many of the white teachers appointed to the schools of Harlem," the investigation noted, "regard the appointment as a sort of punishment."[57]

Meanwhile, within the TU, a Communist-led rank-and-file coalition displaced the union's social-democratic leadership. The Communists and their allies demanded both that the union pay more attention to social and political issues and that it respond more militantly to Depression-era teaching conditions. Despite the exodus of the social-democratic faction and the opposition of school officials to teacher unionism, the TU grew from 1,200 members in 1935 to 6,500 in 1938.[58]

The TU's new leadership made the struggle against school racism a priority. The union's Harlem Committee joined with a number of parent, civic and religious leaders to form the Committee for Better Schools in Harlem. The Committee protested the brutal corporal punishment of black students and secured the construction of Harlem's first new schools in decades.[59] Former Communist George Charney, disillusioned about most Party activities, fondly recalled the Committee and the teachers in it:

> In every school the parents' associations sprang up and flourished, . . . pressing their demands for better schools, more schools, textbook revisions, Negro teachers and principals, free lunches, and so forth. . . . Mothers came [to Committee meetings] *en masse* to organize programs, assign delegations, and join in citywide activities. In every school, white teachers, with the active support of the Teachers' Union, came forward to collaborate with the parents in this inspired effort to transform a community through education.[60]

Alice Citron, a leader in Harlem's overlapping Communist and Teachers Union circles, epitomized Depression-era anti-racist school organizing. In her own classroom, Citron's lessons included original plays drawn from black history, and she compiled bibliographies on black history for other teachers. Furthermore, Citron's notion of schoolwork extended to organizing with progressive whites and black teachers in support of a free lunch program, the celebration of Negro History Week, and the construction of new schools in Harlem.[61]

The TU also protested the Board of Examiner's exclusion of blacks from teaching positions because of "regionalisms" in their speech, noting that the accents of white Southerners were deemed acceptable. At a 1949 press conference, the TU protested discriminatory firings of black substitutes, and charged that because of discrimination against both substitutes and black applicants for regular licenses, the number of black teachers, already small, was declining.[62]

TU offered New York's teachers a rare opportunity to study and discuss black history and culture. *New York Teacher News*, for instance, published a critique of New York City history textbooks by black scholar Carter G. Woodson. The union also maintained a curriculum library on black history and life and offered courses on ways to introduce materials on blacks into the curriculum.[63]

When she began teaching, Zippy Bauman recalls, "I knew nothing. My interest developed through . . . working with the people in the union who knew more about it than

I and who helped steer me and teach me and develop me." Eventually, she and Paul Becker would play a leading role in producing TU's annual Negro History Week supplements, which began appearing in *New York Teacher News* in 1952. The guides, which included articles, bibliographies, lessons, puzzles, and other aids, were distributed nationally as well as in New York, and their appearance was a major union event each year.[64]

The legacy of TU coalitions with black activists, as well as its efforts to include black history and culture in the curriculum, predisposed TCC to view demands for community control as a call for black empowerment rather than as a repudiation of interracial solidarity. As tensions between teachers and the black community grew in the mid-1960s, Ann Matlin urged teachers to "understand the hostility which some children bring along to school." She reminded her colleagues that while they were "victims of the 'system,'" children were "the worst victims of official neglect" and that "when the injustices have been eradicated, these hostilities will disappear."[65] Writing in 1968, former TU officer Celia Zitron suggested the relevance of the earlier efforts to the community control conflict: when "teachers work[ed] for better schools as an integral and welcome part of the community . . . relations between union teachers and parents were cordial."[66]

White Anti-Racism in Theory and Practice

The theory on which TU activists based their campaign against racism originated in the American Communist Party. Extrapolating from the crucial role played by national minorities in the Russian Revolution, Communist analysts declared that blacks living in the United States were an oppressed national group with the right to self-determination in the South's blackbelt. At the same time, they asserted that blacks could supply the missing ingredient needed to construct a revolutionary bloc in the United States.[67] "There can be no proletarian revolution," American Communist Party General Secretary Earl Browder claimed, "unless it is accompanied by the liberation of the Negro people."[68] "The Negro problem," therefore, had to be "part and parcel of all and every campaign conducted by the Party."[69]

The Communists contrasted their view that blacks were an ally of the proletariat rather than a part of it, with the positions of the American Socialist Party, which sought to unify the working class while discounting racial categories.[70] Committed to the evolutionary transformation of society, socialists required no agent capable of telescoping the Marxian laws of historical change. Communists, on the other hand, argued that as the struggle for black self-determination confronted the governing structures of American capitalism, it would provoke a "revolutionary crisis" and lead to the transformation of American society. This view allowed the Party to call for the right to self-determination while opposing its actualization. "We are confident," Earl

Browder noted, that "the Negro people . . . [will decide] to join the United Soviet States of America."[71]

The Communist program found a ready audience among African Americans who came to the Party with race-consciousness and a commitment to black self-determination already formed under the influence of Marcus Garvey and its radical descendent, the African Blood Brotherhood. Moreover, even blacks who were not enticed by the chimera of actual independence found it an appealing metaphor for racial identity.[72]

For whites, too, the call for black self-determination had a powerful effect. Even if the idea of black self-determination in the U.S. has been "justifiably described as a bit of 'fatuous romance,'" historian Mark Solomon argues,

> under the ideological lashing of the Comintern and [their American leaders], Communists were being forced to deal with racial issues and attitudes in ways that were totally beyond the awareness and comprehension of most white Americans. . . . [The conception of an "oppressed Negro nation"] led to the most determined efforts of a predominantly white organization to achieve equality since the abolitionists.[73]

Communist theorizing about the revolutionary role of black nationalism did not fully reveal how radicals would convince fellow white teachers to ally themselves with black nationalism. Activists understood that mere exposure to communist theory might not change the minds of whites who had absorbed and benefited from racism. Instead, TU activists sought to convince white teachers both that anti-racism was a natural extension of white working-class values and that race relations had to be reordered if the schools were to deal with teachers' bread-and-butter concerns.

Summarizing her career for the Communist Party's *Daily Worker* when she had been made a target of New York's McCarthy era witchhunt, Alice Citron claimed, "I was suspended because for eighteen years I fought Jim Crow in Harlem."[74] "The thing that we worked on in those days," Ann Matlin recalls of her years with Citron, "was mostly class size, teacher salaries, physical conditions of the schools, and the right of teachers to organize and speak up."[75] Citron traced her horror of the suffering she witnessed in black Harlem and the "joyless . . . shabbiness" of its schools to memories of the squalor of the immigrant Jewish ghetto of her youth. And she appreciated black militancy because it echoed the activism she "imbibed with my mother's milk" in a working-class Jewish family.[76] TU hoped that militant organizing for conventional union demands would lead teachers to see the role of racism in their conditions.

Communist theorizing on the relationship of black liberation to proletarian revolution and anti-racist activism would supply TCC activists with a logic, a psychological motivation, and an organizing style in their support of community control, without their having to renounce their sense of self-worth as teachers or the spirit of equality, universalism, and justice.

The Big Chill

In the 1950s, New York's Teachers Union was among the principal targets of govern-ment anti-Communist repression. McCarthy-era attacks, together with their own failures, led to the collapse of the Communist Party, the Teachers Union, and the TU-led coalitions against racial inequality in schooling. New York's Board of Education dismissed or forced resignations from several hundred veteran teachers accused of Communist affiliations.[77] The 1949 Feinberg Law, which launched the purge, noted that Communist classroom propaganda was "frequently so subtle as to defy detection." Unable to document classroom misdeeds, investigations focused on political activities outside the classroom. Teachers were questioned about what books they had read, whether they had ever supported the Spanish republic, whether they had ever signed petitions for third parties. Teachers were not allowed to cross-examine their accusers or even know who they were. Above all, school board inquisitor Saul Moskoff claimed, "I always try to get suspects to name more names" to add to the nine hundred he had already accumulated.[78]

Minnie Gutride, one of its first victims, came to symbolize the period. Two days be-fore the 1948 Christmas holidays, as Cedric Belfrage recounts, "two Education Board emissaries appeared out of a snowstorm at the Staten Island school where Gutride, widow of a Spanish war volunteer, was teaching." The officials pulled Gutride out of her first grade classroom for questioning. The TU promised to help defend her, but, threatened with "conduct unbecoming a teacher" and then vilified in William Ran-dolph Hearst's *Journal-American*, Gutride "decided to avoid . . . [being] probed by turning on the gas that night in her lonely apartment." That the McCarthy-era purge was personified in a martyr's suicide rather than a casualty's falling in combat suggests how little will or opportunity radicals had for militancy.[79]

Moreover, in case the firing of hundreds of activists were not enough, the Board of Education made a direct bid to destroy the Teachers Union. The 1950 Timone Reso-lution declared that administrators were no longer permitted to "negotiate, confer, or deal with or recognize [the Teachers Union] in relation to any grievances or any per-sonal or professional problems, nor grant to said Teachers Union any of the rights or privileges accorded to any teacher organization." The ban, which lasted until 1962, cemented the TU's destruction.[80]

Finally, those who participated in TU's anti-racist campaigns, such as its support for the roatation of experienced teachers to ghetto schools, were smeared with being communist sympathizers. When psychologist Kenneth Clark and Judge Hubert De-lany called on New York school officials to investigate the quality of education of-fered to black students, an assistant superintendent dismissed the two as "current favorites of the Teachers Union and . . . their program of creating community dissension and distrust of the public school system."[81] The social democratic Teachers Guild invoked the presence of Communists in its successful campaign to block TU membership in the Intergroup Committee on New York's Public Schools, a coalition of liberal groups that endorsed integration. TU-led coalitions that had worked for years to improve ghetto education evaporated as parents were cowed into ending association with heretical teachers.[82]

The Anti-Racist Revival

In the 1960s, the struggle to integrate New York's schools reinvigorated veterans of the Teachers Union. Reflecting the traditional Communist view that black organizing would spark progressive change in America as a whole, party leader Herbert Aptheker argued that with the 1964 school boycotts, "the Negro people [are] once again . . . leading a battle whose stake is nothing less than the whole theory of popular, mass, effective education."[83] Party theoretician Mike Davidow echoed that white New Yorkers would realize that black activists' "struggle against segregated schools [had given] unprecedented stimulus to the fight for a first-class school system."[84]

In practice, unfortunately, the boycotts failed to justify optimism about the ability of white Americans to transcend their racism. [85] Although Anne Filardo supported the boycott, few white teachers were convinced that they would benefit from black activism. When Filardo and a few other teachers joined the civil rights pickets, "we got away with it because we were generally people who were respected in the schools." And yet, in spite of the other teachers acknowledging the boycotters' militancy in contractual matters, they "didn't connect with [the boycott] at all. . . . They didn't participate in it; they didn't understand what it was about."[86]

Nevertheless, lacking an alternative strategy for convincing white teachers to endorse black militancy, Communists persisted in arguing that militant defense of teachers' bread-and-butter concerns would lead them to radicalism. In 1967, party leader Henry Winston urged radicals seeking white workers' support for black equality to avoid arguments that "smack too much of liberal white moralistic preachments and are not placed in sharp enough class and trade union self-interest terms." Instead, he argued, they should emulate UFT head Albert Shanker. When, Winston wrote, conservative members of the UFT

> threatened to resign from the union due to their union's support of the [Police Civilian] Review Board . . . Shanker could not convince them fully of the merits of the Board. . . . He won them over by pointing out that the UFT was going into contract negotiations and they had in the past gotten the support of Negroes and Puerto Ricans.

The UFT, he continued, again needed the support of these minority groups and if teachers did not support them on issues they felt were important, then teachers could expect nothing in return. With this coalition argument he convinced most of the teachers and none resigned.[87]

At the very time when Communist leaders were arguing that pragmatic activism would convince whites to ally themselves with black insurgency, however, the party's theoretical journal *Political Affairs* described some of the trends impeding unity. Blacks, Betty Gannett noted, were concentrated in unskilled jobs and therefore more likely than whites to suffer high rates of unemployment and job-downgrading as a result of automation and changes in industrial production. This meant that economic growth could not be counted on to provide jobs for blacks or foster their upward mobility.[88] Furthermore, government slum clearance and highway construction policies, together with the efforts of developers such as Abraham Levitt, fostered northern segregation at precisely the moment when activists were celebrating integration in the south. Assessing demographic trends, the New York Party documented the decline of public housing construction for the poor and working-class families and the rise of government subsidies for the middle class.[89]

During the years when the school conflict was growing, social immobility awaited the black and Puerto Rican poor who had come to form the majority of New York's public school students. At the same time, teachers were experiencing literal mobility. Paul and Nettie Becker moved from Brooklyn to Rochdale Village in 1964 and then to the Long Island town of Rockville Center, where developer Abraham Levitt had begun his career.[90] Anne Filardo moved to Midwood, a middle-class Brooklyn neighborhood of big houses and shady lawns. While these activists retained their commitment to black empowerment, for the teaching staff as a whole, empathy with minority students became increasingly unlikely.

In the end, it was not union organizing that provided the model for TCC efforts to build support for community control. Rather, an increasingly bitter conflict with UFT President Al Shanker over UFT support for the War in Vietnam reanimated union activism among the teachers who would form TCC.[91] The 1964 creation of the Teachers Committee for Peace in Vietnam anticipated many of TCC's efforts. Among the committee's founders were Zippy Bauman and Paul Becker.[92] Operating outside of the anti-war movement limelight, the committee's first act was the collection of teacher signatures to run a *New York Times* advertisement opposing the war.[93] While anti-war organizing, together with activism in the civil rights and peace movements, reinvigorated the TU veterans, such activities were distant from teachers classroom concerns. Like militant bread-and-butter organizing, they provided an uncertain strategy for radicalizing white teachers' understanding of racial politics in the schools.[94]

Conclusion

"Everyone," as Zippy Bauman notes, "defined community control according to his own lights." For TCC's leaders, community control signified the legitimate desire of poor blacks and Puerto Ricans to share in determining the education of their children, and of the black community to see its culture as well as the dominant American one honored in ghetto schools.

TCC organizers acknowledged that advocates of community control were guilty of "some terribly provocative stuff. . . . There were," Paul Becker admitted, "a lot people who went overboard."[95] "In their way," Zippy Bauman recalls, some Ocean Hill-Brownsville leaders "were as intransigent as the UFT."[96] Still, TCC activists insisted that there was no contradiction between black activists' race-conscious politics and democratic values. Paul Becker's social studies classroom reflected this belief that recognition of a special place for blacks in American life was compatible with their being "integrated" into the mainstream of American history. Blacks, Becker argued,

> have had such a fundamental role because of the class position they occupy in American [history]. If you don't know this material, you don't know American history. It's not a separate course. It's not like throwing something in. It's not like another ethnic type of situation. You want to teach the contributions of Asians, Jews, Italians, fine. But with black history, it's not black history. It's American history.[97]

As had so often occurred in American history, the black demands for community control would spark the transformation of American life. "Just as reconstruction . . . carried with it [the promise of] . . . enhancing democratic rights for the entire South," Herbert Aptheker argued, "the community control struggle is this generation's 'battle for democracy.'"[98] By embracing black activism, white teachers could both challenge oppressive working conditions they faced in schools and join in democratizing American life.

Anne Filardo drew on her own family's experience in arguing that a coalition of teachers and minority parents to democratize education would benefit white students as well:

> my husband had an experience . . . that I think typifies why that movement for community control [arose]. We had just moved into the neighborhood; [our daughter] was going into the fourth grade . . . and all of the sudden she doesn't want to go to school. . . . So [my husband], a white man, suit, white shirt and tie, [goes to the school and] identifies himself. . . . "I'd like to sit in on my daughter's class." "What do you

mean, you'd like to sit in on your daughter's class? It's not open school week." Imagine if he had been black. . . . Community control would help all parents participate in their kids' education.[99]

In the 1930s, amid the crisis created by the Depression and the working-class militancy it spawned, the call for teachers to cast their lot with those below won countless teachers to embrace black equality. By the late 1960s, deindustrialization and suburbanization created a wedge between blacks and whites, and conservatism was increasingly ascendant in public life. With white teacher unionists more privileged and the black poor more desperate, TCC was unable to replicate TU's success. TCC's failure to attract widespread support among white teacher unionists confirmed both the eclipse of left teacher unionism and the centrality of race relations in that eclipse.

Chapter 5

Up Against the Leviathan:
Teaching for
Democratic Community

Men have unrealized potential for self-cultivation,
self-direction, self-understanding, and creativity.
— STUDENTS FOR A DEMOCRATIC SOCIETY[1]

If there ever are great revolutions there, they will be
caused by the presence of the blacks upon American soil.
— ALEXIS DE TOCQUEVILLE[2]

Liz Fusco responded to the UFT strike by taking a teaching job at Ocean Hill-Brownsville's P.S. 178. Fusco "scabbed . . . consciously and not without much thought." Ocean-Hill Brownsville urgently needed teachers to replace striking union members, and Fusco was convinced that UFT actions were designed only to bolster teachers' race and class privilege. As an experienced high school teacher with no desire to teach young children, Fusco remembers, "I went solely for the politics of it. . . . My being there was a commitment."[3]

Fusco continued to teach at P.S. 178 for the next three years. Then, one day,

there was an incident. A kid from an older class hit one of my first graders in the lunch line. . . . I got very defensive . . . these are my kids. I confronted the kid. Then I was up-stairs after lunch teaching my class, and the kid's mother came and slapped me. . . . She just came up to me and hit me in the face, in front of my students. The whole thing went to [the principal, and he] . . . offered her a job in the school. So I felt really betrayed. Not that I wanted her punished or anything like that, but I just felt like it was capitulation. We weren't solving the problem; we weren't going to deal with anything; we were just going to buy off her hostility. I felt like, "You don't know who I am; you don't know what I've done. All you see is white; you're not giving me a chance." And he didn't give me a chance.[4]

Fusco felt "defeated . . . abandoned . . . powerless."[5] She could have transferred from P.S. 178 to another New York school but did not. After finishing out the year, she left the city to teach in a small New England town.

A veteran of the peace and civil rights movements, Fusco had directed the Mississippi Freedom Schools[6] before coming to New York. She was one of many young, politically conscious whites who poured into the New York City school system in the late 1960s. Whether they came through political conviction or to avoid military conscription, they were supposed to be teaching's best and brightest. *Time* labeled them "teachers who give a damn;"[7] liberal *New York Post* columnist James Wechsler concurred, calling them "Those Who Care."[8]

Teachers like Fusco—young, well-educated, dedicated to social justice—seemed committed to their students in ways that defied the rule-bound behavior of the school bureaucracy and the union contract. They took students on weekend field trips, and spent their evenings visiting students' homes and attending community meetings, all without pay.[9] *Time* and the new teachers themselves shared the belief that their charismatic presence could overcome the fossilized school bureaucracy and its time-serving teachers.

The teachers *Time* admired were not united by membership in any organization. Rather, the ideology that informed their idealism is what distinguished them from their supposedly jaded colleagues. Convinced that bureaucracy and centralized power, as much as economic inequality, distorted American life, they countered the UFT and TCC's defense of workers' solidarity with visions of living personally authentic lives through participation in just communities. Today such educators might be called progressive, radical or democratic,[10] but in 1968, the label most commonly attached to them was New Left.

New Leftists called for radical social change but contrasted themselves with the Socialists and Communists of the Old Left. New Leftists wedded the African American freedom struggle's quest for a beloved community and liberal American ideals of self-sufficiency to Old Left visions of ending exploitation and inequality.[11] Whereas the Old Left was shaped by the immigrant ghetto, the Great Depression, the glory days of the labor movement and the utopian hopes inspired by Soviet Communism, the New Left was shaped by America's growing suburban affluence, an emerging youth culture, McCarthy-era government repression, the looming threat of nuclear holocaust, American military aggression, and the black freedom struggle.

New Leftists advocated activity in decentralized, democratic social movements that simultaneously demanded radical change, engaged the individual in moral action, and prefigured a democratized society. Such activity restored to people the individual autonomy and the interpersonal community denied them by the bureaucratized social order. Participatory democracy, in the words of leading New Left theorist Staughton Lynd, allowed one to move toward "a brotherly way of life even in the jaws of the Leviathan."[12] Echoing Deweyan calls for schools to revitalize both community bonds and democratic commitments, New Left teachers envisioned classrooms that transcended the bitter divisions of American society.[13]

The ideals of the New Left—solidarity with the African American freedom struggle, suspicion of entrenched bureaucracy, the belief that schools could model humane, democratic communities for the wider society—continue to inspire many educators. Popular school reform ideas in the decades following the school conflict such as calls for whole language, authentic assessment, charter schools, and small learning communities echo the New Left's values. This chapter recounts the New Left's fragile, contradictory project of working within the school system to catalyze the total transformation of learning and society. It examines how such hopes foundered in the face of the bureaucratized school system, the racial divisions of American life, and white teachers' ambivalence about their role as teachers in urban schools.[14]

Her Pedagogical Creed

Liz Fusco entered teaching in 1959, after studying literature at Smith College and then completing a Master of Arts in Teaching at Yale. While working as a high school teacher, Fusco's deepening involvement in the peace and civil rights movements reshaped her ideas about the curriculum, as well as teaching her "who makes decisions and how bureaucracies lie and cripple."[15] Then, directing the civil rights movement's famed Mississippi Freedom Schools "totally transformed" Fusco's understanding of education.[16]

Two visions of education were at issue in the Freedom Schools: most professional teachers wanted to bring schooling to the state's disenfranchised black poor; activists such as Fusco wanted to free students from it. Like many activists, Fusco noted how resistant the professional teachers who volunteered in Mississippi were to the movement's pedagogy:

> public school teachers were generally tied to worksheets and all that stuff. . . . I remember people coming down from New York, saying, "Where's the rexograph machine? I can't teach without a rexograph machine" . . . whereas people who hadn't been *trained* to be teachers . . . just took what was there, just rapped with people and said "Let's try this."[17]

Increasingly radicalized by their experience in Mississippi, activists like Fusco sought to abolish school, with its stultifying relations of hierarchy and compulsion and its pre-ordained, routinized and irrelevant curriculum; they envisioned the Freedom Schools not as a better form of public schooling but rather as the institution's antithesis.

The Freedom Schools taught Fusco that the teacher's task was to "blur the focus of what [students came to school] to know." Students were used to relying passively on the school's intellectual agenda. At Freedom Schools, teaching was "having people talk with each other . . . and validating what they said." Teachers relied on questioning to "release" students from the "rigid squelching of initiative and expression." By incorporating students' experiences and taking their insights seriously, Freedom School teachers "activated" students "into confrontation, with themselves and with the world and back again." Combined with the wider black freedom struggle of which it was an integrated part, Freedom School teaching allowed students to face the "intolerability of [their] situation."[18]

In Freedom Schools, white activists had to confront their own notions of education. Teachers, according to Fusco, "[threw] away our assumptions about who teaches and who learns."[19] The gulfs separating students from teachers and from one another, knowledge from action, and school from life were effaced. Teaching was enmeshed in communal activity, and, Fusco remembers, "all my interactions with the community were an extension of freedom school."[20]

Freedom Schooling was based on the optimistic notion that by drawing on their American experience, black students could both come to understand the nature of racial inequality and envision a path to equality and liberation. However, as black activists became increasingly convinced of the intractability of racism and of the indelible scars with which it marked black students, the Freedom School pedagogy of questioning and conversation lost its force. By 1966, black hopes for integration were fading. The emerging ideal of Black Power led to concerns that any white leadership reproduced racial domination, leaving white activists with no obvious role in the movement. Fusco "accepted the reality" that she "was not organizing." After spending two years of directing the Freedom Schools, Fusco left the South.[21]

By the time Fusco left Mississippi in 1966, she had become convinced that even in the movement context, black students were too debilitated by schooling to come together voluntarily and learn by "talking what [they know] into consciousness." The "learning to please the teacher and avoid her wrath" that had characterized Fusco's own privileged education marked students in Mississippi as well. Committed nevertheless to acting on what she had learned about teaching in the South and hoping to reaffirm her identification with the black community and its struggle, Fusco headed to New York.[22]

As a public school teacher, Fusco's struggle to validate students' own language and expression forced her to confront the New York City school system's traditional, ethnocentric notions of grammar and literature. She worked to connect learning to social life, getting her classes subway passes and taking them all over the city. Yet, even these curricular efforts, which left unchallenged the unequal relations embedded in compulsory schooling, got Fusco in trouble.

Before going to Ocean Hill-Brownsville's P.S. 178 in 1968, Fusco taught at two New York high schools. She lasted only a few months in the fall of 1966 at Manhattan's Brandeis High School before the English Department Chairman's displeasure at her using a Bob Dylan song to teach poetry forced her out of the school. The next fall she was hired at Brooklyn's Prospect Heights High School. She was still there the following spring, when Martin Luther King, Jr. was assassinated. When black students in the lunchroom talked of rioting, Fusco suggested to the principal that students be dismissed early in Dr. King's memory. In response, the principal "accused me of starting the riot, because I knew that something was up. So of course I was fired." The UFT staged no walkout on her behalf.[23]

Fusco was as troubled by her high school students as by her bosses. At a March 1968 Vocations for Radicals conference in Boston, she declared that by the time students reached high school, they had "grown dulled, closed up," that "anyone with real rebellion, or even real intelligence" had dropped out. Blinded to the worthlessness of a high school diploma, Fusco's students were too "brainwashed" to respond when she tried to talk about "Stokely and Rap." "Why," they wondered, "doesn't she stop that shit and teach us some grammar?" "How," Fusco reflected, "can you be honest with kids who don't see the real world clearly," students who "won't rebel in ways I try to force them to," who won't make demands based on their "real needs," but who only engage in petty disruptions like interrupting when Fusco took attendance and cutting her class?[24]

Faced with the hostility of her superiors and doubts about her students, Fusco welcomed the chance to transfer to Ocean Hill in the fall of 1968. Her entrance there echoed her arrival in Mississippi in the Freedom Summer of 1964:

> We had a mass meeting with all the teachers in the district. [Demonstration district administrator] Rhody McCoy talked to us. . . . There was an incredible energy about the new people; it was almost like white volunteers coming down to the South. . . . There was a sense of movement activity . . . of camaraderie, and of change, and of innovation . . . and of caring.

Fusco and the other new teachers hoped that community control would spark a wider political movement:

> People would come together around their kids and then they would begin to address the other issues. . . . They would come together as neighbors, and they were neighbors because they were poor, they were trapped in that environment because of racism.[25]

Still, Fusco envisioned little role for white teachers in that coming-together process. Teaching in the district lacked the political connectedness of Fusco's Mississippi work. She attended school and district-wide mass meetings, and was

> politically aware that we were all part of a district and we were all part of a movement . . . but I wasn't organizing; I wasn't involved with parents except if they were parents of my kids.

Assigned to an elementary school, Fusco, a trained high school teacher, focused on "trying to cope with not the race or culture issue, but [with] how to teach little kids."[26]

By the end of her third year in Ocean Hill, the combined pressures of the exhausting demands of teaching, the relentless attacks on community control, and the limited role assigned to white teachers by demands for Black Power transformed her work. Fusco remembers,

> There was no movement like there was in the South; there was no coming together. It was just individual white teachers as if we were in any school. . . . I came to school and I left . . . and I had my own life, and it was me all by myself.

Fusco found solace in a dance class that filled her after-school hours, and like the most jaundiced drudge, when the bell rang to end the day, she "cut out of school."[27]

The absence of a movement left Fusco with little real hope that she could help students change their lives. Finally, slapped by a parent and betrayed by her principal, Fusco had nothing left to hold on to. It was not only that she "decided I couldn't stay in a place that didn't value me;" she had no language with which to demand that white teachers like her be valued. Longing for a teaching job in a rural black district like those in which she had organized in the civil rights movement's glory days but settling for a white working-class town, Fusco left New York.[28]

New Left Teachers in New York Schools

When three hundred and fifty UFT teachers walked out of Ocean Hill-Brownsville to protest the May 1968 action taken against their nineteen colleagues, their replacements brought New Left values of egalitarianism and participatory democracy to the district's schools. Teacher-militant Charles Isaacs was offered a number of teaching jobs, but went to Ocean Hill because he did not "think there is any education in any other part of the New York City school system."[29] Mississippi civil rights movement veteran Sandy Nystrom found the men who came to the Ocean Hill-Brownsville to escape the draft "young and hip and energetic, and they do improve the staff. . . . They have something to offer the kids."[30] Teachers like Isaacs and Nystrom convinced educationalist Joseph Featherstone that there was "more energy and talent" in I.S. 201 and Ocean Hill-Brownsville "than in any other two districts in the city."[31] *Time* was even more effusive, calling the demonstration district "one of the nation's youngest, best-educated and most enthusiastic teaching staffs."[32]

Although Ocean Hill-Brownsville dominated press coverage during the school conflict, New Left teachers were scattered throughout the city.[33] They announced their commitment to breaking down sterile, bureaucratic hierarchies even in the way they dressed. Bronx High School of Science teacher Robert Rossner considered himself one of a "new breed" of teachers. In 1964, he became the first teacher at Bronx Science to sport a beard. By 1968 seven teachers had beards; five of them crossed UFT picket lines. Rossner's colleague Don Schwartz, who broke with the union in 1968, had gained notoriety as the first teacher at Bronx Science to wear a turtleneck.[34]

More profound differences also separated New Leftists from other teachers and teacher activists. The new teachers were disproportionately young, male, and inexperienced. Of thirty-eight teachers who worked with Liz Fusco at P.S. 178, twenty-four (along with the principal) were men; thirty were under twenty-five years old. They were far more likely than other teachers to have been born into affluent families, raised outside of New York and educated at elite institutions. Still, whether they grew up in New York's working-class neighborhoods or its suburbs, whether they attended City College or an Ivy League school, three crucial experiences distinguished them from older activists. The new teachers grew up with the labor movement's ghost, the bomb's shadow, the civil rights movement's beacon.

Even teachers who grew up in working-class families were separated by a gulf of experience and ideology from New York's radical working-class culture of earlier decades.[35] Whereas radical children of an earlier era grew up imbibing epic accounts of victorious struggles, as a child in the 1950s, future high school teacher Susan Metz's household chores included answering the door when FBI agents came around to harass her parents. In the face of government repression, children like Metz were told not discuss home life or politics in school. Unlike her parents, Metz was "never attracted to the Communist Party or its take on human nature. I was . . . a humanist [and] a socialist." The Communist Party, she concluded, "was neither of these things."[36]

During the height of the Cold War, when neither class analysis nor explicit radicalism was permissible political discourse, questions of process replaced questions of ends in political philosophy. Thus, McCarthyism forced activists to fall back on the rhetoric of political participation. Even if demands for participation were profoundly embedded in the Cold War, however, they represented a revolt against it, and were central in the early civil rights movement, in the Port Huron Statement, and in demands for community control. Anticipating the New Left and Feminist Movement, future teacher Susan Metz carried with her "the odd feeling . . . 'If I'm not black, how come I feel like I'm not being heard?'"[37]

Whereas the class-based, organizationally disciplined politics of the Communist Party lacked appeal, the civil rights and peace movements animated the young activists. In the late 1950s, Susan Metz participated in the Youth Marches for Integrated Schools organized by Bayard Rustin, and later she picketed northern Woolworth's branches in support of southern sit-ins. In college Metz was campus Chairman of the Student Peace Union. While in college, Bronx elementary school teacher Vivian Stromberg joined campaigns against strontium-90 and bomb tests. In the early 1960s, Stromberg went south as a freedom rider. Brooklyn teacher Paul Baizerman became involved in protests against racism and the Vietnam War while attending Brooklyn College between 1961 and 1967.[38]

During the teachers' strikes, New Left teachers helped re-open hundreds of schools which UFT teachers had abandoned. The absence of grading, compulsory attendance and all the other paraphernalia of mandatory schooling presented a unique opportunity to create educational alternatives. White JHS 271 teacher and law school graduate "Charlie" Isaacs encouraged students to address him by his first name "to break down the wall of fear that usually exists between students and teacher." Twenty-two-year-old Ocean Hill-Brownsville teacher Barry Ernstoff "jolted his students," as *Time* imagined it, "by jumping rope with them." Committed to breaking students of their "slave mentality" and "agonized attitudes of inferiority," the Columbia graduate and New York University student explained, "We've got to humanize ourselves. Black kids are cynical about any white person's caring for them, and little by little, through affection and honesty, we've got to break that down."[39]

At the prestigious and mostly white Bronx High School of Science, twenty-three teachers crossed UFT picket lines. Their "Liberation School," was governed by a committee of eight teachers and eight students whose decisions were subject to ratification by daily assemblies of all students and teachers. They were convinced that eliminating bureaucratic regulation was a crucial element in creating "that tonic feeling of self-government" and heralding wider social transformation. Students chose their own classes each day; some met in hallways to break down the authority of the classroom. "The corridor," according to one visitor, "said a great deal about the new Science. There is a line painted down the middle, to keep traffic moving on either side; no one was observing it now." A bulletin board proclaimed, "IMAGINATION TAKES POWER." Unlike the temporary school conducted by striking UFT teachers in a nearby Jewish Community Center, Liberation School teachers made no promise to test students on the material covered in class.[40] The values shaping the Bronx Science Liberation School were manifest in its proclamation of solidarity with blacks demanding community control. "The Ocean Hill community is trying to determine its destiny free of the New York City bureaucracy" and "to make its schools relevant to present-day life," Bronx Science teachers and students claimed, "*and so are we.*"[41]

As one Ocean Hill-Brownsville teacher argued,

> When a system gets as big as this city's has, then it is necessary to set up rigid controls and categories to maintain order and control the system. In smaller groups like [Ocean Hill-Brownsville], answerable to the immediate community, there is more freedom—and only with freedom can there be education.[42]

"We are not automatized here," echoed J.H.S. 271 teacher Martin Rachels, "because we're not required to serve a [bureaucratic] system—just the children." By insisting on a centralized union and school system, the UFT, in the eyes of New Leftists, betrayed the children in the schools. "We all get along here," Ocean Hill teacher Floyd Sparrow claimed, "because we all answer to the same authority—the needs of the children—not to some petty or absurd demand of a system."[43]

New Leftists challenged UFT claims that bureaucratic forms of "due process" protected all teachers. During the school crisis, they counted hundreds of teachers who were transferred involuntarily without the union interceding on their behalf. They pointed to cases like that of junior high school teacher Michael Levien, who was told by his principal not to return to the school after he had helped students organize an anti-Vietnam protest off of school grounds. After the UFT leadership declined to exert pressure on the principal, parents sympathetic to the teacher staged a sit-in and won him back his job.[44] On the other hand, when a Harlem junior high school teacher each week awarded to his best behaved student a banana, "due process" protected his job because, as Robert Rossner noted, his racist actions violated no explicit school rules.[45]

The New Left analysis of the school conflict drew on three crucial points. Like the Old Left supporters of community control, New Leftists argued that the UFT walkout was not a strike. New Leftists also argued however that teachers did not occupy a working-class position in society and that the role of schools in oppressing students precluded teachers from portraying their actual work as productive labor.

Although New Leftists tended to think of themselves as pro-union, they rejected the legitimacy of the UFT's actions. A group of Bronx Science teachers leafleted their striking colleagues: "This strike, in contrast with our earlier actions, is *not* a struggle of Labor against Management. It is rather a struggle in which both Labor and Management, fearfully defending the *status quo*, are allied against legitimate and necessary change."[46]

New Leftists argued that the UFT's alliance with school administrators reflected teachers' privileged social position. English teacher Sandra Adickes, who had been active in the UFT from the organization's founding, helped open closed schools on Manhattan's Lower East Side and quit the union during the 1968 strike. When the UFT was formed in 1960, Adickes argued, "the traditional trade union concept . . . was relevant. We were making $4800 a year and the union did a good job in improving conditions." The very success of the UFT changed teachers:

They live in their little worlds, in middle-class enclaves. They automatically see blacks as hostile. They know blacks have suffered and they are afraid they are going to take it out on them. They know they are mediocre, that they are not doing a good job. They think someone is going to find out and get them out. . . . There's no pioneering trade union spirit here any more. It's all bread and butter, salaries and working conditions and job security.[47]

New York's teachers, echoed militant junior high school teacher Dave Silver, were "increasingly suburban . . . middle-class in "outlook and orientation, if not in dollars. . . . The fear of radical change . . . and [of] where their position would be at that point . . . will subdue any feelings of conscience." [48] "A narrow, 'careerist' view of self-interest corrupted the UFT," echoed Charlie Isaacs, "and forced it to oppose quality education in order to protect its membership."[49]

Like Sandra Adickes, Bronx Science teacher Robert Rossner quit the UFT because of its opposition to community control. Comparing teachers to an imagined steel-mill worker with a home, two cars and a pleasure boat, Rossner suggested the synthesis of condescension and compassion which informed New Leftists' notions of proper teacher-proletarianism and their critique of teachers' privileged social status and work. "In America," Rossner argued,

a new phenomenon has come into being: the laboring middle class . . . [whose members] spend [their] time in fear that the underclass will take away what [they've] gotten. [Their] attitudes are as middle class as [their] possessions. The trade union movement has been wildly successful. . . . In short, Old Left has become New Right.[50]

Similarly, in the New Left magazine *Ramparts*, Sol Stern argued that in the UFT's early years, "it was the most adventuresome, the most socially conscious New York teachers who fought the union's battles and took the chances. . . . The teachers with civil service mentalities, those most concerned about job security, were the ones who crossed the picket lines. Today the situation is reversed. . . . it is the radicals who break the picket lines. It is the conservatives, afraid of the black community, panicked about their jobs, who shout 'scab' at those who oppose the strike."[51]

Along with their social and economic privilege, teachers' role in the schools shaped the politics of their work. New Leftists argued centralized bureaucratic institutions were a major obstacle to freedom and that American politics had come to be defined by the divide splitting those who ran the state bureaucracy from those whom it oversaw. The schools were fundamentally oppressive to youth, organized not for learning but for social control. Teachers, according to this argument, enforced the regime of the bureaucratized school system, and the deadening, centralized school bureaucracy infiltrated every aspect of teaching.

Bronx Science teacher Robert Rossner suggested the mind and spirit-killing quality of teaching in a contrast between students and teachers at a 1968 anti-war march:

hundreds of teenagers in a ragged line, carrying signs, chanting, even singing—at any given moment, two songs are in the air at once. A smaller group, older, forms its own uneven cluster nearby, more huddled than the youngsters, moving determinedly but keeping its collective eye on the larger group. No singing from them; strictly listeners.

Even the most radical, anti-institutional teachers, according to Rossner, dressed "sedately" and carried their picket signs "with an academic joylessness."[52]

The New Left *Guardian* was far more hopeful about the actions of teenagers than the work of teachers. The newspaper reported excitedly that within weeks of the end of the teachers strike, high school attendance fell by forty percent as tens of thousands of students went out on a strike of their own. Meanwhile roving bands of high school guerrillas blocked subway lines and attacked schools. At Brooklyn's Clara Barton High School, teenagers beat up the principal and threw furniture out of windows; at Haaren High School in Manhattan, they set off explosions that destroyed the auditorium and two classrooms.[53]

The New Left's attitude was manifest in underground student newspapers. "The main thing that's taught us in school," wrote *New York High School Free Press* editor Howie Swerdloff, "is how to be good niggers, obey the rules, dress in our uniforms, play the game, and . . . DON'T BE UPPITY!"[54] Fourteen-year-old John Jay High School student Alice De Rivera reported to the underground *Leviathan* that she had discovered during the teachers strike and its aftermath that "school was a prison—we were required by state law to be there, but when we were there we had no rights."[55] Referring to the number of high school students enrolled in city schools, another underground paper captured the tenor of the times with the headline, "Free the New York City 275,000."[56] Through its critique of bureaucracy, the New Left invented a means with which to assert that racially oppressed blacks and privileged college students shared an interest in radical social change. It gave little hint, however, what students should do once they graduated. Rather than critiquing the school as prison metaphor, New Left teachers embraced it.

One-time UFT staff member Maurice Berube synthesized the New Left's critique of teachers' privileged social status and its critique of the oppressive nature of schooling. The UFT and its social democratic supporters, Berube argued, "have pictured an America where class friction exists mainly between the haves (rich and corporations) and the have-less (the well off working class and the working poor)." In reality, Berube charged, the battle over community control and school politics more broadly did not reflect the UFT's "schemata:"

[the] liberal public school system was not the corporation of early capitalist America; its managers were former teachers and union members, and it relied on the professionalism of the union. What class warfare has now emerged has been Weberian: between the elitism of professionals in unaccountable welfare state bureaucracies and the client welfare and working-class poor without power.[57]

Racial divisions, rather than those separating proletarians from their bosses, separated teachers from students. "The only members of the lower classes in America today," Robert Rossner argued, "are the unemployed and the [non-]unionized—which means, essentially, the nonwhites."[58] Teacher Sandy Nystrom, who came to Ocean Hill after organizing in Sunflower County, Mississippi, charged that UFT opposition to community control had "done harm . . . not just [to] this community, but to all black people trying to take care of their business."[59]

Convinced of teachers' privileged status and of the oppressive nature of schools, New Leftists were unable to articulate a rationale for their work as teachers. In the aftermath of the strike, the contradiction between the educational and social ideals he brought to school and his daily work within the institution left JHS 271 teacher Stephen Bloomfield wondering

> whether being a radical and a teacher are terms that are mutually exclusive. . . . When a group of radicals meets to discuss the institutionalized educational bureaucracies of New York City, the conclusions reached are that the role of radicals should be to destroy the system. The same conclusions are reached by a group of radicals who happen to be teachers.[60]

La Vérité, l'Apre Vérité

Despite their efforts, New Left teachers could not create a liberatory schooling. In part, any tonic feeling of liberation was tempered by the bitter realization that the strikes' inevitable end would signal the return of the academic *Ancien Régime*.[61] School conditions also discouraged New Leftists, just as they did more experienced teachers. At Ocean Hill's P.S. 178, Liz Fusco and her colleagues worked in classrooms with cracked and missing blackboards, broken widow-panes or no widow shades, inadequate equipment, and debris-filled hallways. The school's old, coal-burning furnaces worked so poorly that inside temperatures at times reached as low as 38 degrees.[62]

Were school conditions not enough to dishearten novice teachers, citywide attacks on community control and the menacing presence of police battalions further distracted teachers from thinking creatively about education. In Ocean Hill-Brownsville, the police were stationed

> on the streets, on the roofs, in the school and in our meetings. . . . The children had to squeeze through police barricades in order to reach the front door. . . . More than one parent was beaten for insisting that she be allowed to bring her child into school.[63]

The actions of fellow educators also isolated New Leftists and heightened their ambivalence about teaching. Although strikes by public employees were illegal in New

York, UFT teachers enjoyed solid support from school administrators. Some district superintendents even paid striking teachers during the strike, while delaying the pay of working teachers.[64] Interactions with striking teachers were even more troubling. Pinned to a locked door by a "screaming, maniacal crowd of teachers" as she sought to cross a UFT picket line, Vivian Stromberg was "terrified. . . . There was something very charged and hysterical about the UFT and the names I was called, like 'nigger lover,' and 'Go back to Russia.'" The strike, Stromberg remembers, "was very racist and very disgusting, very anti-community, which felt like it was anti-me."[65]

Meanwhile, black students, parents and colleagues, recognizing perhaps better than white teachers that the rules of the larger academic contest were created neither in isolated alternative classrooms nor in experimental districts, resisted some innovation.[66] John Casey began his teaching career at a South Queens elementary school during the teachers' strikes. His students knew "they were not in their real classes, with this makeshift organization and this makeshift teacher who doesn't know what he is doing." But for these students, the absence of authority was an excuse to be wild, not an opportunity to be free. As Liz Fusco would recollect, "We had no idea of how *gradually* to move from authoritarianism to liberatory education. We *played* anarchy, and we got it!"[67] Students at DeWitt Clinton High School, a ghetto neighborhood school near Bronx Science, lacked the faith that their school could be liberated. In the words of one student leader, it was "just a prison anyway."[68]

In their efforts to concoct an egalitarian and participatory pedagogy, New Left teachers downplayed the importance of professional expertise. Instead, they relied on their own academic achievements, hard work, and charisma. John Casey "brought the content and attitudes" of graduate study in anthropology and linguistics to his elementary school classroom. He stayed at school until 5 o'clock and then visited kids at home or brought them to his house. He spent weekends with them. And yet, he remembers, such dedication did little to alter the nature of schooling: Come "Monday, they bust my balls. . . . What was amazing was how much the kids were extremely well-organized to be against me."[69]

Despite their efforts to efface the teacher's authority and their disdain for their veteran colleagues, the New Left teachers often fell back on the very pedagogical practices they condemned. Although Ocean Hill-Brownsville instituted a few progressive experiments, district teachers, according to Joseph Featherstone, relied "heavily on phonics, reading workbooks and programmed learning materials." Similarly, *New York Times* education writer Fred Hechinger reported that Ocean Hill's young teachers relied on "conservative methods, tight discipline and the advice of the handful of experienced teachers on the staff." Liberal *New York Post* columnist Murray Kempton expected to see Swahili and Karate lessons in Ocean Hill but instead found a social studies teacher "writing questions on the blackboard about British tax policy on the colonies in 1763." Even militant teacher Charles Isaacs conceded that "although innovation is a major purpose of decentralization, we have a basically traditional program."[70]

The end of the strike simultaneously confirmed the distance separating New Left-ists from their colleagues and reinforced the barriers to the development of a libera-tory pedagogy. The return of the UFT teachers inaugurated a range of harassments, petty and large. A UFT teacher interrupted Charles Isaacs's lesson, faced his class and belched.[71] At Bronx Science, the UFT chapter steering committee voted that the names of teachers who crossed the picket line "be posted on the UFT Bulletin Board for the future reference of the Faculty."[72] A Brooklyn junior high school principal ac-cused teachers who had entered the school during the strike of having "called into question this spirit of loyalty and the family feeling that I have always talked about." She had a stenographer record the teachers' explanations.[73]

New Leftists were convinced post-strike hostilities did not reflect the momentary passions of hostile teachers and administrators but rather exposed the oppressiveness of school itself. "After the strike," John Casey would remember,

> they put me as an assistant teacher to this guy who was a control monster. . . . He's telling me the secrets of the system; he's telling me things I don't want to know—how to abuse kids, corral them, make them stay busy, his dreams of working in a white school.[74]

According to High School Independent Press (HIP) Service correspondent Pasha Brant, the end of the strikes signaled the return of cut slips, late passes, detention lists, absence notes, "the right color permission-to-piss slips," and "disciplinary deans who have had no outlets for their hostility hang-ups."[75] Even when John Casey had his students "focused" and his classroom looking like school, "that was not enough." He "knew" that the class "was probably a death trap. . . . The kids were all going to die—socially, to get wiped out. I was not going to solve the problem and the school was not going to solve that problem. And I knew that." Casey could see "all those little pieces of structure that most teachers use to hold the kids together," but instead of relying on such techniques, he "was anxious to blow them up." What Casey lacked was an alternative. "Very overwhelmed," Casey was left with feelings of isolation and entrapment.[76]

Conclusion

Teacher Frederick Rutberg explained his having crossed the UFT picket lines as "an illegal act, which I consider an act of civil disobedience. It is a personal action; it is deep in one's soul and has to be fulfilled." The teachers who crossed UFT picket lines, Rutberg added, "were not acting as a group but as individuals. . . . We were not being a union and not being an organization."[77] Vivian Stromberg relied on the same quintessentially American belief in the autonomy and power of the individual to condemn UFT president Al Shanker's leading teachers against community control. "Like most other people," Stromberg argued, "most teachers . . . follow. If the leadership had had a broader view and was less grasping for power, teachers would have followed that."[78]

The same purity of purpose that drove New Left teachers to cross UFT picket lines during the teachers' strike and to condemn their colleagues drove many of them to leave the public schools soon thereafter. John Casey remembers "incredible loneliness . . . high absentee rate, drug insanities. People got very alienated very fast." The five friends with whom Casey went through the Board of Education's special training program were all gone by the end of their first year in teaching. Casey himself lasted a year and a half, but "emotionally every day" he "cried to get out." Together with Liz Fusco and Sandra Adickes, he went on to become a professor of education.[79] Charles Isaacs took a job at a community college; Robert Rossner left teaching to become a writer.[80]

New Left teachers' faith in the capacity of the individual, like their ability to see the brutalities committed against kids and to imagine Utopian alternatives, reflected in no small part their own advantages and blinded them to teachers' modest efforts to combat school dehumanization. As Joseph Starobin argues, the New Left

> when confronted by setback or by the slowness in the diffusion of its message among the less swiftly moving mass, looks for the explanation within itself, as though the cure lies in self-purification and as though by some heroic voluntarism, some great act of will, the process of historical change can be forced forward. . . . [This] impatience with humble and ordinary people . . . becomes a form of elitism, because the New Left believes that everything can be accomplished by self, a heightened sensibility, and by defiance of history.[81]

Ironically, the New Left's utopian visions of egalitarian deinstitutionalization heralded right-wing visions of deregulation in the service of privilege that fueled American politics in the decades that followed.[82] Christopher Jencks's almost cynical embrace of vouchers suggests the ambiguities of the New Left stance. Responding to the conflict over community control, Jencks argued that schools could do little to affect the academic achievement of poor black students. Still, he claimed, a voucher program "would diffuse the present attack on professional control over the public system."[83] "Whether they are made by Christopher Jencks, by Paul Goodman, or by Milton Friedman," Al Shanker ridiculed, market "solutions" to educational problems suggest that if we "dismantle the public school system and turn it over to competition . . . all of the sudden, it will become great. . . . Everybody will be happy and everything will be fine."[84]

No doubt, a certain romanticism infused the New Left critique of schooling. Still, as educational historians Robert Lowe and Harvey Kantor have suggested, eliminating oppressive bureaucratic structures as well as unequal resources is a prerequisite to fulfilling the democratic promise of public schools.[85] Idealism, impatience, self-absorption and social privilege all shaped the New Left, and all contributed to New Leftists' absolute faith, against all sociological evidence and all the barriers erected by schooling, that all kids could know "bread and roses and peace and all the splendid possibilities of life."[86]

Chapter 6

The Case Against Community: Bayard Rustin and the Black Proletariat

There is no shame in running, even by night, from disaster.
— HOMER, THE ILIAD[1]

On April 6, 1968, Bayard Rustin received the United Federation of Teachers' John Dewey Award, acknowledging the civil rights leader's incalculable contributions to progressive social activism. A founder of CORE and close associate of Martin Luther King, Jr., Rustin had helped invent the Freedom Rides and had organized the celebrated 1963 March on Washington. Throughout the 1940s and 1950s, he was a leading American pacifist. At the same time, Rustin was the protege of black labor leader A. Philip Randolph and eloquently urged activists to fight poverty as well as racism. "More than anyone else in the postwar era," comments historian John D'Emilio, Rustin "was a bridge linking the African American freedom struggle, peace campaigns, and a socialist vision of economic democracy."[2]

Despite Rustin's long record at the forefront of the African American freedom struggle, by 1968 he had come to conclude that blacks would gain more by aligning themselves with the labor movement than from protests reflecting their racial identity and particular concerns. Moreover, Rustin insisted, just as politics should address economic structures of inequality that transcend race, learning should focus on the search for universal truth. Amid the rancor of the school conflict, this dual commitment to economic democracy and the integrationist ideal isolated Rustin from the vast majority of black activists. Severing ties with old allies, he became one of the UFT's few prominent black supporters in 1968.[3]

Rustin's arguments, grounded in decades of struggle, failed to stem the growing appeal of nationalism among black school activists and the declining hopes for school integration among activists and policymakers alike. And yet, no less than advocates of community control, Rustin addressed the quandary that confronted all black activists once America's commitment to racial equality reached its limits and then begun to recede. The issues Rustin faced—about the relative power of race and class in shaping black life, about the ideal of racial integration in a society that has repudiated it—continue to perplex Americans of good will. This chapter explores the evolution of Rustin's thinking as he struggled with the limitations of race-based politics and pedagogy and of school reform itself in the quest to create social justice for urban youth.[4]

Blacks, Schools, and the Civil Rights-Labor Coalition

As was befitting a talk to teacher unionists upon receiving an award named after John Dewey, Rustin attempted to synthesize pedagogical and social issues in his acceptance speech. He began by attributing to one of his own schoolteachers the expansion of childhood horizons circumscribed by "a home where there was no father" in a community where blacks were segregated. The role of the teacher, as of the political activist, Rustin concluded, was not to affirm the particularities we inherit. Rather, where Dewey's democratic educational theory converged with "the creative labors of the American teacher," education had the possibility of "liberating one from the prison of one's inherited circumstances."[5]

Rustin based his assessment of teachers' work on the belief that all Americans could participate in a shared political life and culture. He discounted the notion that racism had created mutually incomprehensible and hostile worldviews that separated those outside the mainstream from those inside it. Rather, teachers needed to replace "distorted, biased and ultimately racist" versions of American history with accounts that recognized the "notable contributions" of African Americans to the nation's progress. Such an effort, Rustin argued, would "foster the ideal of communication and compassion among all the young people of our society" and enable all students "to know the truth and to be free." The act of teaching was thus "an integral part of the effort to bring about social change and social justice in our society."[6]

Still, Rustin reminded UFT members, classwork did not exhaust teachers' responsibilities. Inadequate funding and sterile bureaucracies invited student failure. Moreover, Rustin argued, students learn to the degree that they have the opportunity to use the knowledge they accumulate.[7] Civil rights movement victories over legally sanctioned segregation had not transformed the circumscribed lives of ghetto blacks, and the automation of industrial work was eliminating the jobs where blacks were concentrated. Only by eliminating "poverty and the problems it creates" would all students share the prospect of productive work and decent lives which generates the will to learn.[8]

Rustin warned his audience that their fate as teachers was inseparable from that of their dispossessed students and promised that social reform would liberate them as well as their pupils. Teachers had to join organized campaigns to transform conditions in both school and society. Only "a coalition between teachers, trade unions, and parent groups," he told the UFT, could "make educational . . . bureaucracies and . . . authorities more accountable" and force changes in the wider social order. Only with such changes would teachers "achieve their full effectiveness and their full potential as professionals."[9]

The Dewey Award speech amplified Rustin's ongoing concern about the role of education in the elimination of racial inequality. Situating educational issues in the fluid political, race, and class relations of the 1960s, he was convinced that black educational progress depended on wider social change and that such change depended on the ability of blacks to ally themselves with progressives among the white majority. His appeal to teacher-unionists to work for social justice thus paralleled his conviction that black school activists needed to maintain ties to the labor movement.

In an earlier age, Rustin argued, immigrants with "a minimal public education" could "find jobs and become part of the productive system." At the time of the school crisis, however, the "automation revolution" left "no room for the uneducated or the semi-skilled." An awareness of this unprecedented need for education, Rustin maintained, "is why the schools have become a primary target of the ghetto activist."[10]

If school reform was the right issue for black activists, community control of curriculum and teacher employment by neighborhood school boards was the wrong strategy.[11] It gave "priority to the issue of race precisely at a time when," with the abolition of legally enforced segregation, "the fundamental questions facing the Negro and American society alike are economic and social."[12] The allure of community control, Rustin argued, reflected the difficult political conditions that confronted black activists in the late 1960s. After a period during which civil rights advances had fed black hopes, America's commitment to racial equality had lost much of its force. As "the pendulum of history" began "to swing downward" toward reaction,[13] black expectations for racial justice shriveled into despair. African Americans responded with "a turning inward" heralded by calls for Black Power.[14]

Community control, in Rustin's eyes, exemplified this new "politics of frustration."[15] Grounded in the "psychological" need for pride in black identity,[16] it offered the illusion of "political self-determination in education"[17] to those "so alienated that they substitute self-expression for politics."[18] Like the earlier separatist movements of

Booker T. Washington and Marcus Garvey,[19] community control and black national-ist politics more broadly "derives not from liberal theory but from the heritage of con-servatism. It is the spiritual descendant of states rights."[20] When stripped of the mili-tant rhetoric that "so often camouflages its true significance," community control institutionalized "one of the worst evils in the history of this society—segregation" and legitimized "the idea that segregated education is in fact a perfectly respectable, perfectly desirable, and perfectly viable way of life in a democratic society."[21]

Such an approach was incapable of meeting the real needs of African Americans. Relying on a lumpenized "black slum proletariat"[22] that lacked the leverage of an in-dustrial working class to exact concessions from society, Black Power invocations of anti-colonial struggle in the ghetto could not "create the preconditions for successful, or even authentic, revolution."[23] Rather, such calls were "utopian for the . . . obvious reason that one-tenth of the population cannot accomplish much by itself."[24] A mi-nority "can only be protected by legal safeguards," Rustin warned. "Before we are per-mitted to impose our will on the majority of Americans we will be crushed."[25]

Even within the black community, Rustin argued, the separatist fantasy of commu-nity control inhibited the struggle for social equality. Discounting working-class pro-ponents of community control, Rustin charged that the leadership of

> the fight for the Negro to completely take over the schools in the ghetto is not the working poor . . . it is not the proletariat. . . . This is a fight on the part of the educated Negro middle class to take over the schools . . . not in the interest of black children, or a better educational system, but in their own interest because they have nowhere to go economically.

Much like projects of ghetto-based black capitalism, community control "deepen[ed] the class conflict within the Negro community" and thus subverted the very commu-nity it invoked. [26]

Whereas advocates of community control echoed the rhetoric of segregation and the logic of class privilege, teachers, according to a pro-UFT advertisement orga-nized by Rustin, demanded "the rights that black workers have struggled and sacri-ficed to win for generations." These rights, due process, job security, and "the right of every worker to be judged on his merits—not his color or creed," were "crucial to Negro advancement."[27]

Community control, Rustin concluded, constituted "a giant hoax . . . being perpe-trated upon black people by conservative and 'establishment' figures." Educators and black parents alike needed to realize that a local school board without "real power, de-mocracy, and the funds to carry out new programs" could not "substantially affect the educational system."[28] And even real power and money would not be enough. "Unless there is a *master plan* to cover housing, jobs, and health, every plan for the schools will fall on its face."[29]

Blacks, Rustin argued, could secure the resources needed to initiate such a master plan only in coalition with other aggrieved Americans. Because quality of life is determined by "the economic and social nature of our institutions,"[30] blacks needed to ally themselves with the institution that most forcefully defended working-class people's economic and social conditions—organized labor. By contrast, the separatism exemplified by the movement for community control was

> the opposite of self-determination, because it can lead only to the continued subjugation of blacks. Real self-determination can only be achieved by a unified black movement joining with other progressive social forces to form a coalition that represents a majority of the population.[31]

Bayard Rustin and the African American Freedom Struggle

Rustin's powerful defense of the UFT and critique of community control estranged him from most black activists in 1968. For decades, though, he had helped shape the main currents of the African American freedom struggle.

Born in 1911, Rustin was raised by his grandparents in West Chester, Pennsylvania. Even as a child, Rustin was both immersed in black politics and culture and exposed to the most tolerant segments of white American society. His grandmother was a community leader and an early member of the NAACP. W. E. B. DuBois, James Weldon Johnson and Mary McLeod Bethune were among the prominent black activists who stayed at Rustin's childhood home when passing through West Chester. The area of Rustin's youth was also home to many Quakers, and school field trips included visits to buildings that had once served as stations in the Underground Railroad.[32]

As a young man in the 1930s, Rustin moved to Harlem. Like the West Chester of Rustin's childhood, Depression-era Harlem exposed Rustin to the cutting edge of black political and cultural life and the segments of white America most receptive to racial equality. Rustin acted with Paul Robeson and sang with Josh White. Through philosopher, progressive educator, and Harlem Renaissance luminary Alain Locke, he met such literati as Langston Hughes and Richard Wright. Locke moreover was a role model for Rustin, a gay man who did not advertise his homosexuality but made no effort to deny it.[33]

Rustin's politics fused commitments to pacifism, socialism and black equality. In the 1930s, when the Communist Party led the fight against racism, Rustin organized a Young Communist League campaign against racial discrimination in the military.[34] Then, following the Nazi invasion of the Soviet Union, the Party backtracked on its commitment to pacifism and racial equality. Disillusioned with the Communists,

Rustin began working for black Socialist labor leader A. Philip Randolph, whose Harlem offices were, in Jervis Anderson's phrase, "the political headquarters of black America."[35]

After Randolph introduced Rustin to the ideas of Mahatma Gandhi, Rustin wedded the philosophy of nonviolent direct action to his analysis of race and class relations. He helped found CORE, and even after the United States entered World War II, Rustin crisscrossed the country proselytizing pacifism. Convicted of resisting wartime military conscription, Rustin continued to lead direct action protests against segregation within federal prisons.[36]

Over the years, Rustin became the preeminent organizer of the civil rights movement. He helped run Randolph's 1941 and 1948 campaigns against discrimination in war industries and the military.[37] During the Montgomery bus boycott, Rustin emerged as an influential advisor to Martin Luther King, Jr., and in the late 1950s he helped organize a series of school integration demonstrations that drew thousands of protestors, in ever larger numbers, to Washington.[38]

Rustin's organizing career climaxed with the 1963 March on Washington, which he directed. The 1963 March echoed the school integration demonstrations of the 1950s in several ways. It simultaneously confirmed the vital role of unionized black workers in the African American freedom struggle and heralded the eclipse of labor leaders by community-based ministers as the movement's preeminent leaders. The growing visibility of churches and liberal, white organizations in the 1950s Washington protests suggested that the achievement of civil rights for all was a moral rather than an economic problem and that its solution would entail few costs to white Americans. Finally, in 1963 as in earlier years, protest leaders embraced anti-Communism in efforts to win support for civil rights.[39]

For all its continuities with earlier protests, however, the 1963 March signified a turning point in Rustin's thought; even as the movement attracted an increasingly broad coalition of supporters, Rustin became increasingly convinced of the need to move beyond demands for civil rights. By 1963, he argued, the "legal . . . foundations of racism in America" had "virtually collapsed,"[40] and economics had replaced race as the most fundamental determinant of blacks' lives.[41] Nevertheless, de facto segregation was spreading in northern schools and slums, and black unemployment was growing.[42] Despite civil rights victories, living conditions of the "great masses of Negroes in the north" were deteriorating.[43]

In the face of these changes, Rustin's proposal for the 1963 March focused solely on economic demands.[44] Although these concerns were honored in the Washington protest's official demand for jobs as well as freedom, class issues faded from prominence during organizing. Martin Luther King, Jr. and many other black leaders, together with liberal white organizations, were committed to the call for civil rights legislation, and civil rights inspired mid-1960s protestors far more than organized labor. Moreover, March organizers included few unionists who might have seconded

Rustin's efforts. Although the UAW supported the March, AFL-CIO president George Meany and eighteen of twenty AFL-CIO executive council members refused to endorse it, and when two hundred activists met to plan the protest, no AFL-CIO representative attended.[45]

Even though the March on Washington failed to highlight class politics, Rustin remained convinced that a progressive coalition could be built upon black demands for full inclusion in American life and labor's demands for economic justice. In its own interest, organized labor would recognize that it could not "hold its own in a reactionary society without embracing the interests of the minority groups because capital is too strong for labor alone."[46] Furthermore,

> [Negro] struggle may have done more to democratize life for whites than for blacks. . . . It was not until Negroes assaulted *de facto* school segregation in urban centers that the issue of quality education for *all* children stirred into motion.

"The task of molding . . . out of the March on Washington . . . a political movement" of blacks, trade unionists, liberals and religious groups, Rustin concluded, "is not simple, but no alternatives have been advanced."[47]

As Rustin hoped, the African American freedom struggle did spread north following the 1963 March. Instead of a new liberal coalition, however, the northern movement adopted the disciplined, nonviolent approach of the triumphant southern one. Hundreds of thousands of northern protestors participated in a series of school boycotts from the fall of 1963 through the spring of 1964.[48] Of these, far and away the largest took place in New York City. Confronted with the monumental task of organizing the protest, boycott leader Rev. Milton Galamison called on Rustin to coordinate the action. More than 400,000 New Yorkers participated in a one-day boycott of segregated schooling, and Rustin called the boycott "just the beginning of a massive popular movement against the many forms of segregation, discrimination and exploitation that exist in this city."[49] New York's newspapers were astounded both by the numbers of black and Puerto Rican parents and students who boycotted and by the complete absence of violence or disorder from the protestors. It was, as a sympathetic newspaper account accurately reported, "the largest civil rights demonstration" in American history.[50]

Arguing that "the movement to integrate the schools will create far-reaching benefits" for teachers as well as students, school boycotters had counted heavily on the UFT urging members not to cross picket lines. On December 18, 1963, Milton Galamison appeared before the UFT Executive Board to urge that the union join the boycott or ask teachers to respect picket lines. The union, however, declined, promising only to protect from reprisals any teachers who participated. When militant protestors announced a follow-up boycott for March 16, 1964, the UFT refused even to defend boycotting teachers from reprisals.[51] At the time of the 1968 school crisis,

Brooklyn CORE leader Oliver Leeds and Afro-American Teachers Association President Al Vann would cite the UFT's refusal to support the 1964 integration campaign as proof that an alliance between the teachers' union and the black community was impossible.[52]

New York teachers, almost all of whom were white, were not the only traditional allies of the civil rights movement who boycotted the boycott. The protest, with its demand for complete integration of the city's schools—a demand that would require white children to attend schools in black neighborhoods—severely strained the alliance between black integrationists and white liberals.[53] White reaction in turn led to a split among boycott leaders.[54] In a letter to black labor leaders, Rustin accused Galamison of extremism and, together with the national leadership of CORE and the NAACP, he left the boycott coalition,[55] while militants blasted civil rights leaders for capitulating to the white establishment.[56]

Together with the civil rights moderates, Rustin made one last effort to promote school integration through mass protest. Coming in the wake of the boycott, the May 18, 1964 March for Democratic Schools represented a move toward moderation in both its program and its form. The May marchers were addressed by white labor officials—long the object of black protest[57]—and representatives of established, mainstream civil rights organizations, rather than the leaders of New York's grass-roots black school-reform groups, who had directed protestors during the boycotts.[58]

Unlike the boycotts with the demands for complete desegregation, the May action called for no more than "maximum possible" integration.[59] This goal was to be achieved through such modest programs as the construction of larger schools and the replacement of junior high schools with middle schools.[60] "Our purpose," the demonstrators said, is to "separate white people of good will from those who would camouflage their prejudices under the slogan, 'neighborhood schools.'"[61] In response, such groups as the Jewish Labor Committee and the United Federation of Teachers, which refused to endorse the boycotts and their demand for complete integration, endorsed the May rally.[62]

Coming on the heels of a segregationist rally that had drawn 15,000, Rustin promised to attract at least as many.[63] Instead, only four thousand protestors showed up, and the Board of Education was no more responsive to the conciliatory May demonstration than to the earlier, more confrontational boycott.[64] Protest politics had reached a dead-end: moderation, needed to win white allies, immobilized black activism.

For Rustin, the school protests reinforced the lesson of the March on Washington. Community-based black activism had dismantled legal mandates to segregate and won southern blacks their civil rights, but such a strategy had become detrimental to the struggle for equality once citizenship had been won. The concerns of newly enfranchised blacks dictated the invention of new forms of activism and a move "from protest to politics." To Rustin, the "lessons of 1964 [were] clear: public protest alone will not wring meaningful innovations from the Board."[65] School reformers needed "a silent partner in this effort—the teachers' union."[66]

The American Federation of Teachers and its New York local, the UFT, had much to recommend them to Rustin. The union had actively challenged racial segregation of the schools and racism within the labor movement. Even before the 1954 *Brown* decision, the AFT had expelled segregated southern locals while the rival NEA maintained them well into the 1960s.[67] When the UFT went on strike in 1967, it demanded changes in educational policy along with improved wages for its members. Although some activists claimed that UFT proposals would increase teachers' authority at the expense of black students' rights, when the strike concluded, Rustin argued that the union achieved what black protestors had not, "a historic breakthrough in the area of parent-teacher participation in programs to improve our school system."[68]

Still, as a civil rights activist, Rustin seemed as much to have become a silent partner as to have found one. Whereas before 1964 Rustin had operated under the aegis of peace groups and black civil rights and labor organizations, after 1964 he headed the A. Philip Randolph Institute. Conceived by Rustin and social-democratic leader Max Shachtman, the black leader's new organizational base depended financially on the AFL-CIO and the UFT.[69] In February of 1968, UFT organizer Sandra Feldman met with Randolph Institute staff to plan a conference of black teacher unionists. Although the UFT role was to be kept hidden, the conference's "ultimate goal," according to Feldman, was to get the union "some vital black leadership and loyalty."[70] In the midst of the 1968 strikes, the Randolph Institute announced plans to move its offices into the UFT building, where it would be the union's only tenant.[71]

With the African American freedom struggle having moved beyond the dismantling of Jim Crow, Rustin was increasingly caught between the demands of the grassroots activists he hoped to lead and the allies he sought to nurture.[72] Campaigns against job discrimination, ghetto housing conditions, police brutality, and *de facto* school segregation directly implicated the movement's erstwhile white allies and proved as likely to create conflicts with white liberals and unions as to encourage coalitions with them. Rustin sensed the difficulties that activists faced as heightened movement expectations for black freedom hit up against the limited willingness of white America to allow it: "Negroes have been put in a desperate situation, and yet everyone—myself included—must urge them not to behave with desperation but politically and rationally."[73]

The full, tragic implications of the need to face racism "politically and rationally" became manifest in the summer of 1964. After a white police lieutenant killed a ninth grader on his way to summer school, Harlem and Bedford-Stuyvesant erupted.[74] Rustin witnessed the police riots that left hundreds of black New Yorkers bloodied and personally attended the wounded.[75] When Rustin urged blacks to disperse and to resist with nonviolence, they shot back "Uncle Tom! Uncle Tom!" He could have responded that common sense rather than the accommodation of racism recommended against unarmed blacks confronting brutal police. Instead, Rustin answered the jeering crowd from a sound truck, "I'm prepared to be a Tom if it's the only way I can save women and children from being shot down in the street, and if you're not willing to do the same, you're fools."[76]

Behind the scenes, in protracted negotiations with New York Mayor Robert Wagner, Jr., Rustin adopted the same accommodationist approach. The son and namesake of one of the principal architects of New Deal liberalism, Wagner responded to the unrest by condemning "mob rule" but not police brutality. Unable to convince the mayor to address the politically explosive issue of police violence, Rustin settled for Wagner's promise to seek ten million dollars from Washington for a jobs program. Fearful that New York's hotheaded black leaders would merely exacerbate tensions, Rustin recruited Martin Luther King to lend legitimacy to negotiations. The riots, like the school boycott, confirmed the limits that circumscribed black dreams of freedom, and, Rustin told Urban League leader Whitney Young, left him "terribly depressed."[77]

Even as he implored black New Yorkers to avoid violence, Rustin distanced himself from the nonviolence both as a strategy for change and as an expression of Utopian hopes for creating a just society. "Despite thousands and thousands who have gone to jail, despite bombings of churches and people, despite the millions of dollars tied up in bail and the millions paid in fines," he explained in a speech to the Fellowship of Reconciliation, "no breakthrough has occurred in the South and in the North Negroes are being increasingly pushed to the wall." Blacks were turning to violence, he argued, because the nonviolent "tactics that have been advocated and used [were] inadequate for dealing with the objective needs." Rustin concluded by repudiating the philosophy of nonviolence that had guided his work and much of the southern struggle for black freedom. No longer would he "tell any Negroes that they should love white people. . . . They don't love them, they have no need to love them, no basis on which they can love them."[78]

Before 1964, Rustin had imagined that civil rights activism would drive segregationists out of the Democratic Party, and thus move the Party and the labor movement to the left.[79] In the wake of the school protest failures and the New York riots, Rustin began to reorient his politics. He and other moderate civil rights leaders feared that the riots would advance Republican Barry Goldwater's presidential campaign and shatter "the whole climate of liberal democracy in the United States." In response, they called for a moratorium on demonstrations during the 1964 presidential election campaign.[80] Rustin himself severed ties with the peace and civil rights activists and organizations with which he had been associated for twenty years.[81]

Rustin further distanced himself from movement activists at the 1964 Democratic National Convention in Atlantic City. In the months leading up to the convention, the focal point of the civil rights movement had been Mississippi, where blacks excluded from the segregated regular Democratic Party had organized the Mississippi

Freedom Democratic Party. MFDP representatives petitioned the Democratic Party seeking to replace the all-white Mississippi delegation in Atlantic City. "How could we not prevail?" SNCC activist John Lewis would still wonder decades later. "The law was on our side. Justice was on our side. The sentiments of the entire nation were with us." President Lyndon Johnson, however, opposed the activists. Seeking to appease segregationists, the Democrats refused to seat the integrated and integrationist MFDP delegation. For Lewis and countless other activists, Atlantic City was "the turning point of the civil rights movement. . . . Until then . . . the belief still prevailed that the system would work, the system would listen."[82]

Whereas Democratic Party actions at Atlantic City drove many young activists to a more radical stance, the realization that white America would not grant blacks full and equal citizenship drove Rustin away from radicalism. He worked to get the MFDP delegation seated but also discouraged demonstrations that might alienate "[the Negro's] friends in the labor movement and Democratic Party." For his efforts, Rustin earned the thanks of President Lyndon Johnson and Vice Presidential candidate Hubert Humphrey. On the other hand, militant organizers and grass-roots activists were enraged. In the eyes of Bob Moses, Rustin had "flip-flopped," and thereafter remained steadfastly on the "conservative side."[83]

The extent of Rustin's retreat from the quest for black equality and freedom was manifest in a 1966 debate with militant SNCC activist Stokely Carmichael. In response to Carmichael's critique of individual white prejudice and institutional racism Rustin argued that blacks needed to align themselves with a white majority committed to progress.[84] Pushed by Carmichael as to why he had supported the Democratic Party in 1964, Rustin said, President Johnson "was the lesser of two evils."[85]

Political analysis was not the only reason Rustin distanced himself from ideologies of racial identity and from the peace and civil rights movements. Being black in white America circumscribed Rustin's life and shaped his politics, but just as America refused to accommodate fully black demands for equality, the peace movement and black community refused to embrace Rustin fully. He was gay, and for his homosexuality, he suffered the scorn of movement comrades as well as the taunts of Dixicrats.[86]

A.J. Muste loved Rustin like a son, but considered the embarrassment caused by what one peace activist labeled Rustin's "personal problem" grounds for dismissing him from a position at the Fellowship of Reconciliation (FOR). When Rustin was convicted of having sex with two white men in 1953, he dutifully resigned from FOR.[87] Scandalized by Rustin's homosexuality and Communist past, black ministers squelched Martin Luther King, Jr.'s efforts to hire him at the Southern Christian Leadership Conference, at a time when Rustin, almost fifty, was counting on King for a regular salary. When Adam Clayton Powell, embroiled in a political dispute with King, threatened to tell reporters that King was having an affair with Rustin, King broke off all contact with his former advisor.[88]

As Rustin cut his links to the peace and civil rights movement, long-standing personal, intellectual and political ties with social-democratic activists blossomed. Social democracy embraced the Marxist concept that the means of production determined social organization but stressed the gradual achievement of industrial democracy through constitutional means. The ideology was particularly attractive to union officials, and social democrats dominated the leadership of the UFT.[89] Confronted with the inability of black protest to address the economics of inequality, Rustin found in social democracy theoretical justification for a race-blind egalitarian organizing. At the same time, the social democratic vision allowed Rustin to respond to and transcend his multiple identities in his political work.

Theorizing that politics reflected universal laws rather than cultural particulars, American social democrats argued that racial discrimination reflected class relations and should be addressed through the class struggle.[90] In many white socialists, race-blindness served to justify blindness to racism, but Rustin did not overlook the impact of race on American life. An accomplished singer of black spirituals, he had "preached the dignity of black skin color," worn his hair "Afro style," and taught "Negro history" long before such things became popular.[91] Furthermore, he was as convinced as anybody that "freedom in America applies to all but Negroes," that "in a million quiet ways, the majority of white Americans go about insulting the manhood of Negroes every day."[92]

Still, Rustin's analysis of urban education drew on social democratic race-blind theory by focusing on the impact of social and economic forces rather than on the presumed attributes of black students. Rustin challenged the rationales of educational programs based on particular qualities or pathologies imputed to the black family, underclass or culture. "A Negro coming out of Mississippi," he argued, is not "'disadvantaged'" compared to the masses of immigrants who came to American cities from Europe. The white ethnics "did not know American culture; they did not know the language; they adopted the names given them by immigration people on Ellis Island." But because American "society was prepared to use [their] muscle power," these earlier migrants found "jobs and become part of the productive system." By contrast, the blacks who populated America's deindustrializing ghettos in the 1960s remained outside the political, cultural and educational mainstream "even though they [knew] the language and culture of the United States."[93]

Educational programs that sought only to remediate the deficiencies in ghetto youngsters mistook the cultural consequences of poverty for its economic causes.[94] "Until we face the need for a fundamental reordering of our priorities," Rustin reminded educators, school reforms would constitute no more than pseudo-solutions to the crisis of ghetto education. The years leading up to the New York school conflict, he noted, had witnessed the introduction of the middle school, pairing, open enrollment, community control, and more useless maneuvers, one after the other. Meanwhile the objective situation gets worse and worse. . . . Until we are prepared to eliminate slums . . . we are going to have inferior education for Negro children. If we turn the schools over to parents and community leaders, they will be no different. As long as we have slums, as long as we have the kind of housing we have, as long as people are not working, the schools will be inferior. It is amazing to me that anyone can think it possible to create an effective way of teaching a child who lives in a ghetto. He simply will not be educated, no matter what gimmicks you use. It's a matter of fundamental change here or nothing.[95]

"Wearing my hair Afro-style, calling myself an Afro-American and eating all the chitterlings I can find," Rustin maintained, "are not going to affect Congress."[96]

Coalition Politics in Post-Liberal America

Despite Rustin's social-democratic invocation of proletarian solidarity and "fundamental change," he recognized that revolutionary change was not on the horizon in 1968.[97] Congress was no more concerned with economic democracy than it was with racial equality. What distinguished organized labor from the black freedom movement was not its power to secure social justice for African Americans but rather its willingness to embrace the domestic and foreign policy agenda of America's political and economic establishment. At a time when race relations and U.S. actions in Vietnam, rather than industrial conflict, were the defining issues of American politics, Rustin and other social democrats cloaked acquiescence to militarism and racial inequality in the mantle of working-class radicalism.

Rustin, for instance, condemned anti-war protestors,[98] while improbably asserting that the government's unlimited resources allowed it to fund fully a real war on poverty without cutting military funding.[99] As the anti-war movement increasingly questioned the ideological underpinnings of U.S. foreign policy, Rustin became increasingly vehement in the anti-Communism that had been part of politics since he left the Young Communist League. Similarly, he denounced black nationalism at a time when the federal government had made manifest its refusal to protect blacks' constitutional rights or to eradicate black poverty. For Rustin, as for white social democrats, calls for blacks to align themselves with the labor movement marked an abandonment and not an affirmation of radicalism. As Rustin became isolated from old allies, he was ever more strongly allied with the very conservatism he denounced.[100]

Rustin's attempt to build a labor-civil rights coalition in his John Dewey Award speech came at an inopportune moment. Days before he was to address the UFT, a white sniper assassinated Martin Luther King, Jr. in Memphis, and for many black activists, hopes for integration were buried along with King. When Rustin was called to Memphis, Michael Harrington, a white social-democratic comrade, stood in for him at the Hilton Hotel, site of the UFT's award ceremony. As Harrington read Rustin's speech, protestors gathered outside of the Hilton. They demanded that Rustin sever his ties with the UFT and condemned the union's opposition to community control, its "racist attitudes [and] policies against black and Puerto Rican children and communities," and its "refusal to oppose the racist war in Vietnam."[101]

The Hilton Hotel protestors were not alone in their beliefs. In the course of the school conflict, increasing numbers of black unionists, as well as educators, ministers, and community activists, opposed the UFT. Harlem Labor Council and UFT official Richard Parrish, who had worked with Rustin in the Washington protests of the 1940s and 1950s,[102] was among the black labor leaders who embraced community control. Although Parrish believed that by remaining in the UFT, black teachers could help heal the rift between the union and the black and Puerto Rican communities, in a September 15, 1968 television interview, he labeled the UFT opposition to community control "a strike against the black community . . . a collusive action of supervisors, teachers and custodians against black parents and students."[103]

As the teachers' strikes wore on, leading black and Puerto Rican unionists repudiated labor solidarity in favor of a racially defined notion of community. Late in October, two hundred labor leaders, including Parrish and Negro American Labor Council president Cleveland Robinson, identified the families of black and Puerto Rican workers, rather than the teacher unionists, as "the victims of this vicious system." The group supported community control "as a means of ending this nightmare that for too long has existed in our communities without redress." Rather than advancing a labor-civil rights coalition, teacher unionists precluded it.[104]

Conclusion

Although the struggle over community control intensified conflict between black activists and organized labor, African American radicals had criticized coalition with the white labor movement for almost as long as social democrats had advocated race-blind proletarian solidarity.[105] In the mid-1930s, for instance, W. E. B. DuBois accepted the long-term desirability of integration and noted that "black and white work together in many cases, and . . . have similar complaints against capitalists." Still, he argued, black workers'

> lowest and most fatal degree of . . . suffering comes not from the capitalists but from fellow white laborers. It is no sufficient answer to say that capital encourages this oppres-

sion and uses it for its own ends. . . . The exploitation [of the Negro comes] from the white capitalists and equally from the white proletariat.[106]

Rather than casting the fate of African Americans with the white labor movement, DuBois's "Negro Nation within the Nation" program advocated fostering black unity, power, and self-respect through black consumer cooperatives, black schools and other segregated institutions.[107]

By the 1950s, DuBois had moved to a closer association with the white Left, but the McCarthy-era government repression of DuBois, Ben Davis, Paul Robeson and other blacks committed to interracial labor radicalism weakened their influence. The declining power of appeals to proletarian solidarity set the stage for the rise of narrowly nationalistic ideologies that repudiated interracial organizing.[108]

Then, in the 1960s, the New York civil rights movement adopted the very goal Rustin advocated; it made employment a central focus. When it did so however, labor unions were among its most implacable foes. The unions in the building trades were particularly notorious for their exclusionary practices. No blacks or Puerto Ricans, for instance, were among the four thousand members of Pipefitters Union Local 638 working in 1963. Of the more than sixteen hundred members of New York's Metal Lathers Union Local 46, two were black.[109] For the thousands of activists who received their political apprenticeships demonstrating at New York construction sites, unions were targets of black protest rather than allies of activists.[110] In a 1969 survey, blacks felt discriminated against in the building trades by a nine-to-one ratio.[111]

Bayard Rustin was well aware of the limits that confronted the black freedom struggle and of the conflicts that separated black New Yorkers from teachers and rest of organized labor. His own efforts at coalition building in decades at the center of the black freedom struggle had exposed the ambivalence with which white labor greeted black allies. Moreover, as Rustin acknowledged in his UFT award speech, the racial, political, technological, economic, and social changes of the 1960s made the challenges facing the schools "more serious than any Dewey was ever asked to contemplate."[112] Still, he argued, conditions in America and its cities left blacks no real alternative to alliance with organized labor.

Rustin offered a powerful analysis of the often unspoken links between teaching practices, school policies, and broader political concerns. In politics, as in pedagogy, he rejected notions of racially defined identity or "community." Instead, Rustin advocated a movement away from particular concerns toward universal principles of truth and social justice. He remained committed to forging an integrated movement even as many black activists responded to the enduring racism in American society with desperate manifestoes of Black Power.

Still, Rustin's efforts foundered amid the very ghetto conditions and urban conflicts he hoped to address. Although Rustin argued persuasively that the new urban conditions created by automation required a rethinking of racial politics, he never explored the need to rethink labor activism itself in light of economic changes. Blacks were confined to New York's deindustrializing ghettos, while white labor, including the city's teachers, fled the city, distancing itself politically, culturally, and indeed physically from alliance with the black freedom struggle. The movement of teachers and other whites to the suburbs both reflected and propelled UFT's growing power in school politics and black activists' defeats. The very power of the UFT on which, in Rustin's view, blacks ought to depend was thus embedded in the racial inequality black activists confronted. Rustin's phantom of a black-labor alliance, no less than dreams of black separatism, constituted an accommodation with the persistence of racism as well as resistance to it.

Chapter 7

Milton Galamison and the Integrationist Ideal

*. . . when you are harried by day and haunted by night by the fact that you are
a Negro, living constantly at tiptoe stance, never quite knowing what to
expect next, and are plagued with inner fears and outer resentments; when
you are forever fighting a degenerating sense of "nobodiness" — then you
will understand why we find it difficult to wait.*
— MARTIN LUTHER KING, JR.[1]

On July 14, 1968, Reverend Milton Galamison, the forty-five year old pastor of Brooklyn's historic Siloam Presbyterian Church, was appointed by New York Mayor John Lindsay to the city's Board of Education. According to teacher-activist Jitu Weusi, Galamison was "the guru . . . of the educational thrust of the civil rights movement" in New York for most of the 1960s. In the judgment of civil rights advocate Carlos Russell, the minister was one of New York's "most capable, relentless and dynamic proponents of integration."[2]

Just as the Reverend Martin Luther King, Jr. supplanted labor leader A. Philip Randolph as the preeminent figure of the black freedom struggle on the national stage, so too Rev. Galamison, rather than Randolph or Bayard Rustin, was the guiding force of the movement in New York City. Under his leadership, school integration became the central focus of New York activists. In 1964, Galamison headed a school boycott for integration whose size dwarfed the celebrated 1963 March on Washington. Integration was crucial, he argued, not because it would bring equal resources to black students but because democracy demanded it. Few leaders did more than Galamison to inspire grass-roots activism and promote grass-roots leadership. This commitment, together with the New York integration campaign's focus on school children, helped enable women to play an uncommonly large role in the movement Galamison led.

Still, Galamison's Board of Education appointment was a hollow gesture. By 1968, white New Yorkers had successfully turned back the black campaign for racial integration, and black activists were seeking to replace the school system rather than to participate in it. Unlike the appointment of Thurgood Marshall to the United States Supreme Court, which enhanced judicial efforts to promote racial equality, Galamison's presence on the school board heralded no government program to further equal education. Rather than marking the culmination of his career as the preeminent civil rights leader of America's biggest city, Galamison's appointment confirmed his eclipse and that of the movement he had led.

Since the days of slavery, the African American freedom struggle has tested American democracy and been an engine of its expansion. The school integration movement in New York constitutes an important chapter of that history. Whereas today, discussions of racial inequality in education often focus exclusively on test score gaps, for Galamison and his fellow activists, academic standards were only one component of a fundamental, moral issue: what kind of schooling does justice demand? This chapter explores the integrationist ideal, which propelled Galamison's activism and that of the countless New Yorkers whose energies he catalyzed.

Although complacent accounts of the victorious southern civil rights movement of the 1950s and 1960s have become a staple of our national mythology and school curriculum, Americans have demonstrated less interest in the ambiguous legacy of civil rights organizing in the north. Milton Galamison's efforts make clear that the north, like the south, was the scene of well-organized and principled activism. Whereas, however, the elimination of southern Jim Crow vindicates invocations of America's democratic ideals, the unfulfilled hopes of northern civil rights activities discourage any easy optimism. In addition to exploring the integrationist ideal that animated school activism, the chapter explores the abandonment of integrationist hopes and the movement's evolution into the struggle for community control.

New York's Civil Rights Movement

Although the Supreme Court's historic 1954 *Brown* decision focused American attention on school segregation in the South, northern activists were also examining the schools. In New York, the Intergroup Committee on the Public Schools, an alliance of civil rights and civic organizations under the leadership of Kenneth Clark, charged that school policies contributed to separate and unequal education in the city. In response, New York's Board of Education affirmed its commitment to integration and recruited civic leaders to help formulate desegregation plans. The Commission on Integration concluded that along with demographic patterns over which educators had no control, school zoning and staffing policies contributed to the creation of inferior, segregated ghetto schools.[3]

The Intergroup Committee's elite leadership was not New York's only source of school reform. Even before the Supreme Court issued the *Brown* decision and the Board of Education endorsed integration, grassroots Brooklyn activists had launched their own campaign against racial inequality in black schools. In order to bring support and legitimacy to their efforts, NAACP Brooklyn Branch Education Committee Chairman Winston Craig and Committee Statistician Annie Stein approached Rev. Milton Galamison. The head of one of black Brooklyn's leading congregations, Galamison had a reputation for outspokenness and militancy. He was convinced that the Intergroup Committee's civic leaders had "pushed as far as they could push," but that opposition from teachers, administrators, white parents and real estate interests blocked efforts "to get a school desegregation plan. . . . These leaders had no troops," Galamison reasoned, "and, of course, they failed." He embraced the grassroots campaign and in December 1955 was elected Chairman of the Brooklyn NAACP's Education Committee.[4]

By the fall of 1956, the Brooklyn NAACP had enlisted hundreds of parents into its campaign, including officers from sixty-four PTAs. Activists documented decrepit conditions, abbreviated school days, the tracking of black and Puerto Rican students out of academic programs, and abuse from bigoted educators in overcrowded ghetto schools. Frequent meetings publicized the Board of Education's failure to live up to its promises. Mass rallies at Galamison's Siloam Presbyterian Church added pressure on school officials. The Brooklyn Branch quickly achieved an array of successes, winning homework assignments for students, gifted programs, libraries, an after-school program, and, for one school, a new roof.[5]

As Chairman of the NAACP Education Committee and then starting in 1957 as NAACP Brooklyn Branch President, Galamison made J.H.S. 258 a focal point of protests and a litmus test of school board commitments. When the school, located near Siloam, opened in the fall of 1955, virtually all of its students were black. As was the case in ghetto schools throughout New York, J.H.S. 258 was staffed by teachers far less experienced than those working in white schools. Activists documented that conditions at J.H.S. 258 and other ghetto schools were the result of deliberate policies rather than of the impersonal trends of urban demographics. In one case, black and white children living in the same apartment building were zoned to different, segregated schools. Organizers suggested numerous ways of promoting integration.[6]

Whereas black activists were becoming increasingly convinced that the school system actively promoted segregation and unequal education, white liberals highlighted the lamentable role of abstract social forces in isolating black children. School segregation, the *New York Times* complacently editorialized, was "not imposed by any kind of official action but by the brutal facts of housing and neighborhood racial patterns." Although New York school officials professed support for integration, school superintendent William Jansen argued that J.H.S. 258's location and the likelihood of violent resistance from white parents made desegregation "impossible."[7]

When Galamison called for Jansen's resignation, NAACP leader Roy Wilkins and Brooklyn NAACP moderates castigated the minister for having compared race relations in New York to those in the south and for having invoked the group's name in his own irresponsible crusade. In addition to being frustrated by what he perceived as the overly cautious approach of the NAACP and many of its members, Rev. Galamison found such organizational chores as membership campaigns and fund raising to be "distractions" from the work of school integration. Despite the Brooklyn branch's successes, in 1959, Galamison resigned from the NAACP.[8]

Galamison's conflict with NAACP moderates in part reflected the dogmatic anti-Communism that the organization shared with much of America in the 1950s. Although Galamison's politics drew not on communist theory but on "the revolutionary aspects of the gospel," his open sympathy for socialism and Marxism, together with his willingness to work with leftists, exposed the minister to attack. In particular, conservatives in the NAACP condemned Galamison for working with civil rights veteran and radical organizer Annie Stein.[9]

No white person was more intimately involved in the struggle to integrate New York's schools than Stein. Before coming to New York, she had lived in Washington, DC, where she organized black maids with the Domestic Workers Union. Working with the United Public Workers, Stein organized a sit-down at the United States Bureau of Engraving and Printing, where hundreds of black women counted dollar bills. Stein was an early target of Cold War repression; a union officer fired from her federal job during the Truman administration's Loyalty Oath purges was charged, among other things, with knowing Annie Stein.[10]

Forced out of the labor movement, Stein contributed the skills she had honed in union organizing to the emerging civil rights movement. Between 1949 and 1952, she led a campaign to desegregate Washington restaurants, in particular the lunch counters at dime and department stores. Working with veteran black activist Mary Church Terrell, Stein devised a strategy that combined negotiations, boycotts, pickets, and "sit-downs" during which interracial groups would occupy tables and counters at restaurants that refused to serve them.[11]

In 1953, Stein moved to Brooklyn, and she deliberated about how to continue her political work. When Mary Church Terrell advised Stein to join the PTA, Stein, according to historian Clarence Taylor, "was shocked by the suggestion. She saw the PTA as an organization of conservative middle class white women who baked cookies." Nevertheless, trusting Terrell's judgment, Stein joined the PTA. As it turned out, the organization proved to be an ideal site for Stein's organizing and provided a crucial arena for the NAACP campaign against racial inequality in the schools.[12]

Throughout the long campaign to integrate the schools, Stein continued to work closely with Galamison, providing the statistical documentation of racial inequality in schooling on which activists relied.[13] Her single-minded but unobtrusive work earned her uncommon praise from grass-roots black activists. Ironically, then, McCarthyite repression of militant labor organizing contributed much to the emergence of militant grass-roots neighborhood organizing in New York.[14]

Having left the NAACP, Galamison, Stein and other militants started a new school integration organization in 1959. The Parents' Workshop for Equality in New York City Schools brought parents and community activists together for meetings and rallies, often at Siloam. Meanwhile, freed from ideological and organizational constraints, Galamison expanded his efforts. For instance, he addressed the annual meeting of the leftist Teachers Union, an organization that the NAACP considered taboo.[15]

Under Galamison's leadership, the Parents Workshop encouraged women to take on leadership roles, and the group crafted a vision that endowed motherhood with a radical civic purpose. "We mothers, grandmothers, [and] aunts," the Workshop announced in a 1963 appeal for support from black ministers, "must round up our families, friends and neighbors and start now to rectify the ills in our community!"[16] The combination of a cosmopolitan integrationist vision with neighborly, out-of-the-limelight organizing would be the hallmark of the New York integration struggle.

Like the NAACP Brooklyn Branch, the Parents Workshop both campaigned for the creation of integrated schools and protested racist practices—ranging from abusive or violent teachers and separate bathrooms to tracking—within segregated ones.[17] The group also demanded the inclusion of Negro history in the curriculum.[18] Although school administrators professed that they were doing as much as they could, protest made possible what the professionals had asserted was impossible. When the Parents Workshop organized two thousand parents to keep their children out of segregated schools, the Board initiated the Open Enrollment Program, which allowed black students to transfer from overcrowded ghetto schools to under-utilized white ones. "New York responded only to the threats and pressures of the people," Galamison concluded. The "lesson to be learned from this" is "that the only course for the people is social action."[19]

Urging blacks to take advantage of Open Enrollment, the Parents Workshop trumpeted the academic, social and political benefits of integration. To supplement the bare Board of Education list of eligible schools, the Workshop publicized schools' racial breakdowns and reading scores, as well as application deadlines for participation in the program. At first, claiming that "such data [could be] interpreted only by experts," the school authorities refused "to release this type of information to a parents' group." Finally, under Annie Stein's leadership, activists documented what seemed to elude school professionals—black students in New York's increasingly segregated schools suffered massively from educational retardation and the longer they were in the system the further behind they fell.[20]

Still, activists had "serious reservations" about Open Enrollment. Although it allowed individual students to transfer out of ghetto schools, it "was not," as Galamison noted, "a desegregation plan. . . . No white children were transferred to the black community; the whole thing was at the expense of the black children's traveling." Moreover, the program was "frustrated on every side." The Board of Education "never disseminated any material that would be helpful to the parents." Principals in both ghetto and receiving schools "sabotaged" the program by discouraging participation. Even as black applicants were being refused transfers because of an alleged lack of space, the board rented classrooms at an under-utilized white elementary school to a yeshiva. School officials blandly dismissed Galamison's protest against "the creeping encroachment of non-public school interests."[21]

The Parents Workshop also aided countless parents who appealed to Galamison for help in dealing with school personnel. Here too school authorities stymied activists' efforts to improve conditions for black children. When Galamison protested student suspensions and instances of teacher brutality, school administrators responded that his concerns were groundless. Galamison had heard only parents' version of events, assistant superintendent Joseph Noethen explained, and he had "not been given all the facts." Nor would he be given them. "You can imagine what would happen to the school program," Noethen advised, "if every problem required a long explanation to someone outside of the situation."[22]

In addition to hostility from school officials, developments in the wider civil rights movement deepened Galamison's militancy. In the spring of 1962, he joined with one hundred ministers and hundreds of other demonstrators to demand that Brooklyn stores with black customers employ black workers. Proclaiming "This is a Community and Not a Plantation" and "Don't Buy Where You Can't Work," the Ministers Movement organized pickets and boycotts in the Bedford Stuyvesant business district, convincing merchants to hire and promote blacks and to contribute funds to community organizations.[23]

In the wake of the Ministers Movement, Galamison helped spearhead a more ambitious protest campaign. Between July 15 and August 6, 1963, at the very time when the March on Washington was celebrating the dream of integrating America, activists demanded that blacks be among those hired to build Brooklyn's massive Downstate Medical Center. White construction workers commuted to the Downstate project from as far away as Pennsylvania. Meanwhile, many black World War II and Korean War veterans, living in Brooklyn and trained as surveyors and bulldozer operators, were refused employment. Led by the Brooklyn chapter of the Congress of Racial Equality, activists squared off against the city's trade union and political establishment with demands that 25% of construction jobs be reserved for black and Puerto Rican workers. Unable to mobilize sufficient support to sustain the protest, CORE approached clergy to join their effort. On July 15, CORE leader Oliver Leeds, Rev. Galamison, and thirteen other ministers initiated a civil disobedience campaign at

Downstate. Over the next few weeks, the Ministers' Committee for Job Opportunities for Brooklyn rallied thousands of protestors and led hundreds in civil disobedience.[24]

The ministers, who included associates of both Republican Gov. Nelson Rockefeller and Democrat Mayor Robert Wagner, anticipated success. Then, Clarence Taylor suggests, as the demonstrations began attracting protesters without ties to Brooklyn's churches, the ministers sensed that the movement was slipping from their control. They approached Gov. Rockefeller about negotiating a settlement. In a three-hour meeting, Galamison and the other ministers abandoned their demand that blacks and Puerto Ricans get 25% of construction jobs. Although Rockefeller offered only to enforce existing anti-discrimination laws, the ministers agreed to call off the demonstrations. Members of Brooklyn CORE denounced Galamison and the other ministers as "sell outs" and "Uncle Toms," and, as the militants predicted, the settlement failed to produce jobs for blacks. Although Galamison resented CORE's accusations, he became increasingly impatient and uncompromising in the wake of the Downstate debacle.[25]

The bitterness of the Downstate campaign, together with black New Yorkers' deepening distrust of the school system, added militancy to school organizing. In 1963, the Parents' Workshop united with the Harlem Parents Committee, CORE and the NAACP to form an umbrella organization, the City-Wide Committee for Integrated Schools, with Galamison as president. The group threatened a massive school boycott unless the school system moved toward integration.

School authorities responded to the activist threat to their autonomy by announcing plans for yet another study of ways to further school integration. "The acid test of our sincerity," Galamison scoffed, "does not lie alone in the appointment of committees and the cataloguing of recommendations. The test of our sincerity lies in the doing of what needs to be done. For this no study is necessary. The problem is segregation. The answer is desegregation." Finally, the board agreed that by Dec. 1, 1963, it would announce a plan and timetable for the achievement of "substantial integration" by September 1964. When December first came and went with neither plan nor timetable, Galamison recruited Bayard Rustin as lead organizer, and preparation for a February 3, 1964 school boycott began.[26]

Activists distributed hundreds of thousands of fliers, made hundreds of speeches and solicited scores of churches for use as freedom schools. They distributed first aid procedures and curricula, and planned hundreds of picket lines at schools across New York. Despite the massive interest it generated among blacks, however, the boycott was not supported by white liberals who had endorsed Southern campaigns for racial equality. Although boycott leaders counted heavily on the UFT support, the union declined Galamison's request that it urge teachers to honor picket lines.[27]

Increasingly infuriated by what he saw as the duplicitousness of school officials and perhaps remembering the militant critique of ministerial restraint in the Downstate protests, Galamison almost taunted white New York in provocative predictions about the February 1964 protest. "Nobody wants violence," he told one television interviewer on the eve of the boycott, "but once we turn a group of people loose in a demonstration, nobody can be responsible for everybody's conduct." School board president James Donovan seized on Galamison's provocative rhetoric to justify inaction. The board, he vowed, would not "react one inch" to protesters' "lawless course of action." Although school administrators had not appeared concerned when protestors documented violence against black children by teachers, Donovan warned that Galamison would be held criminally liable for any harm to boycotting children.[28]

Organizers predicted 50,000 students absenting themselves from school, but on the bitter cold morning of February 3, 44.8 percent of New York's million students stayed out. If Galamison and Rustin were the visible faces of the boycott, it was black women, together with a few white women who were willing to work under the direction of blacks, who did much of the organizing. At the boycott's Brooklyn and Harlem headquarters, dozens of women took calls and gave instructions to picket captains and other boycotters. Women also prepared meals for hundreds of thousands of boycotting children and made up for what activists termed a "shortage of men" on picket lines at hundreds of schools.[29]

In some places educators supported the boycott. George Washington High School principal Henry Hillson, whose anti-racist activism dated back to his days as a Teachers Guild leader and high school teacher during World War II, sent coffee to warm protestors picketing his Manhattan school. At JHS 103 in Harlem, more than half of the teachers joined 1333 of 1415 students in boycotting school. Said teacher Jeanne Robinson, "It's worth it to lose a day's pay and earn a lifetime of dignity and self-respect." School superintendent Calvin Gross was less tolerant. "The boys and girls might better have learned the meaning of human dignity and human rights in their classrooms," he disparaged, "rather than in the streets." School board chairman James Donovan dismissed the protest as a "fizzle" and a "bust."[30]

Although the boycott far surpassed activists' expectations, white liberals' rejection of the demand for integration shaped events more than black organizing. In the face of white opposition, the boycott coalition splintered. Invoking the support of "thousands of parents throughout the city," Galamison tried to force the hand of moderates by announcing a second boycott for March 16. In response, the national offices of the NAACP and CORE, together with the National Association for Puerto Rican Civil Rights withdrew from the Citywide Committee.[31]

Despite the absence of mainstream support, the Parents' Workshop, the Harlem Parents Committee (whose head Isaiah Robinson would follow Galamison on the Board of Education) and a number of local groups, including nine of New York's thirteen CORE chapters, endorsed the second boycott. With boycotters demanding black history curricula and the appointment of black principals along with school integration, Puerto Rican support declined sharply. Malcolm X, on the other hand, lent his support. Galamison's willingness to associate his brand of integrationism with Malcolm further differentiated him from moderate civil rights leaders. Still, without the moderates, the Parents' Workshop and the City-Wide Committee for Integrated Schools were "stripped of agents and organizational support" in what Galamison called "a really vicious sellout." Only 264,000 students stayed out of school.[32]

A third boycott, in the spring of 1965 was limited to junior high schools and "600 schools" for disruptive and disturbed students. It was in those schools, Galamison charged, black and Puerto Rican students who "challenge[d] . . . white incompetence" or "whose mental and emotional problems were beyond the scope" of regular schools were consigned to "educational chain gangs . . . by prejudice, ignorance and ethnocentricism." Playing on cultural deficit theories and white stereotypes of monstrous black men, Harlem activist Thelma Johnson promised a "cultural enrichment program" in which fifteen hundred junior high school boys would visit the lingerie department of the Saks Fifth Ave. department store in order to learn about French textiles, comparison shopping, and the availability of union-made products. Galamison and other boycott organizers were harshly criticized for threatening to turn uncontrollable black delinquents loose on the city. The circle of supporters, like the scope of the action, further narrowed, and the protest campaign had little prospect of success. After six weeks, the boycotters, money gone and resources exhausted, called off the protest.[33]

With little to show for a decade of school activism, protesters confronted the Board of Education at its December 1966 meeting. New board president Lloyd Garrison, the descendent of the famed abolitionist, adjourned the meeting and invited those who had waited hours for their chance to speak to "come back tomorrow." A woman demanded, "Who's going to pay the carfare?" Another cried, "We're infuriated," to which Harlem CORE leader Ronald Clark added, "We've been infuriated for a long time."[34]

The protesters, calling themselves the People's Board of Education, initiated a three-day sit-in at the central Board of Education, and they elected Milton Galamison People's Board President. The People's Board charged that the official Board denied citizens the right to participate in policy-making and provided inferior education to black and Puerto Rican students. The citizens of New York, protesters reasoned, could "no longer permit professionals to run the school system by themselves." The People's Board promised to "help communities to determine their educational needs" so that "parents and community groups" could gain "effective control" of the schools and insure that educators were "accountable for children's achievement." Activists had moved from militant demands for integration into mainstream institutions to militant demands for power over them.[35]

Galamison increasingly vacillated between his "lifelong goal" of helping create a true system of public education and an integrated society, and his growing conviction that racism was "the real religion of America—the one with the most serious and devout following."[36] Even as he tried to convince teachers that by "work[ing] shoulder to shoulder" with parents, they would be freed from "the bureaucracy that shackles them,"[37] he was convinced that many teachers would never "stand shoulder to shoulder" with parents whom they "regard as inferior and inherently despise."[38]

In a political culture corrupted by racism, Galamison and other People's Board organizers refused to accept seemingly neutral bureaucratic procedures or majority rule as democratic. The Board of Education, Galamison maintained, "cannot hold [racial equality in the schools] up to a plebiscite."[39] Activists saw the inflexible moral commitment to equality rather than the give-and-take of practical politics as the measure of democracy. The People's Board of Education, activist Mary Ellen Pfeiffer would remember,

> was really pretty effective. Principals didn't know at what time the People's Board was going to come through their schools, so they kept the teachers really on their toes. It didn't have any kind of legal authority, but the publicity it brought did get teachers to see that [they could not be] reading the *New York Times* instead of teaching.[40]

Operating without legal sanction, the People's Board provided a prototype for the experimental governing boards which would soon be created in Harlem and Ocean Hill-Brownsville. Under Galamison's leadership, the Board served as a training ground for activists like Pfeiffer who would go on to play active roles in the battle for community control.

Through the winter of 1967–68, Galamison remained New York's leading black school activist, and he met weekly with members of the IS 201 and Ocean Hill-Brownsville governing boards and staffs. Still, in May 1968, the Ocean Hill-Brownsville Governing Board did not notify Galamison that it was considering the removal of the nineteen teachers and supervisors. Then, his proposal for a boycott in support of community control was ignored by black activists. As the school crisis reached its climax, militant activists no longer felt a need "to check our strategies with Dr. G." The movement was beginning to pass him by.[41]

It was at precisely this moment in the summer of 1968 that Galamison was appointed to the Board of Education. Although he acknowledged the segregationist potential of community control, Galamison remained convinced that local activism for community power could be wedded to a citywide movement for integration. As a Board of Education member, he simultaneously maintained contact with the governing boards and sought to construct an integrationist pro-decentralization political coalition. Galamison spent a great deal of the 1968 legislative year in Albany lobbying unsuccessfully for "a viable decentralization bill."[42]

An incident early in his tenure on the Board of Education foreshadowed Galamison's failure in Albany. Like other new members, Galamison was given the paraphernalia of office—a spacious office, personalized stationary and a city car and driver. He opted to use his own car and instructed his driver to fill its tank at the city garage. The driver, however, was prohibited from doing so. Even though Galamison was Board of Education Vice President, his intervention had no impact on his subordinate at the garage. Then, when Galamison notified Board of Education Secretary Harold Siegel of his difficulties, the matter was quickly resolved. "If," Galamison concluded, "Board members had to go to staff to get permission for anything . . . the Board members had been functioning as a tail on the kite of the professional staff."[43]

Galamison's inability to fill his car's gas tank exemplified how futile his efforts had become. By the 1969 legislative season, Galamison did not bother going to Albany, having realized "how fruitless my efforts had been." When a "decentralization" bill was enacted in April 1969, the city was divided into thirty-two local school boards with very limited powers. "The community," in Galamison's eyes, "got nothing. The professionals got everything." He called the new law "the most crass and barbarous legislation passed since the days of slavery."[44]

Countless activists energized by Galamison's visionary efforts saw in the intransigence of white institutions an opportunity to create new, black ones. While these activists were forsaking mainstream institutions, Galamison made his peace with them. He established a partnership with Philadelphia minister Leon Sullivan in order to provide young blacks with vocational training. In a building that had once housed Goodwill Industries, Galamison oversaw The Opportunities Industrialization Center. Whereas the Downstate campaign had blamed black unemployment on racist unions and state agencies, the training program suggested that individuals' lack of occupational skills explained black poverty. Old allies scoffed at the million-dollar program. Galamison, in Jitu Weusi's eyes, became "a tool for the system." He then faded from the limelight altogether.[45]

After the UFT's defeat of community control signaled the final failure of the integration struggle, Galamison found Biblical imagery for his emerging pessimism. "Like the children of Noah, stumbling on the prostrate, besotted father," Galamison wrote, "it was during the search for character and decency that Black America discovered that the great white father was inebriated beyond rationality with a racism that negated his capacity to function on any other basis."[46]

Becoming Milton Galamison

Milton Galamison's militant commitment to integration as a means of achieving both self-determination and inclusion was already incubating in his childhood. Decades after Galamison had entered his manhood, he remained livid about the racial indignities of his youth. Galamison was born in Philadelphia in 1923. When he and his brother were still young children, they transferred from a black school in South Philadelphia to the John Barry Public School in West Philadelphia. "The principal, one Mr. Foote," Galamison recalled, wanted to put us each back one grade. He claimed that there was no vacancy in the grades for which we applied. But my brother was in the third grade and I was in the second. And even at this early age we wondered how he could find room in the second grade to demote my brother if he didn't have room in the second grade for me. It was such a transparent hoax. We were well dressed, we had better be well mannered, and we were reasonably intelligent. But this bigoted bully felt that the very sight of two black children justified his demoting each a grade.

After the forceful intervention of their grandmother, the boys were placed in the appropriate grades, but racial slights continued. Despite being an able student and avid reader, Galamison was tracked into a vocational program in high school. Even when he excelled in academic courses and failed at the vocational ones, his program was remained unchanged.[47]

Galamison's family life provided no haven from his heartless school. Abandoned by his father, he found meaning in church. Despite his non-academic high school curriculum, Galamison was able to attend college and then study for the ministry. He served for one year as minister to a middle-class congregation in Princeton, New Jersey, and then spent the remainder of his life as pastor of Siloam Presbyterian Church in Brooklyn. Even before Galamison became a school activist, commitments to social justice marked his ministry. Three months' travel in Africa left Galamison convinced that anti-communism was a cover for colonialism and that "Western civilization . . . is willing to do anything for the black man except get off their backs." He often preached against racism and other forms of bigotry in the U.S. as well. Under Galamison, women occupied an unusually high percentage of decision-making leadership positions in Siloam.[48]

At the height of the Cold War, Galamison urged his congregation to follow the revolutionary example of Jesus, by opposing militarism, the idolatry of property, and the corruption of office holders who sought for themselves rather than the commonweal. Attacks on Communists, he preached, deflected attention from injustices that the Communists fought. Instead, Galamison urged Christians to ally themselves with all those fighting poverty, capitalist exploitation, racism and war.[49]

A trip to address a 1957 Presbyterian Youth Conference cemented Galamison's convictions. Driving from New York to Indiana, Galamison and his family were denied restaurant and hotel service. The experience enraged Galamison. "If you're white," he would reflect, "you don't have to worry about whether you're being discriminated against or not in a situation. If you're black, you *always* have to worry." Whereas whites could concern themselves with poor hotel or restaurant service, Galamison was forced to wonder "if somebody was not going to give my wife and my child food because they were black. This is the difference: You're constantly paranoid. You're constantly on the defense." Whereas a white person could sit calmly unaffected by poor service, Galamison would be "getting ready to throw the sugar bowl through the window."[50]

"No man," Galamison recollected, "wants to be degraded in the eyes of his children. . . . I decided in the course of that trip that if I had to burn this stinking, bigoted country to the ground, my son and his family will never have to suffer the indignities heaped on black people of my generation." Shortly after Galamison's humiliating drive across America, he joined the Brooklyn NAACP's campaign for school integration.[51]

Integration and America

On March 27, 1963, the television program "Court of Reason" featured a debate between Galamison and Malcolm X over integration. On some points, there was little reason to anticipate disagreement between New York's preeminent integrationist and its leading separatist. Galamison, no less than Malcolm, condemned America's "stinking, bigoted" institutions and saw no theological "imperative . . . that this country survive . . . while spitting in the face of God."[52] Still, in the televised debate, Galamison rejected Malcolm's suggestion that blacks separate themselves from mainstream America. "There is nothing in America," Galamison countered,

> which does not belong to me. There is no public office, however high; no employment opportunity, however lucrative; no community, however restricted; no marriage, however interracial, which is not part of my heritage as a citizen of these United States. . . . The soil has been fertilized by our sweat, the factories built on our backs, the machines oiled by our tears, the homes maintained by our servitude and the nation carved by our suffering. When we speak of integration or separation as alternatives, we must consider the degree to which the black is already woven into the pattern of American life. We have been integrated at the level of sowing. It is in the area of reaping that we have been shortchanged. We have paid the fare. The question is whether we should fight for the ride. We have planted the tree. Should we not demand the fruit?[53]

Today, discussions of school integration are frequently reduced to questions of resource allocation or to the truism that black children do not need to sit next to white children in order to learn. Milton Galamison did not dismiss the importance of equalizing school resources or the intellectual capacity of black youth, but he offered a more expansive view of integration as a moral imperative "to live an ideal life," one that required the radical transformation of America itself.[54]

In New York, as in the Jim Crow south, school officials answered the demand for integration by proposing additional resources for ghetto schools. "It's Mississip-plan," Galamison ridiculed. "It's fraudulent; it's separate-but-equal all over again." The problem was not merely that segregationists could never be trusted to provide equal educational opportunity to black youth they despised. Even "if a Negro school were made academically superior," Galamison maintained, it would still be unequal, for it could never adjust the Negro child to the contest of the culture in which he lives. . . . The Negro child will still develop inferiority feelings, and the white child will develop racial arrogance. The Negro school would still be based on segregation, and the white school based on exclusiveness.[55]

Integration, in Galamison's mind required a radical commitment to human equality. Although he had white classmates throughout most of his elementary and secondary schooling, Galamison did not consider his own experience an example of integrated education. "We were baptized in and deluged by whiteness the whole of our most impressionable years," he would recall. "The psychological damage that accrues as the result of such one-sided exposure is devastating."[56] Indeed, in Galamison's mind, the injury inflicted on blacks by the school system was far deeper than that caused by poverty. "The Negro parent," he maintained, "knows [that the school system] is the area in which he's most exploited, or his children are most exploited." [57]

At the height of the 1968 UFT strike against community control, Galamison testified to his transcendent, redemptive vision of integration. From the pulpit of Siloam Presbyterian Church, Galamison compared black America to ancient Israel, exiled in Babylon. "Like Israel," he claimed, "we are a community cut off from the wellsprings of the nation. This is the essence of segregation, to be cut off from the mainstream of life. Segregation is a denial of the basic human right to belong." Basing his October 27, 1968 sermon on the prophet Ezekiel's Vision of the Valley of Dry Bones, Galamison drew an analogy between the scattered, disinterred bones of Israel and

our valley of dry bones all over America, places where we find vast communities of human beings standing by the graveyard of their lost hopes. And the question God is asking about Watts . . . about Bedford-Stuyvesant—the question God is asking is the question we ought be asking ourselves: Can these bones live?[58]

Integration would not merely promote achievement, Galamison argued. It would "resurrect from the academic graveyards the children who are America's future."[59]

If integration offered great promise, it would come at great cost. Unlike many white liberals who assumed that integration could be achieved with relatively little of the burden placed on themselves, Galamison understood that a true program of integration required the radical transformation of American life. Even his "most liberal white friends," Galamison observed, "are horrified at the prospect of real school integration, which might place some inconvenience on white families."[60]

Despite Milton Galamison's ability to articulate eloquently the moral claims of integration, he never discovered a means to win white New York to his cause. Moreover, Galamison called into question the very institutions in which he and other activists demanded inclusion. This steadfast moral commitment to an ideal of humanity rather than to participation in the prosaic processes of majority governance or the institutions of actually existing American democracy sped the transformation of the militantly integrationist movement into militant invocations of a nationalist ideal.

Integration and Community

Galamison's school integration campaign drew on a long tradition of protesting the increasing pervasiveness of racial subordination in what historian Harold Connolly has aptly labeled Brooklyn's "intensifying ghetto." Beginning in the 1920s, the NAACP's Brooklyn chapter protested discrimination and segregation by movie theaters, insurance offices, real estate agencies, banks and stores. Organizers fought the restriction of black New Yorkers to low-wage occupations deserted by whites, including the street-side "slave markets" for black women seeking domestic work. They struggled against barriers to political participation, police brutality, and racism in public schools. Almost a half century before the 1968 school conflict, blacks protested when teachers at Brooklyn's PS 35 divided students into separate black and white glee clubs, with the black chorus restricted to "mammy" songs. Even as he raised the demand for integration, Galamison called upon this tradition of community activism. [61]

Milton Galamison was not alone in his faith in grassroots activism nor his conviction that what Martin Luther King called "a degenerating sense of 'nobodiness'" harmed African Americans as much as poverty. After all, this struggle to reconcile individual autonomy with community bonds and democratic commitments is a quintessentially American dilemma. Like Galamison, many civil rights veterans saw no contradiction between integration and community control. Indeed, civil rights leader James Farmer argued, decentralization and community control constituted

> a forerunner to integration; and, in a larger sense, a partner to integration. . . . . Control of the schools, an exercise in populist democracy, is essential for developing the self-image and self-respect of the black community. Only after the full flowering of the black self-image and after the elimination of cultural biases from all our institutions, can there be complete integration."[62]

"I don't think that black power is segregation," Ocean Hill-Brownsville Governing Board Chairman C. Herbert Oliver maintained. "It's just black power. . . . We feel that unequals cannot really be integrated anyway, so that there must be power in the black community; then we can really talk about integration."[63] Harlem Parents Committee head Isaiah Robinson saw community control as "a struggle where the black community comes into its own and takes a seat at the negotiating table of ethnic groups—for the good of this country."[64]

In practice as well as theory, the integration struggle that brought Galamison to prominence was sustained by an amalgam of the integrationist ideal with grassroots, neighborly organizing. Although rarely in the limelight, activists, most of them black women, worked intensely in scores of neighborhood organizations to transform the schools. Ocean Hill-Brownsville Governing Board member Dolores Torres played a leading role in organizing support for the demonstration district. When something important came up, " the first thing" Torres and other parent representatives did "is grab the phone. We notify the principals, our school liaison people and the parent organization heads." School liaison people visited with neighbors, called parents, solicited support from community organizations, churches, block associations and recreation centers, and finally dispatched sound trucks.[65]

"The late '6os," activist Olivia Taylor remembers, "gave voice to many, many parents who were struggling within their individual schools. . . . You just met people— parents who were walking their kids to school. You went to a district board meeting and you met people that way." Integration provided the moral authority for parents to demand the transformation of their schools.[66]

Neighborhood activists simultaneously heeded the claims of community and the integrationist ideal. "The schools," veteran Galamison associate Thelma Hamilton observed,

> have brought these people closer together than they've ever been. . . . I don't think these people will ever go back to the old apathy that was here before the school thing started. . . . They're beginning to have hope now. They're beginning to see how to work together. . . . They're thinking like a community."[67]

Still, as late as August 1969, the Brownsville Community Council, with Hamilton as its director of educational problems, called for the construction of a mammoth 10,500-student intermediate school in order to promote integration.[68]

During the 1968 UFT strike, local parents, mostly women, opened schools and stayed overnight to prevent, teachers, administrators or custodians from resealing them with new locks. Although many teachers worked in the informally opened schools and Milton Galamison offered assistance from his position at the central Board, "the impetus came from local parents." Neighborhood activism for community control resonated so strongly with black New Yorkers because it, no less than Milton Galamison's visionary integrationism, asserted black humanity in the face of the pervasiveness of racism.[69]

In the 1950s and much of the 1960s, demands for integration had given shape and moral stature to neighborhood activists' efforts to ameliorate black life. With the decisive defeat of school desegregation by white New York, black activists found in calls for community control a new language with which to convey their transcendent purpose. The struggle for community control thus marked the culmination as well as the antithesis of the earlier integration efforts, and "many of the same people who gave the impetus for Ocean Hill had been involved in a number of other struggles." School organizing, East New York activist Olivia Taylor recalled, "was coalition work. Community control was not Black Power until the '68 crisis when the UFT made it so."[70]

Chapter 8

From Community Organizing to Community Control: Sonny Carson and the Redefinition of Black Community

There have been those black Americans who have resisted white America and sought to convince as many as possible of what they knew. These were the field niggers during slavery, Nat Turner, the black abolitionists, Garvey, and in our own time, Malcolm, the hustler on the corner and the high-school dropout.
—JULIUS LESTER[1]

This is me, muh-fuh.
Dig it![2]

According to controversial Brooklyn activist Sonny Carson, one Saturday afternoon in July 1967, the UFT held a dinner honoring Bayard Rustin at New York's Hilton Hotel. At the time, Carson was the little-known leader of the Brooklyn chapter of CORE, an organization Rustin had helped found some twenty-five years earlier. Carson and five other Brooklyn CORE activists, four in dungarees and two in dashikis, entered the hotel's ballroom to confront Rustin and his UFT hosts. The day's newspapers had depicted a feud between union president Al

Shanker and school superintendent Bernard Donovan, and yet the two were friendly at the dinner. "Seated before us," Carson concluded, "was the contradiction that we refused to grasp in Our Community: that even though they might be enemies in the press, they were friends in oppression."[3]

Carson's mission at the Hilton Hotel was not to win Rustin, Shanker or Donovan to an alliance with black activists, nor to prefiguratively represent what a just society might look like. Rather, Carson sought to demonstrate that black men need no longer define their behavior and ideals according to white norms. Whereas Bayard Rustin sought to align blacks to the labor movement and Milton Galamison worked for the integration of American democracy, Sonny Carson had no use for white people.[4] Whereas integrationists of earlier years had relied on students to demonstrate that blacks could fit into—indeed represent what was best about—mainstream America,[5] in the 1960s black nationalists repudiated with increasing militancy the goal of entering white institutions. Sonny Carson sought to construct a new oppositional black identity. Although declining hopes for school integration contributed much to demands for community control, Carson's commitments, no less than the demand for equality, were deeply rooted in the history of African America.

Carson never worked closely with Rev. Galamison despite the centrality of Brooklyn's school politics in the careers of both men.[6] Carson's ascendancy marked the replacement of Galamison's church-based movement by "the guys downstairs—from the streets."[7] Dramatic confrontations superseded community organizing, and faith in the power of schooling gave way to the conviction that public schools served only to control black insurgency. This chapter examines the displacement of integrationism and neighborly organizing by appeals to racial identity.

The Education of Sonny Carson

Sonny Carson grew up on a black block in a predominantly white area of Brooklyn. Whereas neighborhood activities revolved around an African American community, at school he was in enemy territory. The very entry into the school system in kindergarten, Carson argued, was

> the most dangerous period for black people, because this is when it starts—the mechanism for submission to the most sophisticated type of oppression that victimizes black people. . . . Certainly not then, but years later, I began to perceive of this as the most magnificent kind of programming that's ever been devised by any system in the history of mankind. For then it begins. White, white, white, white . . . white, white, white, all through the years. . . . This then was the beginning of my miseducation.[8]

Matters only got worse in junior high school, where Carson was one of about fifty blacks among two thousand white students. Part of Carson's trouble stemmed from his sense of being out of place. Arriving late to music class, Carson immediately noticed that he was the only black in the room. As the students sang "Old Black Joe," Carson felt every eye in the room stuck on him.[9]

Cultural insensitivity was only a small piece of the problem. Carson had an increasingly low opinion of his teachers; he remembered them not taking attendance, being drunk, playing poker, having sex in school. After being charged with throwing a snowball at a teacher, Carson would recall years later, he was taken to the office, assaulted by the principal, and then arrested. The only difference between the police and the criminals, he learned, was the amount of power they possessed.[10]

Although he had been a high achieving student in elementary school, Carson opted for a vocational high school. By sixteen, tired of the "non-acquisition of knowledge they call education," he regularly cut school and shook down fellow blacks in order to buy wine or marijuana. Carson's reputation in high school centered on his fearlessness as a gang leader rather than on his intellectual gifts. Indeed, school served largely to further his gang interests. Through such activities as making knives and zip guns in shop class, he earned a "Ph.D." in self-defense. More important, the need for students to unite in the face of white authorities taught Carson an early lesson in black solidarity: "while there was no cooperation outside [of school] between clicks, there was inside, because we needed each other to make those weapons." Carson deemed the rival gang members' mutual aid and solidarity in high school his "first encounter with community control."[11]

Carson enjoyed considerable success as a drug dealer until his criminal activities landed him in jail. Prison had no more stigma for Carson than the criminal enterprises that got him there. Schools, like prisons, were just one more weapon white America used in its battle against blacks. From a distance, Carson would recall, the rural prison in which he was confined resembled a residential school. "If you looked closely you'd see bars on all the windows, just like in schoolhouses." Thus, he determined, "for my first nineteen years, the school houses were the prisons, and the prisons were the prisons posing as schoolhouses, and the many sides of genocide continued to perpetuate itself, in whatever form."[12]

Carson lacked a way of understanding and expressing his oppression until hearing Malcolm X "brought to light" his "secret yearnings about life." From that day forward, Carson committed himself to the survival of black people.[13] Released from prison, Carson became active in CORE's militant Brooklyn chapter. At the time, Brooklyn CORE was organizing thousands of blacks to protest discriminatory employment practices at Brooklyn's Downstate Medical Center. Then, Milton Galamison and other Brooklyn ministers negotiated a settlement with Gov. Nelson Rockefeller. When authorities failed to deliver black jobs, the African American freedom struggle in New York was transformed. Before the Downstate protests, Brooklyn CORE was half-black, half-white; afterward, it was overwhelmingly black. Moreover, the militants proposed to promote as organizers those whom activist Blyden Jackson called "the guys downstairs—from the streets, the poolrooms, the gangs, the reform schools."[14]

Sonny Carson welcomed the change. Even after he became a political activist, Carson remained unapologetic about his gang days, and his notion of politics echoed the language and mentality of his earlier life. He rejected both the legitimacy of the American political order and the traditional goals of the civil rights movement. Freedom and equality, he argued, only became "a problem to an individual when they seek to be accepted by the system." Rather, the civil rights movement was a "battle between the clicks on a turf bigger than I had ever known."[15]

In 1966, Carson was assigned to Brooklyn CORE's education committee. Among the first issues he confronted was the arrest of sixteen black junior high school students. The students attended a school that was located in a white community and that had an all-white staff. Police charged that on their way home from school, the children had rampaged through subway cars, breaking windows and assaulting riders. Carson interviewed the students and their white principal. Rather than expressing concern about the students' situation, the principal told Carson that the black students caused racial conflict at the school.[16]

The principal's white bigotry did not surprise Carson, but the reaction of the students' black parents did. When they sided with school authorities against their own children, Carson was convinced that white society profoundly distorted black consciousness. Carson and CORE foreswore demands for integration and worked to transform black identity.[17]

Under Carson's leadership, CORE worked during the 1966–67 school year to remove principals it considered incompetent. With considerable parent and teacher support, one hundred and fifty CORE pickets at JHS 258 chanted "Levine Must Go!" Reports that a white teacher had assaulted a sixteen-year-old girl led Carson to investigate teacher violence at Brooklyn's elementary and junior high schools. Convinced that assaults were common occurrences, CORE met with Board of Education and UFT representatives. Activists demanded that five principals be removed, that the principals of all schools in black Brooklyn produce written plans for bringing students up to grade level, and that fifty percent of the teachers be black. CORE also claimed that "The Community" needed some means of controlling the education of its children.[18]

When a principal at the meeting said that "as a Jew" he sympathized with blacks, a CORE member shot back, "You Jews do what's best for you." Superintendent Donovan accused CORE of "racial or religious bigotry." UFT President Al Shanker telegraphed that the union would "not submit to bullying, name-calling, etc." New York's newspapers seized upon the comment—one headlined its account of the meeting "Growing Anti-Semitism in the Black Community." The *New York Times* on the other hand did not mention anti-Semitism. It was more concerned with Carson's suggestion of quotas in teacher hiring.[19]

CORE saw the accusations of black intolerance as a smokescreen to protect the racist system. Responding to charges that black activists failed to appreciate the benefits of integrated schools, Clarence Funnye, the formerly pro-integrationist head of New York CORE, asked,

> are they integrated now? Is there any hope that they ever will be? And isn't locally controlled segregation at least an improvement over the present centrally-controlled (white) quasi-colonial system?"[20]

At a February 1968 press conference, CORE detailed more cases of teacher brutality. Augustus McAllister was hospitalized after having been hit in the eye by a teacher at JHS 162. A youngster at JHS 117 had his hands tied behind his back and his head held under running water by a white teacher. CORE demanded that teachers be prevented from beating kids.[21]

The opposition of white teachers, white school authorities and white media to CORE's efforts convinced Carson that the school problems went beyond individual acts of bigotry. Activists documented the tracking practices, unequal punishments, absence of due process, and racist curricula that systematically victimized black students. As they did so, they exposed also the vacuousness of white liberal invocations of equal opportunity in a race-blind society. On June 24, 1967, Brooklyn CORE staged a sit-in at UFT headquarters, charging that the union abetted the harassment of black students and teachers. Activists demanded that the UFT join CORE efforts to include black history in the curriculum, to remove principals of schools not up to grade level, to increase number of black teachers and principals, and to create independent school boards in black neighborhoods.[22]

Carson's radicalization continued when the UFT went out on strike in the fall of 1967. In addition to bread-and-butter demands, the union demanded policies that would facilitate the removal of "disruptive" children from the classroom. While teachers claimed that rising assaults and the educational needs of the quiescent majority of students demanded changes, CORE, the African-American Teachers Association and a number of civic organizations charged that it was too easy to expel students, not too hard.[23]

Sonny Carson argued strongly against the UFT proposal. If the school system itself brutalized black youth, he reasoned, disruption by students was a rational response to compulsory schooling. He argued that children labeled "disruptive" ought more accurately be called "spirited,"[24] and concluded, "The so-called disruptive children are those who refuse to bend, so they are even more important to our struggle for self-determination than other children."[25]

Carson investigated the education of "disruptive" students at the "600 schools" for unruly and emotionally disturbed students. He visited the 600 school where future Ocean Hill-Brownsville Unit Administrator Rhody McCoy served as principal, and he consulted McCoy, Columbia University professor and I.S. 201 advisor Preston Wilcox, and educator and radical black activist Herman Ferguson.[26]

At a November 9, 1967 meeting with school superintendent Bernard Donovan, Carson and other CORE activists proposed an alternative program for disruptive students. Carson envisioned a program that would rely on the knowledge that existed in the community and which would offer the student "lessons that have some pertinence to his every-day struggle." According to a 28-page plan CORE submitted to Donovan, "rather than be exposed to the dry and uninteresting conventional classroom routine," students would "attack real-life problems." A science class, for example, would explore "how to scientifically eliminate rats from their community." CORE promised to recruit caring teachers, black or white, who met the highest professional standards of excellence, and the group demanded three million dollars to establish two pilot programs.[27]

Then, the press reported that on the record-cold morning of January 8, 1968, the principal of Brooklyn's JHS 117 locked children out of school for being late. CORE had already tried to have the principal removed, and when he was beaten up by black youths who, in the *New York Times'* account, sported "Afro-style haircuts" and "Black Muslim crescent symbols," CORE attracted some of the blame. Council of Supervisory Associations President Joseph Brennen attributed the attack to the school system's capitulation to "small pressure groups" demanding community control. In response, the Board earmarked $1.25 million for added ghetto school security instead of funding new programs to serve disruptive children.[28]

Despite its calls for high professional standards in CORE's proposal, Carson was convinced that "an unskilled, uneducated parent could easily assume the teacher's responsibility." "Shanker and his teachers don't want to educate [the disruptive child]," he reasoned, "and Donovan and his board of no education has always abused him." Parents would do no worse. Apart from the crucial contribution of militant educators like McCoy, Wilcox and Ferguson, CORE shunned middle-class teachers and Board of Education professionals, black as well as white. Teachers, judges, commissioners, and other members of the "so-called elite," Carson argued, were dependent on token patronage jobs created by integration. They resisted independent black thinking and politics.[29]

Black Rebellion and White Racial Fantasies

In the late 1960s, the collapse of the school integration movement lent legitimacy to Carson's politics, and the emergence of outlaw/radicals like Carson as emblems of the black freedom struggle reflected blacks' widespread feeling of alienation from the promise of American democracy. Still, alienation predated 1968. The criminal had long been a stock figure in African-American folk culture, drawing both on trickster narratives handed down from Africa and on the need, in W. E. B. DuBois's phrase, for "outthinking and outflanking the owners of the world."[30]

Carson's own disengagement from school replicated a familiar pattern among black youth, especially young men. Growing up in Spanish Harlem in the 1930s and 1940s, writer Piri Thomas could "always find something to do, even if it was doing nothing. But going to school was something else. School stunk. I hated school and all its teachers." For all the brutality of the police and the judicial system, Thomas distinguished the sympathetic police officer or prison guard, however rare, from the oppressive institution. Teachers, however, wanted to control his mind as well as his body; he identified them wholly with the oppressive schools.[31]

In the late 1940s and 1950s, it seemed to Harlem writer Claude Brown that "whenever I went to school, I got into a fight with the teacher. The teacher would take me to the principal's office. After I fought with the principal, I would be sent home and not allowed back in school without one of my parents. So to avoid all that trouble, I just didn't go to school." Many mornings a truant officer escorted Brown to school. "This," he remembered, "was one way of getting me to school, but he never found a way to keep me there. The moment my teacher took her eyes off of me, I was back on the street." Brown describes the price he was willing to pay in order to defy the truant officer:

> Every time Dad got a card from Mr. Sands, I got bruises and welts from Dad. . . . That yellow card meant that I would walk into the house and Dad would be waiting with his razor strop. He would . . . pause just long enough to say to me, "Nigger, you got a ass whippin' comin'." . . . Each time, the beatings got worse; and each time, I promised never to play hooky again. One time I kept that promise for three whole weeks.[32]

It was not an absence of academic skills or a poor cultural fit that explains Thomas's and Brown's response to schooling. They expended enormous energy in repudiating school; however ineffectively, they were resisting the institution. This resistance did little perhaps to transform schools in ways that served the future possibilities of their black students. Still, whatever the ultimate price blacks might have paid for seemingly destructive behavior or school failure, disengagement from school was a plausible response of students to an institution which they had come to view as unalterably racist.

In the 1960s, future Black Panther Alfred Cain, Jr. attended Brooklyn's Tilden High School. Like Malcolm X, Sonny Carson and many other militant black men, Cain remembered, "At one time I was an honors student but things happened where I got sidetracked." Initially moderate in his politics, "little slurs" from white parents and school personnel "mounted in my subconscious." Things came to a head when black students, a number of them already involved in the Black Panther Party, organized the Afro-American Club. The club invited militant black nationalist teacher Leslie Campbell to address the group. Despite having assured students that they could bring in controversial speakers, the principal called in the police to prevent Campbell from speaking. "After that," Cain exulted, "we never had any peace in the classrooms."[33]

Afeni Shakur also joined the Black Panthers and was one of the New York 21, as the defendants in one of New York's most celebrated show trials were called. As a teenager in the early 1960s, Shakur had enrolled at New York's prestigious High School of Performing Arts, expecting to be able to "relate" to students there. Instead, she found that she would

> just walk up to white children and just hit them, and then I would get angry because they didn't want to hit me back. . . . These were rich kids . . . just coming out of private schools all their lives, and they were being picked up by chauffeurs and all that non-sense, and you know I hated them. I hated them with a passion. . . . I couldn't look pretty, you know, outslick them or outtalk them or anything. The only defense I had was the things I did in the street.

With other members of the Disciples, a gang from her neighborhood, Shakur got drunk every day before going to school. At school, she recalled,

> I would get uptight because I saw this white child who had all these beautiful clothes and who was showing off. And I couldn't stand this so I'd walk up to her and just call her a bitch and smack her, you know, and she would look at me like I was some kind of other life form. And I was.[34]

Unable to adjust to the world of Performing Arts, Shakur left school.

Ironically, even as the Carsons and Cains of the black freedom struggle struck a responsive chord among blacks brutalized by the public schools, they fascinated whites as well. In part, the media attention Sonny Carson received reflected the role he performed in the imagination of white New York. In the 1960s, whites responded to increasingly militant black demands for racial equality both with massive resistance to integration policies and with traditional American images of monstrous black men. Out of this fevered fantasy life, white New York created the image of someone like Sonny Carson even before Carson himself rose to prominence among Brooklyn's black activists.

Carson cited the case of the Harlem Six, which dragged on for nine years from 1964 until 1973, as proof of the intractability of white racism, and it illuminates the symbiotic relationship of white racial fantasies and black activity.[35] The case began as an inconsequential incident when a few children returning home from school swiped some apples and oranges from a Lenox Ave. fruit stand. Police beat the children and then beat a number of teenagers—the *Times* described them as "tough teen-aged members of Harlem gangs"—who sought to intercede on the children's behalf. Two men who protested police actions and a number of young onlookers were similarly beaten by the police; one man lost an eye.[36]

When a white Harlem shopkeeper was murdered two weeks after the so-called Fruit Stand Riot, police charged six young blacks, including three who had been arrested at the Fruit Stand, with the killing. Police and press joined in a campaign, spearheaded by the *New York Times*, to paint the Fruit Stand disturbance and the murder as the opening salvos in a sinister terrorist campaign by "militant and organized bands of Negro toughs . . . who, after being trained to maim and kill, roam the streets of Harlem attacking white people."[37]

A lengthy *Times* investigation concluded that the Fruit Stand Riot had "set the stage for the expansion of anti-white youth gangs, some of whose members call themselves Blood Brothers." The paper traced the Blood Brothers to Malcolm X, the Black Muslims and "black nationalist movements" and reported that the group was "indoctrinat[ing] an increasing number of youths with militant anti-white sentiment." Organized into divisions which communicated with one another by means of "a system of runners," the karate and judo-trained Blood Brothers were a formidable force: "Each night before going to bed [a Blood Brother] spends half an hour jabbing his hand into a pail of gravel."[38]

Despite the *Times*'s tabloid-lurid account, the prosecution made no mention of the Blood Brotherhood at the trials of the Harlem Six. Challenged by the NAACP to make pubic the evidence on which it based its sensational allegations, the *Times* retreated into silence.[39] Nevertheless, in response to the alleged black nationalist threat, the police concentrated a Tactical Patrol Force, limited to judo-trained officers over six feet tall, in Harlem, and community centers operated by the Board of Education began turning over information on suspicious youths to the police.[40]

In jail awaiting trial, the Harlem Six were regularly assaulted by guards who stopped the prison elevator between floors to administer beatings and seek confessions. Urged by their court-appointed lawyers to plead guilty to lesser charges, the Six rose in court to claim that they could not get justice in "this white man's court." For that the judge sent them to a mental hospital to determine their sanity.[41] Malcolm X, traveling in Africa when the *Times* invented the Blood Brothers scare, commented upon his return that blacks were "too quick to apologize for something that might exist that the power structure finds deplorable . . . If it doesn't exist, sometimes it should."[42]

The notoriety of the Harlem Six exemplified the heightened white paranoia which has often followed waves of black protest in America. Whereas *The New York Times* imagined a secret, growing plot of black racists, the black youths arrested at the Fruit Stand considered a white man who interceded in their defense a friend and black police officers their foes. The simplistic racial categories of good and evil belonged to the police and the *Times* rather than to the teens.[43]

The case of the Harlem Six anticipated the school conflict in several ways. In its frenzied racial fears, white New York made no distinction among blacks. Furthermore, the case exemplified the fundamental, interwoven and seemingly inalterable racism of municipal institutions. Police violence against black children traveling between home and school was the cause of both the Fruit Stand Riot and the larger 1964 Harlem Riot. In the eyes of black New York, police violence, like assaults by teachers, was a regular feature in the lives of African American youth. As Paul Chevigny notes, innocence was no protection for blacks confronted by the "brazen unfairness" of the police and the criminal justice system. The presence of police and the use of police-like disciplinary tactics in ghetto schools implicated educators in police racism.[44] To divorce police brutality from the politics of schooling is to treat racism as the effect of discrete incidents of discriminatory behavior, each of which can be remedied by the elimination of intentionally harmful actions. Instead, the case of the Harlem Six reminded Sonny Carson that an interwoven, institutionalized racism permeated New York.

The Politics of Disruption

The persistence of racial oppression in the schools and the wider failure of the movement victories to transform the lives of black New Yorkers led many activists to abandon traditional civil rights remedies and interracial alliances and to embrace Sonny Carson's politics of disruption. The daily demonstrations at Ocean Hill-Brownsville's schools invited UFT charges that community control achieved little more than the promotion of extremism and mob rule. Still, as the *New York Times* recognized, the Ocean Hill-Brownsville Governing Board, faced with a "limited bag of resources," counted "evidence of community support as one of its most important weapons. How to display community support effectively was one of the first and early concerns of those people in the area who had organized for the community control experiment."[45]

However useful it was in the defense of community control, Carson's politics of disruptive protest contributed to the decline of neighborly organizing by local activists. In no small part, CORE enjoyed the attention it received and the success it experienced because it played on white fears of and fascination with black violence. Whereas historians can find many references to Sonny Carson in the *New York Times Index*, the women who had labored for years in Brooklyn's school campaigns did not rate mention.

CORE's campaign to rid black Brooklyn of unfit principals epitomized its relationship with parent activists. CORE entered the dispute surrounding the principal at Brooklyn's JHS 258 only after PTA leader Eualalie Lediyard and other parents had negotiated with school officials for months to remove the school's principal. Once Carson and other flamboyant CORE activists became involved, leadership over the fight passed to them and symbolic gestures took precedence over parental concerns. Carson coyly responded to UFT and Board of Education accusations of threats and intimidation with claims that the organization had threatened no one. Still, CORE claimed "the authority to do whatever necessary to bring about the relocation of the principal," and white New York responded to the threat.[46]

However much Carson sought to appropriate the white image of black criminality, his defense of community control was marked by what historian Nell Irvin Painter has called "the masculinist tradition of black nationalism."[47] It reflected white stereotypes and asymmetrical gender relations, reproducing oppressive identities even as it challenged oppression. "To most of us," observed writer Michele Wallace, "Black Power meant . . . black men . . . taking over the country by brute force, arrogant lawlessness and an unquestionable sexual authority. . . . The media emphasized this definition. It was their selective image of Stokely Carmichael that I fell in love with as a teenager, not the cautious, rational man who defined Black Power as 'proper representation and sharing in control.'"[48]

Still, one should not simply read the gender relations of middle-class white America onto black life and thereby reduce nationalist politics to a vehicle for women's victimization. Decades after the school conflict former African-American Teachers Association president Al Vann would recollect, "Compared to the violence today, those gangs were very tame. In some ways they were a healthy development. They reflected a high degree of organization, had a high regard for the neighborhood. You were only at risk if you didn't live in the neighborhood. Your elders, your seniors, they had no problems. They were well-respected."[49]

Legendary Harlem activist Queen Mother Moore marched in support for community control with younger Black Power advocates such as Stokely Carmichael. Moore argued that the schools perpetrated mental genocide and trained black youth for self-subjugation. "Your educational system," she marveled, "can take an African and turn him into a 'Negro.'" Moore did not "see any special problems for the black woman as apart from her people." Citing the history of lynching, unemployment, and attacks from the judicial system, she argued that the primary job of the black woman was to "understand that her man has been demeaned, emasculated" and therefore "to protect her man, to build him up."[50]

Confrontational politics was not, of course, incompatible with community organizing. Among the groups organizing community meetings on school conditions and supporting community control was the Black Panther Party, established in New York in 1967.[51] The disruptive politics of community control and cultural transformation invested the efforts of neighborly activists with drama and heroism. In repudiating the desirability of integration into white New York, activists like Sonny Carson sustained a celebratory sense of possibility among blacks. Still, Sonny Carson's claim that

CORE represented the community and would do whatever was necessary to enforce its demands disrupted participatory organizing within the ghetto. "Our Community," in Carson's capitalized rendering,[52] was an ideal, for which he spoke. Community as the daily experience of neighborly life was overwhelmed by an abstraction.

Conclusion

Support for nationalism was widespread among blacks and deeply rooted in African-American life.[53] So too, the discourse of school-as-prison and criminality-as-rebellion had deep roots in black culture.[54] Just as the combination of subordination and exclusion, of racial oppression and racial isolation, shaped ghetto life,[55] so too did the combination of extreme surveillance and extreme abandonment[56] shape a culture of resistance in ghetto schooling.[57] If the schoolhouse and prison were indistinguishably oppressive embodiments of American life, then misbehavior in school and disruption outside of it both constituted resistance to black oppression and set the stage for the creation of autonomous black institutions.

By abandoning unreciprocated efforts to integrate American life, black activists in urban schools and communities were able to create some enclaves in which they exercised considerable power. Even for countless blacks who never participated in militant politics or gangs, gang style came to serve as a potent articulation of the black condition.

Ultimately, however, institution building proved more ephemeral than disruption. And the articulation of oppositional identities could not sustain the institutionalization of self-determination. While it repudiated the goal of winning access to mainstream America, the discourse of school-as-prison and the infatuation with criminality failed to articulate a distinctive black politics and culture. At the same time as it marked the racialized alienation of blacks, it reflected values they shared with other Americans.[58] Not surprisingly hip-hop invocations of gangsterism have both provided an outlet for creative energies repressed in ghetto schools and resonated with white suburban youth.[59] Yet, even as white journalists embraced images of New York's ghetto schools as "neocolonial fortress[es]" and "smothered, smoldering prison[s] of futility,"[60] white America retreated from commitments to government programs to foster social equality.

The benefits from the oppositional, disruptive identity promoted by nationalists like Sonny Carson were meager consolation prizes in a larger defeat. The visible presence of black youth—their loudness, to use Signithia Fordham's term—was accompanied by a declining belief in the possibility of participating in mainstream politics.[61] Integrationist leader Milton Galamison unleashed the politics of disruption with his 1965 boycott of the 600 schools. Still, Galamison reflected, "those in the community who yelled the loudest, jumped up and down the most, and elbowed the hardest" failed to advance community interests but rather were exploited by "counter revolutionary" agencies of the white state.[62]

The politics of disruption promoted by black nationalists proved to be a two-edged sword. Being opposed to dominant norms and institutions, it possesses a certain affinity with a radical critique of white supremacy.[63] Still, celebrations of cultures of resistance often minimize the ways students accommodate themselves to oppressive situations. Moreover, a focus on the implicit politics of everyday life in schools risks suggesting that race relations are characterized by fixed identities rather than contested, evolving relationships. And it risks neglecting the role of explicitly political school activism. The career of Sonny Carson suggests both that the degree and shape of resistance varies in time and that resistance has its contradictions as well as its rewards. It suggests the need for educators to address both African America's enduring cultural values and the brutalizing impact of domination in the lives of black youth.

Chapter 9

Visible Men: Black Teachers and the Curricular Implications of Black Power

The general American public at no time had any serious intention of providing, in public or private schools, institutions that had the capacity of preparing [Afro-Americans] for full citizenship; and the vast majority, in any generation since the founding of the Republic—and even before—never was so prepared. Certainly this is one of the chief reasons why this population has not been able to maintain full citizenship; it had been brutalized, degraded, dehumanized, and uneducated, by every instrument of the culture and society.
— HORACE MANN BOND[1]

We are history's amnesiacs, fitted with the memories of others.
— RANDALL ROBINSON[2]

At Ocean Hill-Brownsville's Junior High School 271, a portrait of Malcolm X stared at visitors from behind the desk of Al Vann, the dashiki-wearing assistant principal and president of New York's African-American Teachers Association. Black teacher-activists were struggling to transform public schooling, Vann told students, in order that "you begin to understand . . . that you are a person, that you are of value, that you are of worth."[3] Harlem administrator Merle

Stewart shared both Vann's view that the existing school system annihilated the very humanity of African American students and the hope that a transformed education would enable educators to "creat[e] men and women out of the 'things' which they now are."[4] Similarly, Leslie Campbell called on black educators to ensure that "the black man will no longer remain 'invisible' and content."[5]

This struggle to recover black humanity in the face of racism's brutalizing power echoes across the history of African American life. The goal of African American education, W. E. B. DuBois proclaimed in 1930, should not be "to make men carpenters but to make carpenters men."[6] It was "difficult, virtually impossible," educator Benjamin Mays would recollect of his youth in the Jim Crow South, "to combine manhood and blackness under one skin. . . . To exercise manhood, as white men displayed it, was to invite disaster."[7] So too in the urban North. The price of being rendered "an invisible man," novelist Ralph Ellison suggested in the 1950s, was that "you wonder whether you aren't simply a phantom in other people's minds. . . . You ache with the need to convince yourself that you do exist."[8] This "degenerating sense of 'nobodiness,'" Martin Luther King, Jr. declared a decade later, constituted the black child's unique burden.[9]

Rarely has the struggle against "nobodiness" been pursued with as much force or catalyzed as much educational thought and activism as in the late 1960s. Although massive resistance to racial equality in the liberal north had thwarted black efforts to create an integrated America, activists retained utopian hopes of transforming African American life. Still, as activists became increasingly convinced of the intractability of American racism, nationalism displaced integrationism as the most prominent and dynamic tendency in African American thought.

Unlike integrationists, who had demanded the provision of mainstream educational opportunities, nationalists claimed that even in the absence of segregation laws, American schools systematically subjected black children to "classroom genocide."[10] Abandoning failed campaigns to integrate American schools and society, they worked to promote a black humanity that did not depend on assimilation into the dominant white American culture. They sought to celebrate rather than erase black racial identity. The commitment to transforming black consciousness rendered pedagogical questions central to nationalists' work. Whereas black teachers had played only a marginal role in school integration efforts, during the struggle over community control, New York's black teachers became leading spokespersons for the educational and political aspirations of black America.[11]

This chapter focuses on four of New York's most prominent black nationalist educators. Their efforts to envision new ways of thinking about curriculum and pedagogy, school-community relations, and the role of schooling in the construction of a just society influenced black activists across the United States.[12] In education, as in other arenas, black nationalist thought and action has turned on two crucial axes, the one involving tension between engagement with and separation from the dominant

American society,[13] and the other focused on the relative claims of political contestation and cultural activities[14] in the pursuit of black liberation.

Inevitably, New York's black teachers struggled with both of these pivotal issues. Rhody McCoy saw schooling as a vehicle with which to promote black engagement with American political life; Herman Ferguson sought to promote black political autonomy through schooling; Keith Baird was committed to the inclusion of African American voices in the American cultural mosaic; Leslie Campbell to developing an autonomous black culture. As they wrestled with the sometimes competing, sometimes overlapping claims of political engagement and cultural activity, of interaction with mainstream America and autonomy from it, the four educators suggest the range of black educational thought and action.

The efforts of McCoy, Ferguson, Baird and Campbell belie generic notions of teacher professionalism or voice, even of black teachers' professionalism or voice. Their biographies illuminate not only their relationship to the broader freedom struggle but also the roots of black educational thought in long-standing African American intellectual traditions. The differences among them as well as their agreements demonstrate how conscious political choices and intellectual commitments shape the work of teaching.

Rhody McCoy: Black Nationalism and the Transformation of the School

As the unit administrator in charge of the Ocean Hill-Brownsville community control school district, Rhody McCoy was at the epicenter of the New York school conflict. Navigating between the grass-roots activism that established black community control and the school system that sought to dismantle it, McCoy attempted the quintessentially progressive project of fostering democratic communities by connecting school to life. This project was complicated however by McCoy's conviction that racial divisions structured American society.

McCoy grew up in Washington, DC, where his father worked as a postal worker and his mother cooked for a white family. As a child, McCoy watched, powerless, as his mother set off to walk miles to work on snowy winter days when buses were cancelled in black neighborhoods. The first member of his family to attend college, McCoy studied at Howard University before arriving in New York City in 1949.[15]

In New York, McCoy built a reputation among black school activists for his work in New York's "600 schools," to which the system assigned delinquent and disturbed children who had been expelled from other institutions.[16] McCoy rejected the idea that his students' problems were the result of their own deficits. Rather, black failure was the intended outcome of the school system and the society of which it was a part. Therefore, McCoy reasoned, addressing racial oppression in school and society was the preeminent task facing educators:

> My idea was very simple. . . . Too often we got caught up in saying, "Our kids can't read and write". . .and we lost sight of the fact that we've got millions of our kids who *can* read and write . . . who are basically not educated in terms of what's going on in the real world.[17]

McCoy's commitment to educating students in terms of what was going on in the real world recalls Deweyan notions of progressive education. Schools, for McCoy as for John Dewey, were embryonic communities where people came together to form bonds of social solidarity by the solving of common problems. For both educators, learning intersected with social life; pedagogy and social vision followed the same logic; meaning came from actively solving shared social problems. In today's language, contributing to civic capacity is a primary task of schooling.[18]

Where McCoy differed from Dewey was in the profound racial divisions he saw in American society and in New York's schools. In McCoy's eyes, the racial conflicts that led to community control were very different from the industrial conflict that shaped the society in Dewey's day.[19] In the late 1960s, images of ghetto poverty—decaying buildings, peeling paint, cracked walls, empty lots strewn with glass—approached clichés.[20] But to note this poverty left open why symbols of municipal authority—schools and police—were the objects of black rage rather than those of corporate capitalism. Why rage was black and not proletarian.

According to McCoy, the urban politics of race shaped the black community far more than class conflict. Ocean Hill-Brownsville, he noted, had a larger percentage of welfare recipients than any neighboring area; "it has a frightening narcotics problem that is largely ignored by *health authorities.* Many buildings in the area are uninhabited, while absentee landlords wait to reap huge profits from *Model Cities resales.* The inadequate service of the *Department of Sanitation* makes the neighborhood's physical appearance horrendous."[21] The state rather than the factory created and maintained the ghetto.

The very community at issue in the dispute over community control, McCoy argued, was a creation of the state. Ocean Hill-Brownsville originated when "the poverty program came in and redistricted the lines, and there was a little political gerrymandering and so forth." Suddenly, right in "the heart of Bed Stuy and Brownsville, two of the most volatile communities in the city . . . Ocean Hill-Brownsville was created by a politician."[22]

Government action, rather than the appropriation of their labor, alienated the "demoralized, poverty-ridden" inhabitants of Ocean Hill-Brownsville. "The city takes no notice of them," McCoy argued in activists' August 1967 proposal to formalize community control. "They are simply not seen—the invisible people. . . . These people are obscure, unnoticed—as though they do not exist."[23]

Still, a dialectic operated. The people of Ocean Hill-Brownsville were a "community" rather than a mere administrative convenience because

there's been an internal struggle for survival, and they've had common goals and interests. . . . They were involved in struggles with poverty programs, with political machines.
There's been a sense of community round fighting some of the bureaucratic impositions
such as hospitals, welfare and so forth.[24]

The phenomena that McCoy noted were the culmination of the transformation of
American cities in the years following World War II, and no city exemplified these
changes more than New York. From the mid-1950s until the late 1960s, as historian
Joshua Freeman notes, runaway shops and automation eroded the city's blue-collar job
base and culture. Meanwhile, public and private white collar employment and
government-sponsored white-collar suburbs—jobs and neighborhoods from which
blacks were largely excluded—grew rapidly. Together with McCarthy-era government
attacks on labor organizing, changes in urban life transformed racial politics.[25]

The new political economy of education was announced in the very architecture of
school buildings that became the focus of demands for community control. Abandoning the old scholastic factory design, Harlem's I.S. 201 was built windowless, as if to
defy the neighborhood in which it sat. Similarly, Ocean Hill's I.S. 55 was a mass of
brick with doors and windows almost invisible, a foreboding building in the neo-
fortress style. The schools, in Joseph Featherstone's phrase, were "colonial garrisons in
suspicious and hostile neighborhoods."[26] An educational approach grounded in a vision of cooperative, productive labor might have made considerable sense in John
Dewey's industrial-age world, but it made far less in Rhody McCoy's.

McCoy was not however without hope. The activism that led to the creation of
community control epitomized the process through which the dispossessed could
come together to overcome their invisibility. Ignored by their local school board,
residents "banded together" to form the Ocean Hill-Brownsville Independent
School Board:

> An unauthorized committee sanctioned by needs moved toward action. . . . First, a chant
> for representation at the local board level, then, a demand for change in the architectural
> design of a building, and, finally, a request for consultation in the selection of principals: a
> once nebulous group attained structure, purpose, authenticity, support, and recognition.

A community defined itself in the course of political struggle and, with the inaugura-
tion of community control, sought "to become architects of the educational fate of its
children."[27]

As unit administrator of Ocean Hill-Brownsville's schools, McCoy sought to preserve the sense of collective problem solving. "One danger I was constantly working
to minimize," he stressed, "was the pressure of individual demands." Instead of focusing on their "little Johnny," McCoy encouraged parents to see "twenty-five little
Johnnies, all in the same boat. . . . I tried to have people think of common needs, to
view the schools as an interdependent totality—a whole school system."[28]

Community activism would lead to black achievement not only because it would force the school system to provide needed educational resources but primarily because it would change blacks' relationship to the schools and supply a motivation and a capacity to learn. New York's schools, McCoy had observed, produced "imageless children who take no special interest or pride in academic achievement.[29] Allowing people to become visible, according to McCoy's analysis, was appropriate action in pedagogy, as in politics.

At first, McCoy was optimistic that he could bridge the gulf between the system and the street, and "work with both worlds" to create an educational program that white teachers and the black community could accept.[30] In the course of the school conflict, however, McCoy became increasingly pessimistic. Changing the relationship of black children and communities to the schools required changing the role of teachers as well. Rather than defining the needs of black children, teachers were "to interpret and translate . . . into . . . professional jargon" needs articulated by the black community. This relegated educators "to the ranks of the followers" who lent "stability" and "sophistication . . . to changes which they have not produced." It was a role that New York's educators resisted with all the power they possessed.[31]

In the end, McCoy judged the experiment in community control by the pragmatic, Deweyan standard of learning through action that solves problems. Did the black community have enough power to affect the course of events and in so doing to learn from its actions? At community meetings, McCoy noted, "mothers would stand up in the back of the auditorium" and ask,

"Can you put my child into the right high school?"
I'd say, "No."
They'd say, "Where do you get the decision from?"
I'd say, "Down at Central Headquarters." . . .
"Do you have money to put these kids on busses to do something?"
"No."
"Where do you have to go?"
"Have to go to the Central Board."
"Whose game are you playing? . . . As long as the Man has control, nothing's going to change."[32]

Community control, McCoy realized, was suffering the same fate as the 1964 New York school boycotts demanding integration and the 1966 effort to abolish the Board of Examiners, which used racist pronunciation tests to exclude minority educators from supervisory positions. "Each futile movement to reform the New York City schools," McCoy observed, had been charged with "creating its own impotence out of a failure to build workable and political coalitions." Rather, he concluded, any strategy blacks adopted would have been ineffective; any strategy white teachers adopted would have succeeded: "the crucial variables are not those related to tactics or goals but rather to the political and economic resources which the opposing groups possessed." What was at issue was not any "vituperous desire to deny black and Third World people their rights" but the need "to protect the social and economic benefits of racism." Because "education can be translated into socioeconomic power," McCoy concluded in the wake of the school conflict, "no white community is about to educate its black population."[33]

Even worse, blacks lacked the ideological and organizational resources to alter their fate:

> lacking an economic and political power base to bargain from, the community is forced
> not to bargain at all; forced out of the system, the community must chose to either allow
> that system to perpetuate genocide against its children, or to exercise the only power it
> has: . . . [the] futile and self-defeating weaponry . . . of violence and disruption. . . . Black
> people are not permitted to operate the system, but they can, for short periods of time,
> prevent the system from operating.

McCoy foresaw only "a rather protracted death sentence" for young black minds, the result of "a predetermined script, established by racist, capitalist America."[34]

What McCoy learned for himself from the struggle for community control was that his effort to "work in both worlds" was untenable. He concluded that as a professional educator, he "had been in the system too long" and was "imbued with the bureaucratic system."[35] Unlike other leading black educators, Rhody McCoy had relatively few connections to the broader black movement. Following the defeat of community control, McCoy judged his career of commitment to professionalism and educational reform a failure. He left the city and after a few more years, left education and political activism altogether.

Herman Ferguson: Schools and Black Nation Building

At the time of the battle over community control, Herman Ferguson was already convinced that blacks would never achieve full citizenship in the United States. Rather, he saw school politics as a means of creating political autonomy for blacks. Like Rhody McCoy, Ferguson figured prominently in press accounts of the late-1960s school wars. New Yorkers knew him as an assistant principal who had been indicted for conspiring to assassinate moderate integrationist civil rights leaders Roy Wilkins and Whitney Young.[36] Soon thereafter, he addressed a February 1968 Malcolm X memorial at Harlem's I. S. 201, a school at the center of the battle over community control. "To die takes only a split second," Ferguson reminded students in an assembly that also featured James Baldwin and Betty Shabazz. "If you can't do anything at all," he urged, "take someone with you. . . . Get a gun and . . . use it at the appropriate time. . . . The hunting season is approaching."[37]

Ferguson's repudiation of nonviolence and integration extended to his educational ideas. "The whole phenomenon of white supremacy," he argued, was "spread and fostered and supported through the educational system." To counter the inculcation of subordination, Ferguson proposed a "black survival curriculum" of "self-determination, self-control and self defense." It aimed to produce a new black student who would "not be found dying in far-off places in an army that represents the same forces that oppress and exploit him daily. He will know exactly where his battlefield is."[38]

If Ferguson had his way, martial arts training and target practice on the school shooting range would form black students' core curriculum:

> Inasmuch as a good course in weaponry must include basic information from such disciplines as math [muzzle velocity and windage, for instance], physics, chemistry and biology, and since his physical training will deal with developing his neuro-muscular system to a high degree of efficiency, a total curriculum could be planned using these two areas as the core.

Moreover, conducting self-defense and weaponry classes in Swahili and Yoruba would serve to make the "study of original languages more functional and to motivate [the student] to master his native tongue." Even home economics would inform students how the black community could survive when white America cut off supplies. Thus, the entire school day would serve to delegitimize students' American identity and provide the framework for an independent black one.[39]

Still, the proposal to create paramilitary boot camps constituted only one element of Ferguson's educational vision. Because racism's brutalizing impact twisted the consciousness of black youth, teachers could not rely on students constructing an understanding of American life out of their experience. Instead, Ferguson called for a teacher-centered, lecturing pedagogy. The school day would start with a pledge to the red, black, and green flag, and perhaps LeRoi Jones's "We Are Beautiful People." Reading classes would focus on biographies of Nat Turner, Marcus Garvey, Stokely Carmichael, and other leaders. Hallway loudspeakers would "continuously bathe" the black student "with the quiet sound of Malcolm X speaking, LeRoi Jones reading one of his poems, Aretha Franklin singing a soul song, and other heroes speaking to him and *filling* him with a constant pride in his blackness."[40]

Rhetoric like Ferguson's, in which millennial hopes for black liberation intersected with desperate fears about black survival, became increasingly common in the late 1960s. In their own eyes, nationalists' invocations of violence were a response to the genocidal white assault on black America. In fact, Ferguson borrowed the hunting imagery of his Malcolm X memorial speech from retired U.S. Army Colonel Rex Applegate, whose textbook on riot-control was used by police departments around the country. "Just put [police] teams . . . all of them marksmen, with fine guns . . . on the street," Applegate suggested, "and let them go hunting." Applegate's advice reflected the increasing sophistication with which police were preparing to combat ghetto insurgency. Indeed, many of the weapons used by police anti-riot squads were originally developed for use in Vietnam. As Philadelphia police chief Frank Rizzo put it, "I consider myself an expert on guerrilla warfare."[41] Police plans, Herman Ferguson concluded, were part of "a plot, a conspiracy on the part of the U.S. government to completely destroy black people—a final solution the majority of white people would find acceptable as well as desirable."[42]

Other black nationalists denounced racism in what struck many whites as hysterical harangues, but white New York found the mild-mannered Ferguson particularly disturbing. He was a sober man who picked his words carefully and whose idea of flamboyant dress extended no farther than a subdued sports jacket. "Whether Herman Benjamin Ferguson is or is not a dangerous firebrand," the *New York Times* puzzled, "his appearance, manner and speech are those of a disciplined school teacher." He suggested the banality of hating whites, and raised the specter that black New York found his views normal and rational. [43]

Before the 1960s, Ferguson's activities had offered only hints of his eventual militancy. Still, his experiences, both preceding his entry into teaching and while a teacher led him to see racial identity and conflict as preeminent characteristics of American society. Ferguson was born in Fayetteville, North Carolina, where a commitment to education was instilled in him by his parents, both teachers for whom a local black elementary school was named.[44] The attentiveness of Ferguson's own teachers to black history and culture contrasted sharply with the virtual absence of such topics from New York's classrooms. "In the South," Ferguson would remember,

> as part of our curriculum in the high school, they taught Negro history, and all the teachers were black and all the students were black; and in spite of the fact that we were not getting [what] the white students were getting in terms of money . . . there was still a degree of pride and self-respect that one got from having black teachers who were really interested in you and [from] learning about . . . Negroes who had achieved.[45]

After attending Ohio's Wilberforce University, Ferguson settled in New York and went into teaching. "Because it was New York City . . . [and because] the requirements for getting into that system were so stiff," Ferguson expected to find "quality education going on." Working as substitute teacher in schools all around the city, however, destroyed Ferguson's naive visions of educational quality and equality:

> In a white school . . . the teachers were more demanding, the discipline was higher, and there was real teaching and learning going on, and the administration seemed to be more concerned.[46]

Meanwhile, in black neighborhoods,

> the schools were rundown; the teachers by and large were uninterested. . . . Black kids were not being educated or being miseducated, being thrown out of the system. . . . These kids would be labeled as delinquents, slow learners, and . . . would be put into special classes. . . . They would have the kids do things like make shoe-shine boxes and . . . teach 'em how to wash cars. . . . Decisions were being taken and things were being done because these were black kids.[47]

Despite the obvious evil of the Southern racial caste system, Ferguson was left to conclude that his own schooling had been in many ways superior to that which occurred in New York.

At first, Ferguson's conclusion that the black community needed to take responsibility for the education of its children did not preclude his belief in the possibility of blacks participating in and contributing to American society. He worked for a decade within New York's famously Byzantine personnel system to gain administrative jobs for black educators. At the same time, Ferguson was an early member of the United Federation of Teachers and actively supported its efforts to bring trade unionism to school work.[48]

In the 1960s, however, the wider course of race relations, together with continuing disillusionment with New York's schools and the failure of efforts to gain administrative positions for blacks, reshaped Ferguson's thinking. His political activism began shortly before the March on Washington in the summer of 1963. In cooperation with New York's municipal government, a number of unions were building a huge cooperative housing project called Rochdale Village near Ferguson's home. Ferguson joined the Rochdale Movement, which protested the virtual exclusion of black construction workers from the mammoth project.

The Rochdale Movement was one of several New York protest campaigns aimed at integrating construction jobs at public and semi-public projects. Whereas the March on Washington sought to build an alliance of blacks and organized labor to make demands on the government, in New York City, labor and government were united against black economic and political power. Just as civil rights activists under the leadership of Milton Galamison made little progress in their long campaign to integrate New York's schools, black protesters gained little from their protests at Rochdale Village and similar projects. Although Ferguson preserved his professional demeanor following the collapse of the Rochdale Movement, he grew increasingly disillusioned in its wake.[49]

Ferguson and other frustrated activists turned to Malcolm X for advice and support. Under Malcolm's tutelage, Ferguson came to identify himself as a black nationalist and a revolutionary Pan-Africanist, and he moved from demands for civil rights in America to demands for human rights in the colonized ghetto. By 1964, Ferguson chaired the Education Committee of Malcolm's Organization of Afro-American

Unity, and he helped organize the OAAU's weekly Liberation School. The school's curriculum drew on the model of political education developed in the freedom schools of the southern civil rights movement but replaced their focus on citizenship with a radical vision of Pan-African internationalism.

Rather than defining blackness in terms of color, genetics, geography, or culture, Ferguson, like many black nationalists in the late 1960s, articulated a political notion of blackness as colonial relationship to Euro-American domination. "The black revolution," Malcolm argued shortly after his break with the Nation of Islam, "has been taking place in Africa and Asia and Latin America; when I say black I mean non-white—black, brown, red or yellow."[50] Liberation school lessons in African and African American politics and history, according to OAAU educator James Campbell, stressed a "worldview which sees [African Americans] in relation to the broad struggle of peoples around the world who are being victimized by capitalism."[51]

Ferguson became increasingly alienated from the programs with which the public schools responded to racial inequality. As an assistant principal at PS 40 in Queens, he refused to support the school's More Effective Schools (MES) program. Proposed by the United Federation of Teachers as the solution to the underachievement of black students, MES avoided the question of integration. Instead, it called for allocating added resources to inner-city schools. Critics like Ferguson charged that the provision of supplementary resources and services ascribed black academic failure to deficits in the students rather than to the workings of a racist system. If, on the other hand, teachers were part of the machinery of racism, smaller class size and added resources would only increase the power of the schools to harm black children.[52]

Ferguson considered his doubts about the intentions of his fellow teachers—the vast majority of whom were white—confirmed in 1967, when the United Federation of Teachers (UFT) went out on strike over demands that included a policy allowing teachers to more easily remove "disruptive" students from their classrooms. Ferguson and other black teachers were convinced that the incompetence and racism of teachers rather than behavior of students caused most classroom disruption. In response to the 1967 strike, he helped lead the African American Teachers Association's organizing of parents to open schools closed by striking teachers.[53]

Ferguson's activism outside of teaching continued to expand as well. In part because of growing frustration with race relations and in part because of the presence of police agents provocateurs, Ferguson and other black nationalists became increasingly extreme in their demands for political separation from the United States. While Ferguson's militancy won him surveillance and harassment from the police (including J. Edgar Hoover's naming Ferguson as a primary target of the FBI's illegal campaign to discredit radicals),[54] it won him respect from black educational activists. When his 1967 indictment on charges of conspiring to kill Whitney Young and Roy Wilkins prevented the Ocean Hill-Brownsville community control project from making Ferguson a principal, he was hired as a consultant instead.[55]

Then, at the February 1968 Malcolm X memorial, Ferguson argued that the federal government was "stockpiling ammunition and weapons and training riot-control troops . . . [to use] against us and we should be prepared to defend ourselves."[56] Newspapers clamored for action against the black teachers who participated in the Malcolm X assembly, and Board of Education told the I.S. 201 Governing Board, which employed Ferguson, that it would not receive official recognition until it fired its indicted advisor.[57]

In June 1968, an all-white jury convicted Ferguson and another black activist of being part of a terrorist cell. (The third member and chief prosecution witness was an undercover cop who organized the alleged plan and supplied the materials for its execution.[58]) The conviction further radicalized Ferguson. He served as Minister of Education of the Republic of New Africa, a group that proposed guerrilla warfare to win the creation of an independent black nation in the southern states and/or northern ghettos. Arguing that the destruction of the community control had proved that blacks would never control their own lives within the United States, Ferguson helped organize a March 21, 1969 plebiscite in which Ocean Hill-Brownsville residents voted on whether to become part of the Republic of New Africa. The vote led to Ocean Hill's sending six delegates, including Ferguson, to the Republic of New Africa's National Council of Representatives, in Detroit. An announcement of the group's Brooklyn effort was a highlight of the Detroit meeting, and Ferguson was elected Deputy Speaker.[59]

With the defeat of community control, Ferguson was more convinced than ever that within the United States, blacks and whites

> exist as two separate nations. . . . The whole thing was to get across . . . as a possible solution to our problems, actual separation into a nation which we already are. . . . What we were talking about was using community control . . . as a training ground for actual nationhood.[60]

The defeat of community control, however, left Ferguson little room to fight for separate black nationhood in New York's schools. Awaiting sentencing on his murder conspiracy charge, Ferguson jumped bail and spent the next two decades in exile.

Keith Baird: Nationalism and Cultural Pluralism

Veteran educator and activist Keith Baird served on the election commission for the 1969 Republic of New Africa Ocean Hill-Brownsville plebiscite in which Herman Ferguson played a leading role. The call for political sovereignty, Baird suggested, should not be "dismissed as a fatuous dream. For such a claim enunciates and dramatizes the question asked by Frederick Douglass speaking before the Anti-Slavery Society in 1847: 'What country have I?'"[61]

Still, Baird offered a distinctly different vision of black nationalism from Ferguson's. The task facing educators, Baird believed, was

> fundamentally cultural in its implications, and I use the word cultural being cognizant of the origin of the word. "Culture" is related to development: how a person comes into, and maintains itself in, being. So that even the political aspects then become, as it were, subservient to that. Politics have to do with who gets what, but who you are is something else and much larger. That is why the cultural aspect is much more important.[62]

Baird never abandoned hopes that authentic understanding of Africa's cultural legacy could foster full African American participation in mainstream American life.

Although New York's newspapers showed far less interest in Baird than in Ferguson or McCoy, as director of African American and Latin American Studies for the Ocean Hill-Brownsville community control school district, he was uniquely positioned to articulate a nationalist curricular vision. The curriculum Baird developed for Ocean Hill-Brownsville included educational innovations ranging from a gifted program and an art program for potential drop-outs to closed circuit television, educational film, and machines for teaching math. Still, in Baird's eyes, the techniques and technologies teachers used were far less critical than the ends that guided them. By introducing Swahili and African art, history and counting games, as well as Spanish and Puerto Rican history, Baird insisted, schools could help restore cultural and human identities which had been devastated by enslavement and colonization.[63]

Baird acknowledged the impact of political forces on education and black community life, and he combined extensive civil rights movement activism with schoolwork.[64] Still, Baird was, in his own words, "principally a scholar-activist—with a very strong emphasis on scholar." More than any other activist educator of his day, Baird stressed the role of academic inquiry in securing equality and human rights for African Americans.[65]

Serious cultural studies, Baird argued, not only promoted black equality, they offered a means of avoiding the bitter tensions between white teachers and black activists that marked the battle over community control. School protests, in Baird's eyes, "had to do with the assertion of African people of their identity and their educational rights. [They] did not threaten my professionalism as an educator." African American "parents' aspirations for quality education for their children," he reiterated in his capacity as an editor of the civil rights movement journal *Freedomways*, "do not conflict with the need of the teaching profession to protect rights won by trade unionism."[66]

Baird's curricular vision reflected both his experience and his understanding of racism. Born in Barbados, Baird, like many from that island, tended toward Anglophilism. As a child he studied and later as an elementary school teacher he taught a curriculum that was "quite British." Nevertheless, like many West Indian intellectuals who admired English culture, Baird's thinking combined Fabian reformism with a commitment to independence and the recovery of Africa.[67] Baird's earliest political memories date from when he was six. His grandfather was a Garveyite, and Baird began accompanying him to meetings.[68] One Empire Day, Baird told his grandfather that he had learned in school that he was a British subject: "Grandfather responded, 'British subject; you mean British object. When you grow up, someone will ask you, "Are you English?" and you will respond, "I am not English, I am African."'" Garveyism, Baird credits, "gave me great sense of identity. It has a lot to do with my consciousness."[69]

Growing up in a black society also did much to inoculate Baird against the internalization of racial subordination. When he moved to New York in 1947 at the age of twenty-four, Baird applied to Columbia University because "nobody had told me that I shouldn't expect to be admitted and it had never occurred to me that I would not be admitted." Although he "was aware" that because he was "an African person," he "was not going to be able to walk in the door of an employer and [be hired] merely on the basis of my ability," Baird did not allow racism to crush the sense of identity and possibility nurtured in his youth.[70]

In preparation for a career in the ministry, Baird had studied Latin and Greek, and at Columbia, Baird continued his language studies. Having read that the New York school system needed teachers for Spanish-speaking students, Baird decided to study Spanish. Then, while pursuing graduate studies in Romance philology, Baird took Uriel Weinreich's course, "Languages in Contact." Weinreich, a noted linguist and Yiddish scholar, argued that creolization resulted in new languages formed by the contact of older ones rather than in deformations of established European languages. This concept offered Baird a way to think about the languages and societies of the Caribbean as vibrant, legitimate cultural creations rather than as the shadows of European civilization.[71]

In addition to his early experiences and academic training, Baird's understanding of African history and culture was enormously influenced by Afro-Caribbean writers such as J. A. Rogers and, especially, Richard B. Moore.[72] A founder of the African Blood Brotherhood and then one of the first black members of the United States' Communist Party, Moore combined Marcus Garvey's race-consciousness and anti-colonialism with militant demands for socialism and full democratic rights in the U.S.[73] Baird's training in linguistics made him particularly receptive to Moore, who, in the words of Franklin W. Knight, "more than any other individual . . . educated the American public in the proper semantic distinctions between 'black,' 'Negro,' and 'Afro-American,' terms [which previously had been] used interchangeably in the Afro-American community."[74]

As a trained sociolinguist, Baird stressed that our language directs how we think of the social world. What one calls oneself and is called shapes who one is. "By defining to their own satisfaction the identity, status, and destiny" of the Africans they enslaved, Europeans and Euro-Americans, Baird argued, "used communication as an instrument of control to maintain their ascendancy over the oppressed."[75] Whites' oppressive power to name and define African Americans began with slavery but did not end with its abolition. "The word Negro, with its opprobrious origins, its historic servile denotation, and its declassé connotation," according to Baird, remained "the name and the concept of the subhuman. In brief, Negro is a slave name." It denied that African Americans "were people with a historical and cultural identity."[76]

This deprivation of cultural identity was the African American's unique burden:

> Of all the various ethnic groups comprising the American population . . . that group . . . which has its origins in Africa [is the only one] not generally referred to by a group name that connects the members of the group with land, culture, and history. . . . Conceptually, this disassociation of the African individual from soil (Latin *humus*) was a means of rendering him less than human (Latin *humanus*).[77]

Liberation, Baird argued, required that African Americans cease to label themselves as non-persons. Calling oneself African American instead of Negro made "a very important semantic and therefore epistemological difference." It "made a connection to a homeland and to a sense of historical and cultural continuity absolutely manifest and indisputable." (By this standard, the increasingly popular term "black" was little better than "Negro." Although at least on "a level of semantic parity" with white, black still "tells only how the people look, not who they are. . . . It describes them physically but deprives them of cultural identity."[78])

Baird began his New York teaching career in 1953, but it was the blossoming of New York's school integration movement that offered him the opportunity to enact his ideas. During the 1964 New York school boycotts, Baird worked at the freedom school in the church of protest leader Rev. Milton Galamison and then with the Harlem Parents Committee, one of New York's leading grass-roots school reform organizations. Although the school boycotts reflected the 1950s–early 1960s civil rights movement's demands for integration and assimilation, Baird took his freedom school lessons in a different direction. Without knowledge of one's own history, he argued, a person is dehumanized and made the object of another's will. The recovery of one's history, then, was a prerequisite to democratic citizenship. Together with Richard B. Moore and historian John Henrik Clarke, Baird introduced freedom school students to such great African civilizations as Egypt, Kush, Meroe, and Zimbabwe.[79]

Following his freedom school teaching, Baird worked from 1965 until 1968 with John Henrik Clarke and OAAU liberation school educator James Campbell in the Heritage Program of HARYOU-ACT, an agency that had been created by psychologist Kenneth Clark to address the problems of youth in Harlem. "Social service cannot be relevant to the pathology of the ghetto, except to reinforce it," Clark had argued, "if it encourages even subtly the dependency of the people in the ghetto."[80] Education which would help youth devise ways to address their social problems was therefore integral to HARYOU-ACT's work.

After the staunchly integrationist Kenneth Clark severed his ties with HARYOU-ACT, the organization began to supplement classes in organizing skills and the analysis of contemporary problems with the development of students' cultural and historical awareness. In March 1967, Baird's youth leadership class explored the connections among African music, Caribbean Calypso, and African American jazz. Two months later, the class considered the activities of Denmark Vesey, Sojourner Truth, Carter G. Woodson and Mary McLeod Bethune. Other lessons introduced Harlem youth to such scholars as W. E. B. DuBois, J. A. Rogers, Melville Herskovitz, and Basil Davidson. Baird also taught Swahili courses at HARYOU-ACT.[81]

"The challenge of African American cultural nationalism," Baird would explain, "is to reclaim in all its multi-millennial grandeur and sweep and depth of human experience, the African cultural heritage which is the natural birthright of every African individual whether on the ancestral continent or in the Diaspora."[82] Such study, he maintained, promoted a sense of community and identity which enabled youth not only to envision themselves as agents of social change but also, by producing "a positive appreciation of differences among people in a polyethnic and multicultural society," to imagine their integration into the mainstream of American life.[83]

Although Baird and other Heritage Program teachers included "team teaching, audiovisual aids, and other modern teaching techniques" in their lessons, helping African American youth rethink how they defined themselves and their place in the world required conveying to students a language and body of knowledge they lacked. Therefore, Heritage instructors relied on a lecture/discussion format much like that of conventional high school history classes.[84]

The Heritage Program was widely celebrated not only in New York City but also around the United States. The Norwalk, Connecticut Negro History Committee had Baird lecture on "Pan-Africanism—Theory and Practice." "Africa's Golden Past," a record made by Baird and John Henrik Clarke, was used by SNCC organizers in Alabama. Baird was invited to address the National Council of Negro Women's 1967 Project Womanpower conference on "the missing pages of history." In part because the format of the Heritage Program curricula resembled that of the public schools, Baird and his associates fielded a steady stream of inquiries from public schools. [85]

Baird's growing reputation also led to his being invited to address over one thousand educators at the American Federation of Teachers' 1966 conference on Racism in Education.[86] Urbane, erudite and cosmopolitan, Baird quickly won his audience. His speech offered teachers an alternative to then—and now—popular cultural deficit theories which attributed black academic failure to a lack of mainstream knowledge, values and attitudes.[87] Rather, Baird suggested, African Americans were isolated by a lack of awareness of their own identity.[88]

Baird concluded his speech by introducing a resolution, inspired by Richard B. Moore's 1960 pamphlet, *The Name "Negro"—Its Origins and Evil Use*, that the terms "African American" or "Afro-American," which simultaneously acknowledged the cultural legacy of Africa and asserted "a claim of [American] citizenship," be used instead of Negro or black. The resolution, which passed after some controversy, was typical of Baird's insistence that altering the way Americans used language—an essentially educational project—would transform race relations.[89]

Then, as Ocean Hill-Brownsville's director of African American and Latin American Studies, Baird initiated lessons in African history and culture, urging teachers to center the study of African American life on "ethnic identity, [and] historical and cultural continuity." By describing African Americans in ethnic terms, Baird challenged the reliance on dichotomous racial terms common in the United States:

> "Ethnic" and "national" have essentially, for me, the same connotation. . . . Unlike the Republic of New Africa, I do not use nationalism in the sense of setting up a separate national entity. The term "nation" has in its root the same notion as native, natural, and so on, the Latin *natio* corresponds for me to the Greek *ethnos*.[90]

Rendering African Americans more like Jewish Americans or Italian Americans, Baird argued, did not preclude participation in American society and politics. Rather, it "encourages and facilitates it, because it means that one comes to the council of humanity not empty-handed."[91]

This view that African identity could contribute to participation in American life shaped the way Baird organized the curriculum in Ocean Hill-Brownsville. Rather than separating black culture from the mainstream of American culture, his curriculum promoted African American studies as an integrated aspect of American studies:

> We aren't concerned with putting one culture over another, but with supplying the missing pages of black culture. . . . We want to integrate cultures by expressing diversity that is inherent in unity. We will infuse every phase of the existing curriculum with Afro-American and Hispanic studies.[92]

At the same time as Baird introduced the study of Swahili, the number of courses in French and Spanish was expanded as well. A group of fifty Puerto Rican parents declared that the district's bilingual program had both taught their children English and Spanish and given them "a sense of self-identity."[93]

Baird's pluralist nationalism was not without critics. Responding to Baird's 1966 motion to have teachers replace Negro with African American, Black Muslim Minister James X argued that the new term was no better than the old. If Negro had a "slave connotation," the integrationist aspirations of hyphenated Americanism were equally "fictitious."[94] An identification with Africa, writer Harold Cruse echoed, was "motivated more by a psychology of non-identification with the American Negro status and accommodation to American white bourgeois values, than with other essentials of the American Negro struggle."[95]

Meanwhile, other activists charged that Baird's pluralism excessively distinguished blacks from other Americans. HARYOU-ACT founder Kenneth Clark caustically rejected the efforts of the organization's Heritage Program to recover students' African roots. "The American Negro," Clark argued,

> is inescapably American. In spite of the psychological appeals of identification with Africa, and the temporary props to a sagging ego which can be found in occasional discussions and seminars about 'our African heritage,' the American Negro is no more African than he is Danish, or Irish, or Indian. He is American. His destiny is one with the destiny of America. His culture is the culture of Americans. His vices and virtues are the vices and virtues of Americans. His dilemmas are essentially the dilemmas of Americans. He cannot escape this stark fact, in spite of understandable attempts to evade the bitter reality that he has been treated, more often than not, as an alien in his own land.[96]

Self-definition was, moreover, only one element in determining the status of African Americans. Perhaps Baird's most potent critics were New York's white teachers and citizens. Amid the bitter strife between teacher unionists and community activists over the control of New York's schools, Baird offered a way to reconcile teachers' professional aspirations with activists' demands. Possessing a strong African-American voice yet "conversant with European culture" and able to work harmoniously with whites, Baird embodied the kind of pluralism, cosmopolitanism and teacher professionalism that he sought to promote. If white New York sought to find an African American voice committed to fostering intergroup harmony and black participation in the mainstream of American life, it could not have done better than to celebrate Baird's efforts.

Few white teachers or other white New Yorkers, however, embraced Baird's stance or even demonstrated interest in it. In 1967, he ran for president of the United Federation of Teachers, heading a slate of candidates that challenged the union's opposition to community control. Teachers, however, used the vote to endorse the union's increasingly uncompromising stand.[97]

Ironically, cultural pluralism gained far more popularity in the years following the school conflict than it enjoyed in 1968. Largely bereft of utopianism and decoupled from both scholarly inquiry and political activism, "multiculturalism" became a preferred curricular response to racial differences.[98] Keith Baird's pluralism, however, was more politically and intellectually ambitious than is common today. Although Baird continued in the decades following the school conflict to educate African and European Americans about Africa's contributions to the world's cultural heritage, his quest to wed the recovery of African American identity with engagement in mainstream American life remained unfulfilled.

Les Campbell: Schools for a New Culture

Whereas Keith Baird's lessons on African American culture served as a means of cementing the place of blacks in American life, Leslie Campbell turned to cultural nationalism because of what he saw as the impossibility of equal participation in American life. As the struggle for black community control of the public schools wound down in defeat, Campbell spearheaded the establishment of "The East," a network of educational and cultural agencies that were independent of the public schools and other government programs.

The "crown jewel" of the East was Uhuru Sasa Shule (Swahili for Freedom Now School), created for militant youth who had been suspended or expelled from public schools. Campbell recruited African American Teachers Association members to serve as instructors and convinced activist Rev. Milton Galamison to provided space. On February 1, 1970, the Uhuru Sasa opened with sixty youth, aged fourteen through nineteen. Soon, the school added an elementary school and its enrollment climbed to two hundred.[99]

In many ways, Uhuru Sasa's curriculum resembled that proposed by Herman Ferguson. Students took courses in self-defense, political education and nation-building. Assemblies began with students pledging allegiance to the red, black and green flag, and ended "with songs and chants praising the black man and the struggle for liberation." Students attended political rallies and lectures by Herman Ferguson, Stokely Carmichael, Black Panther Safiya Bukhari and other radicals.[100]

Still, after white teachers succeeded in their campaign to dismantle community control, hopes that radical activism could transform the political position of the black community receded. "The glue that held everything together" at Uhuru Sasa, according to Campbell, was "the cultural nationalism of Kwanzaa architect and black studies pioneer Maulana Karenga."[101]

"Walking into the East," the editors of the black nationalist journal *Imani* reported, "is like entering a new black world. You are engulfed by the aroma of fragrant incense as you gaze upon entire walls of colorfully painted murals of black heroes and symbols." The notes of jazz musicians in jam sessions joined with voices of community meetings to announce the "spiritual unity of blackness. . . . In an age of alienation, frustration, and 'revolutionary suicide,'" *Imani* suggested, Campbell and his comrades had demonstrated that is was still possible for blacks to "give new meaning to their lives."[102]

"Big Black," as the six-foot six–inch tall Campbell was sometimes called, served not only as Uhuru Sasa's head teacher but also as its "spiritual leader," a role he proclaimed by changing his name to Jitu Kasisi Weusi, Swahili for Giant Black Spiritual

Leader. Under his leadership, the school's curriculum, *Imani* explained, was "rooted in the seven principles of blackness." Thus, for instance, polite respect for teachers was a way "to value the traditional knowledge of elders." Uhuru Sasa relied on Cuisinaire rods and other hands-on learning aids appropriate to the non-linear logic and active learning style it attributed to black people, rather than public school pedagogy designed with the linear logic and passive learning style of whites in mind. Unlike Jewish students, who thrived on "monotonous, boring" lectures, the East's newspaper *BlackNews* reported, black children could not tolerate "stiff learning."[103]

The defeat of community control was not the only source of Campbell's campaign to transform the culture of the black community. Born in Brooklyn in 1939, Campbell was the child of a Communist activist who introduced his son to such figures as Paul Robeson and Benjamin Davis at Party affairs in Harlem. In high school, Campbell participated in the campaign of the Communist–led Labor Youth League to protest the murder of Emmett Till. Although Campbell would eventually reject the Communist approach to black politics, through the Party he was exposed at an early age to the view that interracial working-class solidarity did not require the political or cultural assimilation of the black community.[104]

Just as Campbell was coming of age, however, the Communists' own activities and McCarthy-era repression combined to diminish the Party's role in interracial organizing. Arrested under the Smith Act, Campbell's own father spent several years in prison. Meanwhile, Cold War attacks on radical workplace organizing gave new importance to community activism. Campbell's mother epitomized this focus. In addition to serving for a number of years as a PTA president, she was active in the United Parents Association and the reform wing of her local Democratic Party club.[105]

While Cold War politics undermined Communist leadership in the struggle for racial equality, it encouraged demands for racial integration. Participating in the 1957 and 1958 marches on Washington for school desegregation and civil rights, Campbell met Bayard Rustin, who was the chief organizer of the marches. Rustin in turn introduced Campbell to Minnijean Brown, one of the nine students who had integrated Little Rock, Arkansas's Central High School in 1958. Rather than explicating the virtues of integration, Brown recounted to Campbell being forced to leave Central High and move to New York City after altercations with racist white students. "One nigger down and eight to go," her white classmates chanted following Brown's dismissal. Brown's description of the months of violent abuse that had preceded her expulsion shook Campbell, and it mirrored his own sense of racial isolation as one of a handful of blacks attending New York's 6,000 student Brooklyn Technical High School.[106]

After four college years in which he engaged in little political activism, Campbell found work as a social studies teacher at Junior High School 35 in Brooklyn's Bedford Stuyvesant neighborhood. The school reinforced Campbell's ambivalence about the movement for racial integration. JHS 35 was "a 99% school—99% of the students were black or Puerto Rican." Although civil rights activists cited conditions at JHS 35 as evidence of the need to integrate New York's schools, the staff included a core of "young, dynamic, strong" black teachers. Working with them reinforced Campbell's skepticism about demands that black teachers and students be dispersed into white schools.[107]

At the same time, Campbell could not ignore New York's grassroots school integration movement, led by Rev. Milton Galamison. Campbell's mother and her family were members of Galamison's church, and Campbell had been impressed with the preacher's militant sermons since his youth. In 1963, Campbell started attending the Monday night meetings of Galamison's City-Wide Committee for Integrated Schools. When the coalition launched its 1964 school boycott demanding integration, Campbell and fellow JHS 35 teacher Al Vann organized almost total participation by the fifteen hundred students at their school. As they participated in the boycott, Campbell, Vann and other teacher activists became convinced of the special contribution a black teachers' organization could make to the struggle for racial equality in New York's schools. They founded the African American Teachers Association.[108]

Integration was not without its critics however. At the same time as he was working with the school integration movement, Campbell was making weekly pilgrimages to Louis Michaux's celebrated Garveyite bookstore in Harlem. One weekend, he recalled, "I looked across the street from Michaux's and standing on this ladder talking to the people was Malcolm X. His voice is like a drummer that I wanted to hear. . . . Malcolm's voice was like a live source."[109]

Malcolm's influence, work in New York's schools and the wider evolution of the African American freedom struggle all propelled Campbell ever more fully back into political activism. Unlike the 1950s, when the Communist Party had promoted "moderate, middle of the road" interracial organizing, Campbell "just gorged [himself] on a steady diet of nationalism" in the 1960s:

> I didn't see how we were going to get integration. And it sort of had a confining element to it. Like we got to get to some place where we will have "black and white together," or we don't have any Utopia. . . . I couldn't visualize that. Like when you go to sleep can you dream this? No, I can't dream that.[110]

Campbell's understanding of black nationalism echoed that of Malcolm X. Black Power, Campbell maintained, was

> the power of the non-white peoples. It means we no longer need to be integrated into the white world to be relevant. We have the dynamic within our own body politic to be important world-wide, to be well-respected, to be recognized. . . . What Malcolm does is that he takes you away from this whole premise of ghetto, of slum, of downtrodden neighborhood, and he transforms this premise into one of community. Where one is weak the other is strength.[111]

Campbell's understanding of education mirrored his definition of black identity as a political phenomenon:

> What we have operating here is a colonial educational system where the goods and services are being supplied to the colony by the outsiders (devils). Outsiders reap the benefits ($) and privileges (pensions and other goodies) of this system and all the colony receives is a yearly flow of functionally illiterate youths who fulfill the need for a cheap labor force and for Vietnam War cannon fodder.

Neither the irrational biases of teachers nor cultural differences between them and black students were the main source of failure in ghetto classrooms. Rather, Campbell argued, the white teacher "despises our children, our community, our culture, and most of all, the goals and aspirations of our people."[112]

Campbell's militancy won him increasing recognition from black nationalists and increasing notoriety among whites. When he defied a Board of Education directive prohibiting teachers from bringing their classes to the Malcolm X memorial at Harlem's I.S. 201, school superintendent Bernard Donovan suspended Campbell, but Afro-American Teachers Association leader Al Vann praised his "courageous stand against the death-dealing techniques [of] the school system."[113]

As a compromise punishment, Campbell was transferred from JHS 35 to Ocean Hill-Brownsville's JHS 271. Rhody McCoy alternately struggled to bridle Campbell's militancy in order to placate school authorities and relied on Campbell to pressure the system. Among black teachers as well as whites, Campbell quickly gained a reputation for extremism and militancy.[114] Spearheading black teachers' demands for equal representation on the JHS 271 faculty steering committee even though they were a minority of the staff, Campbell dismissed an alternative one-teacher-one vote plan as "a step backward in the fight for black self-determination."[115] Meanwhile, he decorated a hallway bulletin board with pictures of "black heroes and heroines," quotations from black radicals, and a large anti-war poster with a picture of Uncle Sam and the slogan, "Uncle Sam Wants You, Nigger."[116]

Campbell's notoriety climaxed on Dec. 26, 1968, when he read an anti-Semitic poem by one of his fifteen-year-old students on the radio program of black nationalist writer and talk show host Julius Lester. Although Campbell stressed to listeners that he was reading the poem in order to expose the hateful sentiments generated by the school conflict, he also asserted that it "tells it exactly the way it is" and had "a tremendous sense of truth." When the UFT and a New York tabloid publicized the poem a few weeks later, Campbell's reputation was set.[117]

Meanwhile, Campbell's tenure at JHS 271 proved short-lived. Although the battle for community control had demonstrated that a "downtrodden community, faced with a crisis, using its own resources, could hold a city-wide apparatus at bay for six months," it also demonstrated that eventually the black community would lose the fight to control its public schools. The community control governing boards were abolished, and the African American Teachers Association lost its capacity to fight after a white teacher unionist applied to join the organization and then broke the group's treasury by suing when he was denied membership.[118] With his black comrades fleeing New York's public schools, Campbell's jubilation because of the unity of the black community was joined by the anguish of its defeat. He too retreated from the schools.[119]

Uhuru Sasa promised to preserve unity and jubilation, even in the face of political defeat. In the end, however, Campbell was no more able to establish an island of radical black culture outside of the public schools than community control activists had been able to redistribute power within the school system. Amid the changing priorities and growing poverty of the black community and declining government support for programs in it, in 1985 the East and Uhuru Sasa closed their doors.[120]

Ironically, at the moment Uhuru Sasa was closing, the school, with its attentiveness to the history and culture of Africa and the African Diaspora, was providing a model for a rapidly growing number of black independent schools. Weusi took little comfort in the rise of independent Afrocentric schools, however. "Independent black schools are being used as the bait," he charged, "[to] wean monies from public education. . . . Black schools have to realize the situation they're in and not play into the hands of those who are trying to do away with public education." Weusi, who had never foresworn radical political activity, returned to the public schools, serving as an assistant principal at Brooklyn's JHS 258.[121]

Conclusion

Through Black Power, Julius Lester observed, "blacks asserted their right to speak for themselves, define for themselves, and organize themselves. . . . It was a clarion call, awakening the dead and giving life to the unborn."[122] Although Rhody McCoy, Herman Ferguson, Keith Baird and Leslie Campbell intensely debated the nature of race relations and schooling, profound areas of agreement united them.

Like myriad black teachers and educational activists, McCoy, Ferguson, Baird and Campbell all charged American schools with an almost complete refusal to educate black children. Abysmal reading scores, graduation rates, and other common measures of educational failure capture only the most superficial aspects of this indictment. "Until the [black] child gets to school," writer James Baldwin observed in a defense of community control, "his circumstances, however wretched in appearance, however hard in fact, are coherent." In contrast, Baldwin argued, the school assures him . . . that he deserves his condition. . . . When the school is finished with him . . . he is ready for the streets, the needle, the jail, the army, the garment center, ready to be used in nearly any way whatever, always assuming that white people—for that is absolutely all that Americans are to him by now: white people—have any use for him at all.[123]

Like the integrationist civil rights movement that preceded it, black nationalist school activism of the 1960s produced what Adolph Reed, Jr. has labeled "moments of transcendence . . . openness to alternative possibility."[124] Whatever their differences, Rhody McCoy, Herman Ferguson, Keith Baird and Leslie Campbell agreed on the need for schooling that allowed black youth to interrogate their brutal world and imagine utopian alternatives to it, rather than one that discouraged such inquiry. The large ambitions that Ferguson, Baird, Campbell and McCoy had for themselves and their students reflected not only their immersion in the wider struggle for black liberation, but also their engagement in central currents of black thought as it developed across the twentieth century.

In many ways, our political, moral, and social imagination has atrophied rather than expanded in the years since 1968. We have fallen far from transcendent hopes. The four educators portrayed in this chapter suggest instead that one cannot imagine or create fundamental alternatives to inequitable systems of schooling without participating in movements to imagine and create an alternative to the inequitable society that schools serve.

In their curricular activism, McCoy, Ferguson, Baird and Campbell were all cognizant of the impact of oppression on the psyches of black youth, but they were equally convinced that what James Baldwin called African America's "endless struggle to achieve and reveal and confirm a human identity" has been a source of America's richest and most original art.[125] If, they suggest, black educators could not ignore white racism, neither could they reduce their work to a response to white racism. The source and meaning of black educational thought and activism lie neither in responding to white supremacy nor in asserting the free agency of the black community but in the interplay of these two contradictory impulses. This delicate, fragile, always threatened balancing act remains the task of those who would promote racial justice in the schools.

Chapter 10

Schools and Social Justice in the Post-Liberal City

Justice, justice
shall thou pursue.
—DEUTERONOMY: 16, 20

Attending a 1967 conference on the future of Harlem's I.S. 201, historian David Tyack found the mutual recrimination of teachers and black activists a "shattering experience." Few of the contestants, Tyack felt, "could hear what others were saying. . . . Few were willing to credit the opponent with good will. . . . People who needed to be partners in social justice were shredding each other's morale."[1] Echoing Tyack's experience, virtually every commentator in subsequent decades concluded that no event in New York's recent history "evokes such despair as events . . . in 1968."[2]

This study documents the depth of the chasm that appeared between whites and blacks during the 1968 conflict and the way it rippled through the schools and urban life. At the same time, however, it demonstrates both that 1968's divisions had deep historical and ideological roots and that even at the bitterest moments of the school conflict images of monolithically antagonistic black and white opinion masked a multiplicity of beliefs.

If, as Rhody McCoy concluded, the outcome of the school conflict was completely determined by the unequal "political and economic resources" with which blacks challenged "the social and economic benefits [whites derived from] racism,"[3] ideas and ideals would not matter. The very division of this book into two halves, the first white, the second black, reflects the power of racial inequality in school politics and life. Still, the very existence of diverse views among blacks and whites challenges fatalistic notions that school politics is predetermined by social inequality. An understanding of the racial politics of education, like an understanding of the racial dynamics of the classroom, must account both for the enormously powerful social, political and economic structures of inequality and for the capacity of people, individually and collectively, to reshape and redefine their worlds.

What Was Won

The school conflict ended in a victory for the teachers' union and a defeat for black activists. In the spring of 1969, New York State ratified the UFT victory. A union-endorsed "decentralization" law abolished the community control demonstration districts. The central Board of Education retained the power to approve textbooks, curricula, and school construction; the Board of Examiners retained a large role in teacher hiring; the Chancellor, who replaced the Superintendent, was given power to suspend or remove community boards. In addition, the central board of education retained complete control over New York's troubled high schools.[4] UFT President Al Shanker called the new law "a good piece of legislation," while Brooklyn civil rights leader Milton Galamison claimed, "we couldn't have gotten a worse bill in Mississippi."[5] In crushing the demonstration school districts, the UFT guaranteed itself a prominent role in school affairs and municipal politics.

The new law established between thirty and thirty-three "community" school districts containing a couple hundred thousand residents and lacking the media or political institutions of an independent city. Indeed, the only organization with the resources to consistently sway the many "community" school board elections was the United Federation of Teachers. Designed to insulate the school system from black activists, the "Community School Board" elections worked as planned. In Ocean Hill-Brownsville, voter turnout fell from 25% in 1967 to 4% in 1970. Although in a few areas with strong community organizations, persons of color, women and grassroots activists served on community boards, the new "community boards" were dominated by white male professionals.[6] In a school system where only a minority of students were white, whites formed a majority on 25 of 32 boards, including that of Manhattan's District 3, where whites were 19% of students and Brooklyn's District 13, where only one student in twenty was white.[7] Although the huge new districts were designed to preclude effective community mobilization, they allowed school authorities and political elites to maintain that the success or failure of schools serving poor children of color was now in the hands of the communities from which the schools drew their students. By 1980, *The New York Times* would claim that decentralization was an experiment that was tried and, alas, had "failed to fulfill hopes that it would significantly raise educational achievement of schoolchildren."[8]

Moreover, even though the demonstration districts were eliminated, the rhetoric of community control was taken up by opponents of racial justice. When a few dozen black students were bused into Brooklyn's Canarsie neighborhood in 1972, ten thousand white students boycotted classes for a week. On the first day of the boycott, two thousand Canarsians rallied in support of the segregated status quo. An Orthodox rabbi invoked Canarsie's right to "community control" as he told the crowd, "What's good for the goose is good for the gander," and a PTA leader acknowledged, "We thought the boycotts during the Ocean Hill-Brownsville crisis were terrible, but we whites learned from the black militance."[9]

The school conflict also catalyzed the transformation of electoral politics. As historian Jerald Podair has observed, the more conservative candidate has won almost every New York mayoral election since the 1960s; the city of LaGuardia, Wagner and Lindsay became the city of Koch, Guiliani, and Bloomberg.[10] The invocation of community control in defense of social inequality was not limited to New York. President Richard Nixon used calls for "local community" power in education in a bid to reduce federal funding for urban schools.[11]

The class and racial hostilities of the wider society, in the words of historian Michael Katz, are "integral, not incidental" to the structure of public schooling.[12] Marjorie Murphy notes that at the very time when the newly founded UFT was winning concessions from the school system, black school activists, mobilizing as large a percentage of their constituency as the UFT, "had little to show for their efforts."[13] The defeat of community control did not create inequality but rather confirmed and intensified a political imbalance that had been growing throughout the decade.

The contrasting results of teacher organizing and black activism reflected the evolving conditions of urban and national life. In the years leading up to the school conflict, new urban patterns created by automation and the relocation of industrial production confined blacks to New York's deindustrializing ghettos, while highway construction and urban renewal programs destroyed old neighborhoods and promoted suburbanization.[14] At the same time, city agencies faced declining municipal resources and national economic policies which de-emphasized social welfare.[15] As economic growth gave way to uncertainty, teachers became increasingly skeptical of claims that their interests aligned with those of the poor.

In 1968, schools were a central arena in which notions of race, class, and government were reshaped. Preeminent among the achievements of teacher unionists was their role in heralding the transformation of race-blind standards of equal treatment from a means to justify demands for racial equality into a way to oppose it. The UFT argued that by prohibiting discriminatory acts with conscious perpetrators, racism would be eliminated and equal opportunity ensured. Conversely, to favor a black job applicant over a white one because of race would be as racist as refusing to hire blacks. This race-blind standard of justice had informed UFT support for the civil rights struggle against legally enforced segregation in the South, but with the elimination of Jim Crow laws, it suggested the fundamental fairness of a school system and society profoundly marked by racial inequality.

Despite the UFT victory in the battle over community control, black activists could point to significant achievements as well. They were able to create autonomous black schools and other institutions and dramatically increased curricular attention to black history and culture. New York school activists contributed much to helping discredit the once-popular liberal notion that African America had produced no distinctive and noteworthy culture. As black nationalists repudiated the integrationist ideal, they laid to rest notions that black culture was merely a distorted version of white America life. The school crisis did much to help convince African Americans that black, no less than white, could be beautiful.

The efforts of black activists also helped undermine both the notion that racism was reducible to isolated acts of wrongdoing and the notion that the school and social systems were just. Racism was readily visible in the pervasive inequality and subordination that enveloped the ghetto. Such racism required no conscious act and the elimination of individual bigotry was insufficient to address it. Even as it marked the decline of integrationist hopes, the creation of the community control school boards provided an arena for the development of minority political leaders.

What Was Lost

The most profound impact of the school conflict lies not so much in what each side could claim to have won but in what each side had lost. Despite the UFT victory, teachers paid a substantial price in the school conflict. Their organized clout, coming at the expense of the movement of racial justice, discouraged interracial coalitions for better education, subverted the notion that schools could help construct an equitable society, and exacerbated feelings of demoralization in teachers' daily school work. In spite of the UFT's clout, some 10,000 teachers, most of them white, lost their jobs in New York's 1975 Fiscal Crisis.[16] Similarly, although black activists mobilized the rediscovery of African American culture, the flowering of racial pride and consciousness never translated into an effective movement for racial justice. The vast majority of black children remained confined in impoverished and demoralized schools. Educational enclaves in which blacks exercised considerable power were meager consolation prizes in a larger defeat.

Lack of clear winners and losers is also evident when one takes gender as well as race into account. With androcentric notions so embedded in the views of UFT leaders and black nationalists, it is not surprising that women were more likely than men to cross the black-white divide. For a decade, Annie Stein was a close associate of Rev. Milton Galamison, and she played an important role in black community activism. Teachers for Community Control had far more women in leadership than did the UFT. Black community organizers Thelma Hamilton and Mary Ellen Pfeiffer embraced community control without ever abandoning hopes for integration.

Interests were not uniform and clear, and because of their ambiguity, they alone did not make history. A summary of the economic and social changes of the post–World War II years which suggests that material interests and their ideological consequences were unambiguous is therefore misleading. Even if a conflict between black activists' and white teachers' interests inevitably existed in New York, the way activists understood and responded to that conflict was by no means predetermined.

Whites and blacks brought to the school conflict ideas that had long shaped American political activism. UFT leaders understood community control through the lens of race-blind social democratic theory, which subsumed race relations under class analysis, even as they embraced notions of teacher professionalism. Teachers for Community Control sought to build working-class militancy while honoring the independence of black activism. New leftists subsumed issues of class under identification with the black freedom struggle. The Jewish Teachers Association reduced issues of race to the claims of ethnicity.

Like his UFT allies, Bayard Rustin sought to incorporate blacks into the white labor movement and, through it, fight poverty and protect blacks from the worst abuses of an increasingly conservative nation. Milton Galamison saw in community control a means of asserting the full humanity of blacks, an integration into the human family rather than into the institutions of American life. Keith Baird was a cultural pluralist who saw the celebration of the achievements of African culture as fully compatible with Afro-American participation in American life. Herman Ferguson and Sonny Carson saw no such hope for black participation in white America, and viewed community control as a step in the development of separate and independent political and cultural institutions for blacks. When he came to Ocean Hill-Brownsville, Rhody McCoy saw in community control a way for the African American community to transform both itself and the institutions which dominated it.

The varied ideals that energized educators were like rivers coursing subterraneously before appearing unexpectedly above ground. Immersion in social movements and ideals that shaped the twentieth century afforded school activists the intellectual and political tools with which to understand and shape, however incompletely, the crisis of their times. This engagement of teacher and community activists in political and intellectual life beyond the schools provides a model for those who would reform the schools today.

Unexpected dialectics propelled the school conflict in unanticipated ways. Just as McCarthyism drove Annie Stein out of the labor movement and Milton Galamison out of the NAACP, it led to the formation of alternative organizations like the Parents Workshop with militant grass-roots tactics over which national organizations had little control. Furthermore the very redbaiting which discouraged radical class analysis encouraged an ideology of democratic participation. Interests impelled no single response to school politics from blacks or whites. Although activists' visions were inevitably grounded in history, they were not dictated by it.

The Past and the Future of Schooling and Social Justice

The legacy of the 1968 school conflict figures centrally in the latest scheme to reform New York's schools. On June 12, 2002, New York abolished the 32 community school boards created in the wake of community control and transferred their powers to the central board of education. In turn, the central board was itself placed under the direct control of the mayor.

New York is not alone in granting mayors greater authority over urban school systems. Over the last decade, reformers in such cities as Boston, Chicago, Cleveland, Oakland, and Washington have embraced mayoral control in hopes of raising student achievement levels and promoting efficient school management.[17] The turn to mayoral control represents a recognition on the part of researchers and reformers that the sustained improvement of urban schools requires more than curricular and organizational innovation. It also demands the creation of political and financial support for public education. Transferring school governance from independent boards of education to the mayor's office, proponents argue, will foster the creation of broad coalitions needed to revitalize urban public schooling.[18]

Political scientists have labeled the spirit of cooperation needed to tackle difficult and controversial social problems such as educational inequality "civic capacity." They recognize that obstacles to the development of civic capacity in matters of urban schooling are great.[19] The development of a sense of common purpose that transcends individual interests and the execution of a shared plan for urban school improvement inevitably confront racial divisions.[20] White communities resist reforms that threaten their children's academic advantages. Long experience with white domination discourages minority parents from seeking ties with white communities and with the white corporate and political elites who control resources for schools. Meanwhile, educators often view the involvement of others as outside interference. Finally, the enhancement of civic capacity requires that participants in school reform discuss explicitly their varying goals and understandings. As this study demonstrates, such discussions are exceedingly difficult.[21]

In theory, mayoral control can facilitate political organizing and thus enhance civic capacity to improve urban schools. In reality however, mayoral control of New York's schools has diminished civic capacity for school reform. Rather than promoting interracial coalition, mayoral control has served as a vehicle for promoting racial division. Arguing that the creation of New York's community school districts had been a capitulation to vicious and incompetent black demagogues intent on plundering the city's schools for personal gain, *New York Times* pundit James Traub hailed mayoral takeover as the greatest achievement of Republican Mayor Michael Bloomberg's regime.[22] The claim by Traub and other proponents of recentralization that black community activists are particularly given to corruption is an odd one in an era which has witnessed a parade of corruption scandals—S&L, Enron, Arthur Anderson—involving white national elites. It is odd too because New York's own history is full of corruption scandals involving central school authorities.[23] Rather than building a multiracial, multi-class coalition to create exemplary democratic schools, the Bloomberg administration has followed the pattern of other mayoral takeovers—the promotion of a pared down curriculum and tied to narrow, quantifiable goals and high stakes tests, cost savings, privatization, and reliance on corporate elites to plan and lead educational changes.[24]

Although pro-business, pro-gentrification policies, outcome-based systems of accountability and a narrowing of educational goals are not inherent in mayoral control, the mayors who have been granted power over the schools have consistently been advocates of such approaches. Mayoral control has frequently facilitated attacks on civil rights era gains by blacks. In Boston, the school board created by mayoral control voted to end busing and return to neighborhood schools. Minority groups protested that mayoral control had diminished their role in educational affairs. In Chicago and Oakland, mayors have used their power over the school to promote gentrification.[25]

Given the politics of mayoral control, it is not surprising that researchers have been unable to document consistent academic gains from the mayoral takeover of the schools. Nor are administrative reforms certain. Unlike most U.S. cities, Baltimore relied on mayoral control of the schools in the decades following World War II. Nevertheless, it experienced the pattern of miseducation, mismanagement and racial conflict that mayoral control promises to eliminate. Rather than galvanizing support for school improvement, Baltimore's mayors generally avoided the political costs of leading reform. Finally, mayoral control, which has commonly been promoted by pro-business mayoral administrations and state legislatures with few links to minority communities, has done little to win added resources for underfunded urban schools.[26]

Decades of sustained attacks on New York's community boards left them with little legitimacy and opened the door for elimination of this vestige of community control.

Even though mayoral control emerged as an attack on minority power, it is possible that the high visibility of mayoral politics will foster the creation of coalitions rather than conflicts. However, given the inherent fragility of civic capacity, it is equally plausible that mayoral control will contribute to the further erosion of public schooling. At the very least, for mayoral control to promote civic capacity and contribute to the creation of equitable schools, those interested in school reform will have to confront the varying visions they bring to their work; they will have to confront the myriad political ideas and ideals advocated in 1968.

The New York school crisis revolved around invocations of community and their relationship to universal standards of truth and justice. The uncompromising division between the vast majority of teachers and the communities from which they drew the majority of their students renders problematic invocations of classroom communities or of schools' ability to contribute to the construction of wider communities. Whether one takes community to signify the received particularities of ethnic traditions or the feelings of social solidarity growing out of shared experience, the 1968 school conflict presents a challenge to educators who seek to create a sense of community in or by means of the schools.

Racial antagonisms and economic inequality mark American society today just as they did in 1968. The dilemmas that activists confronted so dramatically in 1968 continue to shape conditions in school and society, but public commitment to social justice is even more wanting.[27] A politics committed to diminishing poverty and to incorporating all into a vibrant public life may again animate American politics. It will need to address the complex, sometimes contradictory nature of social relations, and to utilize the range of intellectual resources that activists possessed in 1968.

Instead, today's racial politics of education reflect how much we have narrowed our vision since 1968. Efforts to combat racism in schools that focus on closing the racial achievement gap have largely abandoned the goals of civic and intellectual participation in the broader society.[28] Whites invoke race-blind standards of fairness to claim that they oppose discrimination and to justify their inattention to it. Market mechanisms in school assignment and local community governance of individual schools are largely divorced from any broader movement for the redistribution of resources and opportunities. The cruel deceptiveness of strategies of individual mobility is mitigated only by their almost inevitable improbability.

The widespread disinterest of whites today in racial justice has its own deep roots in American history. Although Americans once thought liberalism to be an invincible national ideology,[29] United States politics were never uniformly liberal and divisions had always existed within the liberal amalgamation. Elite reformers, for instance, often placed more faith in technical expertise, consensus politics and the emancipatory potential of education and less faith in redistributive programs than did labor organizers. Furthermore, liberalism did not preclude ethnic self-identification and the celebration of ethnic cultures. By the same token, the grievances that generated grass-roots support for liberalism before the school conflict have not disappeared, and many activists have retained the conviction that the United States can accommodate each American, whatever his or her inherited statuses, in a common public life.

This study does not propose discover through the examination of the 1968 conflict a policy to rectify today's inequalities. Rather, it suggests a range of ways of thinking about and debating schooling that can help us clarify our own ideas and challenges.

Notes

Chapter 1: Worldviews in Collision

1. Langston Hughes, "Same in Blues," in *Selected Poems* (New York: Alfred Knopf, 1959), 271.
2. W. E. B. DuBois, *The Souls of Black Folk* (Chicago: McClurg & Co., 1903), 1.
3. A third district, Two Bridges, was not a focal point of the conflict.
4. See for instance Phillip Lopate, *Against Joie de Vivre: Personal Essays* (New York: Poseidon Press, 1989), 289–93.
5. M. D. Usdam, "Citizen Participation: Learning From New York City's Mistakes," *Urban Review* 4 (Summer 1969): 9–12; "Decentralization and Community Involvement in Local School System," *National Education Association Research Bulletin* 43 (Mar. 1970): 3–6.
6. Mwalimu J. Shujaa and Hannibal T. Afrik, "School Desegregation, the Politics of Culture, and the Council of Independent Black Institutions," in Mwalimu J. Shujaa, ed., *Beyond Desegregation: The Politics of Quality in African American Schooling* (Thousand Oaks, CA: Corwin, 1996), 254–55; M.A. Farber, "An 'African Centered' School: How the Idea Developed and Why It May Fail," *New York Times*, 8 Feb. 1991, A13.
7. William Ayers and Michael Klonsky, "Navigating a Restless Sea: The Continuing Struggle to Achieve a Decent Education for African American Youngsters in Chicago," *Journal of Negro Education* 63 (1994): 12–13; Fred Hess, *School Reform Chicago Style* (Newbury Park, CA: Corwin Press, 1992), 87.
8. David Rogers, *110 Livingston Street: Politics and Bureaucracy in the New York City Schools* (New York: Random House, 1968), 483, 486–87.
9. Richard Mudder, "City Will Receive $126 Million More in Albany Accord," *New York Times*, 29 Mar. 1967, 1; "Notes and Comments," *The New Yorker*, 21 Sept. 1968, 39.
10. Mario Fantini, "Community Control and Quality Education in Urban School Systems," in *Community Control of the Schools*, Henry Levin, ed. (Washington: Brookings Inst., 1970), 52, 72–3; Mudder, "City Will Receive $126 Million;" "Notes and Comments;" Teacher's Freedom Party of the UFT (Ralph Poynter, chairman), "Anatomy of a Cop-out: Harlem vs. Shanker," *Liberator*, Jan. 1968, 17.
11. Fantini, "Community Control," 61; Fred Hechinger, "The Neighborhoods Demand Control," *New York Times*, 19 May 1968, IV, 9.
12. Rogers, *110 Livingston Street*; John Leo, "Study Finds Pathological Bureaucracy in Schools: Charges System 'Sabotaged' Desegregation Plans in the Early Sixties," *New York Times*, 24 Oct. 1968, 50; Mario Fantini, Marilyn Gittell, and Richard Magat, *Community Control and the Urban School* (New York: Praeger, 1970); Rhody McCoy, interview, in *Why Teachers Strike: Teachers'*

Rights and Community Control, Melvin Urofsky, ed. (Garden City, NY: Doubleday, 1970), 118; Marilyn Gittell, *Demonstration for Social Change* (New York: Institute for Community Studies, 1971); Fantini, "Community Control," 46; Mark Maier, *City Unions: Managing Discontent in New York City* (New Brunswick, NJ: Rutgers University Press, 1987), 127; Maurice Berube and Marilyn Gittell, eds., *Confrontation at Ocean Hill-Brownsville: The New York School Strikes of 1968* (New York: Praeger, 1969), v.

13. *Toward the Integration of Our Schools, Final Report of the Commission on Integration* (Board of Education of the City of New York, 1958), 25.

14. Clark, a psychology professor at City College whose work had influenced the *Brown* decision, contended that in New York, as in the South, segregated schooling left black students with a sense of inferiority and limited their education. Gerald Markowitz and David Rosner, *Children, Race, and Power: Kenneth and Mamie Clark's Northside Center* (Charlottesville: University of Virginia Press, 1996), 98–99.

15. Although one may distinguish integration from narrower policies of desegregation, movement activists and policy analysts often elided the two, expecting that as legal barriers to interracial contact are eliminated blacks would inevitably assimilate into the mainstream of American life. (See Diane Ravitch, *The Troubled Crusade: American Education, 1945–1980* [New York: Basic Books, 1983], 126; Diane Ravitch, *The Great School Wars, New York City, 1805–1973: A History of the Public Schools as Battlefield of Social Change* [New York: Basic Books, 1974], 252–3, 278.)

16. Rogers, *110 Livingston Street*, 15; John Theobald, "Education," in Lyle Fitch and Annmarie Hauck Walsh, *Agenda for a City: Issues Confronting New York* (Beverly Hills: Sage, 1970), 170. An elementary school was considered segregated when more than 90 per cent of its students were black and Hispanic. In the fall of 1955, 42 New York City elementary schools—about 10 percent of all elementary schools—were segregated. By 1963, the number had risen to 134. In 1960, 41% of black and Puerto Rican students attended segregated schools; by 1965, the figure had risen to 49%. (Ibid., 15–16; Ravitch, *Great School Wars*, 253, 257, 268.)

17. Richard Montague and Alfred Hendricks, "The Battle for the Schools," *New York Post*, 2 Feb. 1964, 22. Although many whites who opposed school integration were not liberals, in 1964, many whites who had supported the Southern civil rights movement opposed the New York boycott. The opposition of these white liberals propelled the transformation of school politics.

18. Rogers, *110 Livingston Street*, 27.

19. Martin Mayer, "Frustration Is the Word For Ocean Hill," *New York Times Magazine*, 19 May 1968, 59.

20. Kenneth D. King, "Attitudes on School Decentralization in New York's Three Experimental School Districts," (D.Ed. dissertation, Teachers College, Columbia University, 1971), 32–36.

21. "Crisis Erupts Over Decentralization Projects," *United Teacher*, 11 Oct. 1967, 9.

22. Rogers, *110 Livingston Street*, 483, 486–87.

23. Allen Matusow, *The Unraveling of America: A History of Liberalism in the 1960s* (New York: Harper and Row, 1984), 243–271; and Fantini, "Community Control," 52, 72–3.

24. Zippy Bauman, interview, New York City, 14 Sept. 1990; Paul Becker, interview, Rockville Center, NY, 16 Sept. 1990.

25. Fantini, "Community Control," 61; Fred Hechinger, "The Neighborhoods Demand Control," *New York Times*, 19 May 1968, IV, 9.

26. Ibid.; "Fact Sheet Ocean Hill-Brownsville School District," *Scope Bulletin*, Sept. 1968 (Emergency), 1; author's personal copy.

27. New York state law prohibited strikes by all public employees.

28. Sol Stern, "'Scab' Teachers," *Ramparts*, 17 Nov. 1968, 21; Carter, *Pickets, Parents and Power*, 31, 47-8.

29. "Why the New York Urban League Backs the Ocean Hill;" Ad Hoc Committee for Justice in the Schools, "Due Process . . . Civil Liberties . . . and the Public Schools" (advertisement), *New York Times*, 24 Nov. 1968, 7E.

30. Barbara Carter, *Pickets, Parents, and Power: The Story Behind the New York City Teachers' Strike* (New York, Citation Press, 1971), 2.

31. Ad Hoc Committee, "Due Process . . . Civil Liberties . . . and the Public Schools;" "Letter of Transfer," in *Confrontation*, 33.

32. Albert Shanker, interview, in *Why Teachers Strike*, 37.

33. Leonard Buder, "Most City Schools Shut," *New York Times*, 10 Sept. 1968, 1. On October 22, 1968, Board of Education reports from 28 of New York's 33 school districts showed 316 of the city's 900 schools open, with 5,513 of 57,000 teachers and 62,927 of 1,129,000 pupils in attendance. Leonard Buder, "City to Ask Court for Aid in Ending Dispute," *New York Times*, 23 Oct. 1968, 1, 32. The vote for the first of the three strikes was 12,021 to 1,716; by the third strike the margin of support had declined to 6,042 to 2,128. Perhaps what is most remarkable is how many of New York's 50,000 teachers, whether because they were satisfied with the UFT's direction or alienated from the union, opted not to vote. Ted Bassett and Philip Bonosky, "Protest wave hits 3d Shanker strike," *Daily World*, 15 Oct. 1968, 5.

34. "Anti-Semitism in the New York City School Controversy: A Preliminary Report of the Anti-Defamation League of B'nai B'rith," *United Teacher* Special Supplement, 22 Jan. 1969, c; Bill Kovach, "Racist and Anti-Semitic Charges Strain Old Negro-Jewish Ties," *New York Times*, 23 Oct. 1968, 1.

35. Becker interview; Robert Rossner, *The Year Without an Autumn: Portrait of a School in Crisis* (New York: Richard W. Baron, 1969), 164; Kovach, "Racist and Anti-Semitic Charges."

36. Judge William Booth, "Racism and Human Rights," in *Black Anti-Semitism and Jewish Racism*, Nat Hentoff, ed. (New York: Richard W. Baron, 1969), 118.

37. Rossner, *The Year Without an Autumn*, vii.

38. Leonard Buder, "Brooklyn Schools Shut in Decentralization Dispute," *New York Times*, 16 May 1968, 41.

39. "Charge Editorial is Racist," *United Teacher*, 22 Jan. 1969, 9.

40. "'Hoodlum Element' Said to Run Schools," *New York Times*, 12 Feb. 1968, 17. The New York Civil Liberties Union argued that "the UFT had used 'due process' as a smokescreen to obscure its real goal . . . to discredit decentralization and sabotage community control." The community boards noted that teacher strikes were themselves illegal and demanded, without success, that the letter of the law be adhered to by all participants in the school conflict. (New York Civil Liberties Union, "The Burden of Blame: Report on Ocean Hill-Brownsville Decentralization Controversy," 28 Oct. 1968, 16; David X. Spencer, Chairman, I.S. 201 Governing Board, "Dear Friend," 3 Apr. 1969, Isaiah Robinson Papers.)

41. David Selden, *The Teacher Rebellion* (Washington, DC: Howard University Press, 1985), 153-4.

42. Melvin Zimet, *Decentralization and School Effectiveness: A Case Study of the 1969 Decentralization Law in New York City* (New York: Teachers College Press, 1973), 26.

43. "The Legislature," *New York Times*, 2 May 1969.

44. John Theobald, "Education," in Lyle Fitch and Annmarie Hauck Walsh, *Agenda for a City: Issues Confronting New York* (Beverly Hills: Sage, 1970), 171.

45. C. A. Tesconi," The Crisis of the Triumph of Liberalism," (keynote address at the 1979 meeting of the American Educational Studies Association), *Educational Studies* 11 (1980): 239–250; Steve Fraser and Gary Gerstle, eds., *The Rise and Fall of the New Deal Social Order, 1930–1980* (Princeton: Princeton University Press, 1989). In the eyes of elite liberal reformers, government, through the scientific application of resources created by economic growth, would abolish poverty without redistributing wealth. This New Deal liberalism was sustained by the belief that American capitalism, free from a feudal past and growing boundlessly, allowed social problems to be solved without fundamental social change. "When the cost of fulfilling people's aspirations can be met out of a growing horn of plenty—without robbing Peter to pay Paul," enthused economist Walter Heller, "ideological roadblocks melt away and consensus replaces conflict." Alan Matusow observes that the very definition of poverty as an absence of money rather than as a relationship of inequality reflected the promise that poverty would be eliminated without recourse to redistribution of wealth. (Heller quoted in Godfrey Hodgson, *America in Our Time: From World War II to Nixon, What Happened and Why* (New York: Doubleday, 1976), 484; Matusow, *The Unraveling of America*, 217–221.)

46. Joshua Freeman, *Working Class New York: Life and Labor Since World War II* (New York: New Press, 2000), xiv. In the wake of the school crisis, New York City's system of higher education was also attacked, and amid the widely held misperception that with Open Admissions, City University served primarily the black and Latino poor, a long tradition of free tuition was ended. (Sherry Gorelick, "Open Admissions: Design for Failure?" *Politics & Education*, Summer 1978, 11.)

47. John Hull Mollenkopf, "The Postindustrial Transformation of the Political Order in New York City," in Mollenkopf, *Power*, 225, 227; Norman Fainstein and Susan Fainstein, "Governing Regimes and the Political Economy of Development in New York City, 1946-1984," in Mollenkopf, *Power*, 161–180; Freeman, *Working-Class New York*, 170–72.

48. Jeffrey Mirel, *The Rise and Fall of an Urban School System: Detroit, 1907–1981* (Ann Arbor: University of Michigan Press, 1993).

49. Jonathan Rieder, *Canarsie: The Jews and Italians of Brooklyn Against Liberalism* (Cambridge: Harvard University Press, 1985), 16, 19. Their fears were not unfounded even if their analysis was mistaken: by 1966 blue collar wages in the United States had stagnated and would within a few years begin a dramatic decline. See Hodgson, *America in Our Time*, 482.

50. Hodgson, *America in Our Time*, 416–17.

51. Ibid. See also Michael W. Miles, *The Odyssey of the American Right* (New York: Oxford University Press, 1980), 301–339.

52. Wayne Urban, *Why Teachers Organized* (Detroit: Wayne State University Press, 1982).

53. John L. Rury and Jeffrey Mirel, "The Political Economy of Urban Education," *Review of Research in Education* 22 (1997): 49–110.

54. In 1968, the vast majority of teachers were white, and the concerns of white and black teachers differed. While the notion of antagonistic labor-management relations was central to the thinking of most white activists, few blacks were preoccupied by labor relations within the community-controlled schools. Although New York had sizable Chinese, Puerto Rican and Dominican populations, few activists from these communities played significant roles in 1968. They did not challenge the prevailing view that defined school politics in terms of black-white conflict.

55. Much of the scholarship on New York City has followed the UFT's stance, attributing New York's problems to white liberal pandering to black extremism. See Charles Murray, *Losing Ground: American Social Policy, 1950–1980* (New York: Basic Books, 1984); Jim Sleeper, *The*

closest of Strangers: Liberalism and the Politics of Race in New York (New York: Norton, 1990); Tamar Jacoby, *Someone Else's House: America's Unfinished Struggle for Integration* (New York: Free Press, 1998); Vincent Cannato, *The Ungovernable City: John Lindsay and His Struggle to Save New York* (New York: Basic Books, 2001).

56. Michelle Fine, ed., *Chartering Urban School Reform: Reflections on Public High Schools in the Midst of Change* (New York: Teachers College Press, 1994); Bruce Fuller, ed., *Inside Charter Schools: The Paradox of Radical Decentralization* (Cambridge: Harvard University Press, 2000). 1–11.

57. On the limits of school reform see Richard Rothstein, "Out of Balance: Our Understanding of How Schools Affect Society and How Society Affects Schools," (Chicago: Spencer Foundation, 2002).

58. Carole Hahn, *Becoming Political: Comparative Perspectives on Citizenship Education* (Albany: SUNY Press, 1998). On the other hand, an extensive literature addresses the impact of cultural diversity on citizenship itself. See for instance Nancy Rosenblum, *Membership and Morals: The Personal Uses of Pluralism in America* (Princeton: Princeton University Press, 1998); Will Kymlicka, *Politics in the Vernacular: Nationalism, Multiculturalism and Citizenship* (New York: Oxford University Press, 2001); Richard Shweder, Martha Minow and Hazel Rose Markus, *Engaging Cultural Differences: The Multicultural Challenge in Liberal Democracies* (Russell Sage Foundation, 2002); Paul Kennedy and Victor Roudometof, eds., *Communities across Borders: New Immigrants and Transnational Cultures* (Routledge, 2002); Reneo Lukic and Michael Brint, eds., *Culture, Politics and Nationalism in the Age of Globalization* (Ashgate, 2001).

59. Andy Hargreaves, "Revisiting Voice," *Educational Researcher* 25 (Jan.–Feb. 1996): p. 12–19.

60. For a similar perspective, see Paul Willis' depiction of working-class lads in *Learning to Labor: How Working Class Kids Get Working Class Jobs* (New York: Columbia University Press, 1981). For works suggestive of the ideological and material contexts that have shaped teacher unionism, see Wayne Urban, "Teacher Activism," in *American Teachers: Histories of a Profession at Work*, Donald Warren, ed. (New York: Macmillan, 1989), 190–209; and Marjorie Murphy, *Blackboard Unions: The AFT and the NEA, 1900–1980* (Ithaca: Cornell University Press, 1990). For an exploration of the historical ambiguities of community participation and the complexities of parent and community activism in schooling, see Carolyn Eisenberg, "The Parents' Movement at IS 201: From Integration to Black Power, 1958–1966" (Ph.D. Dissertation, Columbia University, 1971).

61. Daniel Perlstein, "Teaching Freedom: SNCC and the Creation of the Mississippi Freedom Schools," *History of Education Quarterly* 30 (1990): 297–324; Elizabeth Aaronsohn, Interview, Willamantic, CT, 12 Sept. 1990; Deuteronomy: 16, 20.

Chapter 2: Race, Class, and the Triumph of Teacher Unionism

1. Joseph Epstein, "The New Conservatives: Intellectuals in Retreat," in *The New Conservatives: A Critique from the Left*, Lewis Coser and Irving Howe, eds. (New York: Quadrangle, 1974), 13.

2. Peter Milliones, "Both Shanker and McCoy Fear Growing Racial Unrest in City," *New York Times*, 9 Nov. 1968, 20.

3. Sandra Feldman, "N.Y. City Decentralization" (Part II), *New America*, 15 Apr. 1968, 5.

4. Maurice Goldbloom, "The New York School Crisis," *Commentary*, 1969, reprinted in *United Teacher*, 5 Feb. 1969, 14; Michael Harrington, *Toward a Democratic Left: A Radical Program for a New Majority* (New York: Macmillan, 1968), 78.

5. Henry Hampton and Steve Fayer, *Voices of Freedom: An Oral History of the Civil Rights Movement from the 1960s through the 1980s* (New York: Bantam, 1990), 496.

6. Sandra Feldman, "N.Y. City Decentralization," *New America*, 31 Mar. 1968, 5.

7. David Selden, *The Teacher Rebellion* (Washington: Howard University Press, 1985), 150; "UFT Spends $220,000 on Ads During Strike," *New York Times*, 16 Nov. 1968, 7.

8. Fred Hechinger, "A Conflict With No Easy Solution," *New York Times*, 22 Sept. 1968, IV, 2; Leonard Buder, "Shanker Rejects Offer to Protect Ocean Hill Staff," *New York Times*, 25 Sept. 1968, 1.

9. UFT, advertisement, *New York Times*, 13 Sept. 1968.

10. "Crisis Erupts Over Decentralization Projects," 9.

11. Albert Shanker to Parents, 6 Sept. 1968, in Philip Taft, *United They Teach: The Story of the United Federation of Teachers* (Los Angeles: Nash Publishing, 1974), 189. See also "UFT Fights for Democratic Due Process," *United Teacher*, 29 May 1968, 3; UFT, advertisement, *New York Times*, 13 Sept. 1968.

12. Leonard Buder, "McCoy Defies Donovan's Order," *New York Times*, 18 Sept. 1968, 32.

13. The UFT's liberalism extended beyond racial matters. The union, for instance, supported the 1964 Berkeley Free Speech Movement. (AdCom Minutes, 16 Dec. 1964, in *United Teacher*, 4 Feb. 1965, 13.)

14. On the conflicts between Communists and Socialists within the Teachers Union, see Robert Iversen, *The Communists & The Schools* (New York: Harcourt, Brace and Co., 1959).

15. Charles Cogen, "The President's Column," *United Teacher*, June 1960, 6.

16. "A Meeting for Shachtman," *New America*, 31 Dec. 1972, 8; Merry Tucker, interview, New York City, 11 Sept. 1990; George Altomare, interview, New York City, 20 Dec. 1991; Deborah Meier, interview, New York City, 11 Sept. 1990; John O'Neill, "The Rise and Fall of the UFT," in *Schools Against Children: The Case for Community Control*, Annette Rubinstein, ed. (New York: Monthly Review Press, 1970), 180; Selden, *The Teacher Rebellion*, 15, 29; Feldman, "N.Y. City Decentralization," 5 fn. 8; Eugenia Kemble, "What's Wrong With Congress?" *New America*, 25 Aug. 1968, 4; Jeannette DiLorenzo, interview, UFT Oral History Collection, United Federation of Teachers Papers, Robert F. Wagner Labor Archives, New York University (hereafter UFT Papers); and Maurice Berube, "'Democratic Socialists' and the Schools," *New Politics*, Summer 1969, 58; Israel Kugler, "A Life in the Workmen's Circle," *Labor's Heritage*, Oct. 1991, 36–49; Marjorie Murphy, *Blackboard Unions: The AFT and the NEA, 1900–1980* (Ithaca: Cornell University Press, 1990), 150–174; *United Teacher*, Nov. 1963, 11; and Fred Hechinger, interview, in *Why Teachers Strike: Teachers' Rights and Community Control*, Melvin Urofsky ed. (Garden City, NY: Doubleday, 1970), 348–49.

17. Iversen, *The Communists & The Schools*, 112; Ruth Jacknow Markowitz, *My Daughter, the Teacher: Jewish Teachers in the New York City Schools* (New Brunswick: Rutgers University Press, 1993), 111.

18. Iversen, *The Communists and the Schools*, 194. See also Iversen, 101; Taft, *United They Teach*, Chapter 2; Celia Lewis Zitron, *The New York City Teachers Union, 1916–1964: A Story of Educational and Social Commitment* (New York: Humanities Press, 1969), Chapter 2.

19. David Hollinger, "Ethnic Diversity, Cosmopolitanism, and the Emergence of the American Liberal Intelligentsia," *American Quarterly* 27 (1975): 144–145. For a discussion of how the impulse toward universalism among New York's teachers resonated with an assimilationist current in Jewish American life, see Chapter III.

20. Founded in 1935, the Teachers Guild had 1,400 members five years later. Despite the 1940 and 1941 AFL decisions to rescind the charter of the Teachers Union and grant it to the Guild, the social democratic group enrolled fewer than ten percent of teachers in 1947, a percentage that had not increased when the Guild gave way to the UFT in 1960. Taft, *United They Teach*, 46, 55–56, 70, 81. The legacy of the old left informed the very structure of the UFT. Shanker and the UFT inner circle, writer Irving Howe argued, "blends the cohesiveness of Bolshevik organization with the style and politics of conservative 'laborism.'" Beginning in the mid-1960s, Shanker's Unity Caucus controlled virtually all union offices, and UFT bodies considered policy proposals on the basis of caucus as well as union interests. At a 1969 UFT Executive Board meeting, for instance, UFT leader Jules Kolodny argued against establishing a committee to evaluate the UFT's structure because it might give the impression that "Unity Caucus has a fission." Executive Board Transcript, 29 Sept. 1969, 104–110, box 2, Executive Board Transcript file, UFT Papers. The mingling of Caucus and union business did not begin in response to community control. In Aug. 1963 the union's AdCom appointed Shanker to be UFT representative to the AFT's Progressive Caucus. AdCom minutes, 13 Aug. 1963, in *United Teacher*, Oct. 1963, 11.

21. Iversen, *The Communists and the Schools*, 201–4. The Guild conspired not only with such conservative unionists as New York State Labor Federation leader George Meany and AFL head William Green, but also with New York's notorious Rapp-Coudert Committee and Martin Dies' House Un-American Activities Committee. Participation in anti-democratic government activities would continue when the Guild became the UFT. Among Shanker's first acts upon being elected AFT president was the establishment of a program for AFIELD, an agency created by the CIA to disrupt militant trade unions around the world. William Edward Eaton, *The American Federation of Teachers, 1916–1961: A History of the Movement* (Carbondale: Southern Illinois University Press, 1975), 79–121; George Schmidt, *The AFT and The CIA* (Chicago: 30; Lois Weiner, "Shanker's Legacy," *Contemporary Education* (1998): 197

22. DiLorenzo interview.

23. Albert Shanker, interview, New York City, December, 1991; Altomare interview; Selden, *The Teacher Rebellion*, 89, 90–91. "Albert Shanker: 'Power Is Good,'" *Time*, 22 Sept. 1975, 17; Alden Whitman, "The Rise and Rise of Albert Shanker," *New York Times*, 15 Jan. 1975, 59; A. H. Raskin, "He Leads His Teachers Up the Down Staircase," *New York Times Magazine*, 3 Sept. 1967, 28; A.H. Raskin, "Today, the Teacher's Union," 72. The particularities of the garment industry shaped the youths of Shanker, George Altomare, and other teacher unionists. As Arthur Liebman notes, it "typified the worst features of industrial or quasi-industrial capitalism." Arthur Liebman, "The Ties That Bind: The Jewish Support for the Left in the United States," *American Jewish Historical Quarterly* 66 (1976): 288.

24. Selden, *The Teacher Rebellion*, 16.

25. Altomare interview.

26. Selden, *The Teacher Rebellion*, 47–8, 68, 109.

27. T. M. Stinnett, *Turmoil in Teaching: A History of the Organizational Struggle for America's Teachers* (New York: Macmillan, 1968), 159. In 1962 the AFT became a member of the AFL-CIO's Industrial Union Department. AFT President Megel called the IUD money and organizers "invaluable" in the UFT's campaign to represent New York teachers. (Ibid., 57, 181.)

28. Stinnett, *Turmoil in Teaching*, 7; James Carey, "Address," *Addresses and Proceedings* (One-hundredth Annual Meeting, Denver, July 1962), Washington, DC: National Education Association, 1962, 48–49.

29. DiLorenzo interview.

30. Markowitz, My Daughter, the Teacher, 153.

31. In the UFT's 1962 strike, 7500 junior high school teachers and 7200 elementary school teachers honored picket lines. Selden, The Teachers' Revolt, 18, 25; Stinnett, Turmoil in Teaching, 59–60.

32. Altomare interview.

33. Thomas Brooks, Toil and Trouble: A History of American Labor, second edition (New York: Dell, 1971), 307.

34. Joseph Lyford, "April 11, 1962: Day of Dignity," United Teacher, Apr.–May 1962, 4.

35. John Scanlon, "Strikes, Sanctions, and the Schools," Saturday Review, 19 Oct. 1963, 51.

36. "AFL-CIO Leaders Back Teacher Union," New York Times, 17 Sept. 1968, 41.

37. Bayard Rustin, "Conflict or Coalition? The Civil Rights Struggle and the Trade Union Movement Today," Address before the AFL-CIO Constitutional Convention, 3 Oct. 1969, UFT Publications Collection, UFT Papers.

38. Benjamin Klebaner, ed., New York City's Changing Economic Base (New York: Pica Press, 1981), 2, 128. Klebaner estimates that private sector employment grew by a modest 102,000. Similarly, Charles Brecher et al. estimate that manufacturing jobs declined from 947,000 in 1960 to 826,000 and service sector jobs grew from 609,000 to 782,000 between 1960 and 1969. By 1989, service jobs would outnumber manufacturing ones three-to-one by 1989. Charles Brecher, et al., Power Failure: New York City Politics and Policy Since 1960 (New York: Oxford University Press, 1993), 7, 194.

39. Klebaner, New York City's Changing Economic Base, 2.

40. Stinnett, Turmoil in Teaching, 22–23.

41. Stinnett, Turmoil in Teaching, 7.

42. Ibid., 24; Raymond Hertan, Municipal Labor Relations in New York City: Lessons of the Lindsay-Wagner Years (New York: Praeger, 1973), 11. Increasing numbers of strikes followed increased union membership; the thirty-three teacher strikes in 1966 surpassed the total of the entire preceding decade. Brooks, Toil and Trouble, 304, 310–11.

43. "Teamwork: Key to UFT Victory," United Teacher, Jan. 1962, 2 (see also "Labor Support Helped UFT," United Teacher, Oct. 1963, 1.

44. Charles Cogen, "President's Column," United Teacher, Dec. 1963, 4; Business Week, 30 Dec. 1961, quoted in Stinnett, Turmoil in Teaching, 56.

45. David Selden, "Class Size and the New York Contract," Phi Delta Kappan, Mar. 1964, 283–87; Selden, The Teacher Rebellion, 82.

46. Taft, United They Teach, 181, 216.

47. Rossner, The Year Without an Autumn, 65, 124–5, 134; Rose Shapiro, interview, UFT Oral History Project; Lenora Berson, The Negroes and the Jews (New York: Random House, 1971), 318. See also Leonard Buder, "Lindsay Rebuked in School Dispute," New York Times, 17 May 1968, 1.

48. Rossner, The Year Without an Autumn, 95. See also 64, 67 74; Robert Lichtenfield, interview, Greenwich, CT, 27 Dec. 1991.

49. Myrna Katz Frommer and Harvey Frommer, It Happened in Brooklyn: An Oral History of Growing Up in the Borough in the 1940s, 1950s, and 1960s (New York: Harcourt Brace & Co., 1993), 231–33.

50. Jack Bloomfield, "Exclusive: The Untold Story of Ocean Hill" (reprinted from New York Daily Column and the Knickerbocker, undated), Teachers Action Caucus Papers, Box 1, folder 2, Tamiment Institute Library, New York University. Although UFT officer John O'Neil claimed that

collective bargaining had been a great step forward for teachers, in his eyes, it had not radically changed their relationship with administrators. John O'Neil interview. On teachers organization officials gaining promotion within the school system, see William Wattenberg, *On the Educational Front: The Reactions of Teachers Associations in New York and Chicago* (New York: Columbia University Press, 1936), 165.

51. Executive Board Minutes, 28 Nov. 1967, and 26 June 1968, Executive Board file, UFT Papers.

52. Minutes of Chapter Committee, Flushing High School, 21 Nov. 1968, Executive Files: Albert Shanker, UFT District Representatives, 1968–1979, UFT Papers.

53. Sandra Feldman, "The Growth of Teacher Consciousness: 1967," (New York: League for Industrial Democracy, no date), 4.

54. Sandra Feldman, "UFT and UPA Join in 'Self-Help' Clinics to Educate Parents," *United Teacher*, 5 May 1967, 2.

55. Feldman, "N.Y. City Decentralization," (Part II), 6.

56. "UFT Fights for Democratic Due Process," 3.

57. Albert Shanker, "UFT Statement on Decentralization" [fall 1968], 5, Box 1, folder 1, TAC Papers.

58. Wasserman, *School Fix*, 309.

59. Bill Kovach, "Racist and Anti-Semitic Charges Strain Old Negro-Jewish Ties," *New York Times*, 23 Oct. 1968, 1.

60. Jervis Anderson, *A. Philip Randolph: A Biographical Portrait* (New York: Harcourt Brace Jovanovich, 1973), 148–9.

61. Albert Gordon, "Freedom Ride," *United Teacher*, Oct. 1961, 7; "Our Gal Rebecca," *United Teacher*, Sept. 1962, 3; *United Teacher*, Sept. 1963, 2, 8; Rolland Dewing, "Teacher Organizations and Desegregation," *Phi Delta Kappan*, Jan. 1968, 257–60.

62. Gunnar Myrdal, *An American Dilemma: The Negro Problem and Modern Democracy* (New York: 1944), lxxi, 928–9.

63. "UFT's Record of Gains."

64. "Executive board minutes," *United Teacher*, 24 Jan. 1964, 7.

65. Harrington, *Toward a Democratic Left*, 78.

66. Jerald Podair, *Like Strangers: Blacks, Whites, and New York City's Ocean Hill-Brownsville Crisis, 1945–1980* (Ph.D. dissertation, Princeton University, 1997), 226. Simon Beagle (Chairman, UFT Committee for Effective Schools), "Honestly, It's Not a Miracle," in Stanley Wanat and Michael Cohen, eds., *Before the Fall: A Discussion of Schools in Conflict with Community* (Ithaca: Cornell University, 1969), 79; Simon Beagle, "Analyzes Various Problems Facing 'More Effective Schools' Program," *United Teacher*, 18 Feb. 1965, 7; Elizabeth O'Daly (Assistant Superintendent, More Effective Schools), "Results of MES," *United Teacher*, 8 Sept. 1965, 13; "UFT Proposals Focus on Ghetto Education," *United Teacher*, 6 Jan. 1967, 2–3. Unfortunately, MES was not particularly effective. John Theobald, "Education," in Lyle Fitch and Annmarie Hauck Walsh, *Agenda for a City: Issues Confronting New York* (Beverly Hills: Sage, 1970), 177.

67. New York City Commission on Human Rights, *Selection of Teachers and Supervisors in Urban School Districts* [Transcript of hearings held January 25–29, 1971] (New York: author, 1972), 342. As Shanker predicted, by the 1990s, Jews had become a minority among New York's teachers, while the percentage of black or Hispanic increased substantially. When a 1991 early retirement plan led 221 of the city's approximately 1,000 principals to retire three-fourths of the retirees but only half of their replacements were white. Benjamin Ginsberg, *The Fatal Embrace: Jews and the State* (Chicago: University of Chicago Press, 1993) 157.

68. Nathan Kantrowitz, *Ethnic and Racial Segregation in the New York Metropolis: Residential Patterns Among White Ethnic Groups, Blacks, and Puerto Ricans* (New York: Praeger, 1973), 27; Nancy Foner, "The Jamaicans: Race and Ethnicity Among Migrants in New York City," in *New Immigrants in New York*, Nancy Foner, ed. (New York: Columbia University Press, 1987), 207.

69. Shanker, interview, in Urofsky, *Why Teachers Strike*, 180.

70. See Kenneth D. King, "Attitudes on School Decentralization in New York's Three Experimental School Districts," (Ed.D dissertation, Teachers College, Columbia University, 1971), 36. For a particularly powerful statement of this argument as it applies to American race relations since the 1960s, see Orlando Patterson, *The Ordeal of Integration* (Washington: Civitas, 1997). One of the problems with the claim that frustration caused black behavior is that American society has always frustrated black hopes. According to Julius Lester, "Black Power was merely the next step in a logical progression, not the outpouring of frustration that the press tried to make us believe." Julius Lester, *Look Out, Whitey! Black Power's Gon' Get Your Mama* (New York: Grove Press, 1968), 30.

71. Sheila Rule, "Exhibition on Blacks and Jews Protested," *New York Times*, Apr. 19 or 20, 1992 or 93.

72. Bel Kaufman, *Up the Down Staircase* (Englewood Cliffs, NJ: Prentice-Hall, 1964), 32, 54, 58–60, 71, 152, 168, 270, 291, 304, 314.

73. Lichtenfield interview. A self-contained community of over 50,000 people, Co-op City was one of several large housing projects built by the UFT and other unions in the 1960s. Although it opened at the end of the UFT strike, thousands of white families from the Bronx had signed up to move into the complex, hastening a wider movement of whites from the area. "Co-op City Opens for 50,000," *United Teacher*, 4 Dec. 1968, 18; David Rogers, *110 Livingston Street: Politics and Bureaucracy in the New York City Schools* (New York: Random House, 1968), 53.

74. Herb Goro, *The Block* (New York, Vintage, 1970), 61.

75. Lichtenfield interview; Deborah Meier to Editor, *United Teacher*, 20 Mar. 1968, Meier interview; Richard Piro, *Black Fiddler* (New York: William Morrow, 1971), 79–80.

76. Goro, *The Block*, 36, 49.

77. Lichtenfield interview.

78. Hampton and Fayer, *Voices of Freedom*, 490.

79. Piro, *Black Fiddler*, 7, 9.

80. Selden, *The Teacher Rebellion*, 156.

81. A. H. Raskin, "He Leads His Teachers," 4.

82. "14 Civic Groups Charge Pupils Are Often Unfairly Suspended," *New York Times*, 6 Apr. 1967, 33.

83. Anne Filardo, interview, New York City, 14 Sept. 1990; Zippy Bauman, interview, New York City, 14 Sept. 1990; Paul Becker, interview, Rockville Center, NY 7 Sept. 1990.

84. Although AFT locals have established hundreds of partnerships with districts, foundations, universities and corporations, the efforts have remained at the margins of teacher unionism. Moreover, the "new unionism" makes no claims about the nature of teachers' work that were not already raised in the 1960s and has not focused on issues of racial inequality. On the new unionism, see Nina Bascia, "Teacher Unions and Educational Reform," in Andy Hargreaves, et al., eds, *The International Handbook of Educational Change* (Dordrecht: Kluwer, 1998).

85. Albert Shanker, "American Schools Are Envy of the World," speech reported in *New York Teacher*, 24 Jan. 1982, 16; in Ira Shor, *Culture Wars: School and Society in the Conservative Restoration, 1969–1984* (Boston: Routledge & Kegan Paul, 1986), 13.

Chapter 3: The Ambiguities of Identity

1. The prophet Nathan tells King David of a man with untold flocks and herds who nevertheless took a poor neighbor's one ewe lamb. David responds that the man had no pity and must surely die. Referring to David's having killed Uriah the Hittite and taken his wife, Nathan explains, "Thou art the man."

2. Bill Kovach, "Racist and Anti-Semitic Charges Strain Old Negro-Jewish Ties," *New York Times*, 23 Oct. 1968, 1; Earl Raab, "The Black Revolution and the Jewish Question," in *Black Anti-Semitism and Jewish Racism*, Nat Hentoff, ed. (New York: Richard W. Baron, 1969), 37; Albert Vorspan, "Blacks and Jews," in *Black Anti-Semitism and Jewish Racism*, 201; Anne Filardo, interview, New York City, New York City, 5 Sept. 1990.

3. Robert Rossner, *The Year Without an Autumn: Portrait of a School in Crisis* (New York: Richard W. Baron, 1969), 39; Sol Stern, "'Scab' Teachers," *Ramparts*, 17 Nov. 1968, 21.

4. Louis Harris and Bert Swanson, *Black-Jewish Relations in New York City* (New York: Praeger, 1970), 110, 132, 151, 226, 228.

5. David Rogers, "The Jewish Teacher in the Ghetto School," *Dimensions in American Judaism* (Summer 1969), 6, 8; Ruth Jacknow Markowitz, *My Daughter, the Teacher: Jewish Teachers in the New York City Schools* (New Brunswick: Rutgers University Press, 1993), 182–3; George Altomare, interview, New York City.

6. *Jewish Teachers Association Bulletin*, 1961–1967, *passim*; *Morim* (Bulletin of the Jewish Teachers Association), 1967–1970, *passim*. The JTA was formed in 1926 and until the school crisis focused on social programs. "It was," one teacher would remember, "a good place to meet men, and they had excellent dances." Deborah Dash Moore, *At Home in America: Second Generation New York Jews* (New York: Columbia University Press, 1981), 102; Markowitz, *My Daughter, the Teacher*, 126.

7. Marc Dollinger, *Quest For Inclusion: Jews and Liberalism in Modern America* (Princeton: Princeton University Press, 2000). While many Jewish intellectuals remained committed to Jewish traditions or communal life, even they embraced liberal ideals. Horace Kallen, *Individualism: an American Way of Life* (New York: Liveright, 1933); Carole S. Kessner, ed., *The "Other" New York Jewish Intellectuals* (New York: New York University Press, 1994).

8. Historical accounts of black-Jewish relations, most by Jews, have tended to follow UFT's lead, portraying a period of cooperation followed by conflict or black betrayal. In one major bibliography of black-Jewish relations, black anti-Semitism is a major category; Jewish racism is not. Robert Weisbord and Arthur Stein, *Bittersweet Encounter: The Afro-American and the American Jew* (Westport, CT: Negro Universities Press, 1970), Jonathan Kaufman, *Broken Alliance: the Turbulent Times Between Blacks and Jews in America* (New York: Scribner, 1988), Murray Friedman, *What Went Wrong?: The Creation and Collapse of the Black-Jewish Alliance* (New York: Free Press, 1995); Lenwood G. Davis, *Black-Jewish Relations in the United States: A Selected Bibliography* (Westport: Greenwood, 1984). A growing body of scholarship however has examined changing Jewish attitudes toward blacks within the context of Jewish life and Jews' place in American society. Michael Rogin, *Blackface: White Noise: Jewish Immigrants and the Hollywood Melting Pot* (Berkeley: University of California Press, 1996); Jeffrey Melnick, *A Right to Sing the Blues: African Americans, Jews and American Popular Song* (Cambridge: Harvard University Press, 1999); Dollinger, *Quest For Inclusion*; Seth Forman, *Blacks in the Jewish Mind: A Crisis of Liberalism* (New York: New York University Press, 1998).

9. John Hatchett, "The Phenomenon of Anti-Black Jews and the Black Anglo-Saxon: A Study in Educational Perfidy," *Afro-American Teachers Forum*, Nov.-Dec. 1967, 1.

10. Weisbord and Stein, *Bittersweet Encounter*, 151.

11. Leo Blond, "Black Anti-Semitism in New York City," *Phi Delta Kappan*, Nov. 1968, 177. Although the original Latin term meant simply "unbelieving," by the middle ages, it had taken on anti-Semitic connotations, a usage confirmed in the Church rituals and later in the translations offered in prayerbooks. In response, Pope John XXII banned the prayer in 1959. Shlomo Simonsohn, *The Apostolic See and the Jews* (Toronto: Pontifical Institute of Medieval Studies, 1991), 9; Richard Barrie Dobson, *The Jews of Medieval York and the Massacre of 1190* (York: St. Anthony's Press, 1974), 20; Marie-Thérèse Hoch and Bernard Dupuy, *Les Églises Devant le Judaïsme. Documents Officiels, 1948–1978* (Paris: Cerf, 1980), 350–352.

12. Marie Syrkin, "The Hatchett Affair at N.Y.U.," *Midstream* 14 (Nov. 1968): 6; Weisbord and Stein, *Bittersweet Encounter*, 153–157; Leonard Dinnerstein, *Uneasy at Home* (New York: Columbia University Press, 1987), 236.

13. Lenora Berson, *The Negroes and the Jews* (New York: Random House, 1971), 430; Vorspan, "Blacks and Jews," 195.

14. Although New York's Jews included persons with differing origins, genders, beliefs, etc., Jewishness, like "blackness" or any group identity, is not merely a fiction or a description of the most common attributes of group members. Rather, such identities are a means to assert and enforce collective interest. Amid evolving social conditions, both Jews and non-Jews have contested the meaning of Jewish identity. In 1968, the UFT and its allies dominated these discussions.

15. Vorspan, "Blacks and Jews," 198; Harris and Swanson, *Black-Jewish Relations*, 31.

16. Weisbord and Stein, *Bittersweet Encounter*, 169–70. On the deceptiveness of other leaflets, see Fred Ferretti, "New York's Black Anti-Semitism Scare," *Columbia Journalism Review*, Fall 1969, 21.

17. Murray Schumach, "Striking Teachers Get Death Threats," *New York Times*, 16 Nov. 1968, 26.

18. Milton Galamison, "The Ghost of McCarthy" (typed version), [c. 1969], 18–19, Milton Galamison Papers, Box 12, folder 73, Schomburg Center for the Study of Black Culture, New York City Public Libraries.

19. "Incitement and Assaults reported," *United Teacher*, 1 May 1968, 4; "Another View of the 271 Scene," *United Teacher*, 1 May 1968, 4.

20. Henry Raymont, "Teachers Protest Poem to F.C.C.," *New York Times*, 16 Jan. 1969, 48; "UFT Raps Anti-Semitic Poem," *United Teacher*, 22 Jan. 1969, 9; Julius Lester, "A Response," in *Black Anti-Semitism and Jewish Racism*, 229–232; Galamison, "Ghost of McCarthy," 19; Herman Mantell to Nelson Rockefeller, 20 Jan. 1969, in *Morim*, Feb. 1969, 6.

21. Galamison, "The Ghost of McCarthy," 21.

22. Jerry Weiss, et al., "Anti-Semitism? A Statement by the Teachers of Ocean Hill-Brownsville to the People of New York" (advertisement), *New York Times*, 11 Nov. 1968, 55. See also Edith Evans Asbury, "Jewish Teachers Back Ocean Hill," *New York Times*, 2 Nov. 1968, 24; David Selden, *The Teacher Rebellion* (Washington: Howard University Press, 1985), 153; Ferretti, "Black Anti-Semitism Scare," 22; Lionel Lokos, *The New Racism: Reverse Discrimination in America* (New Rochelle: Arlington House, 1971), 344.

23. Keith Baird, interview, 3 Oct. 1991.

24. Arnold Forster to Editor, *Columbia Journalism Review*, Spring 1970, 61; Nat Hentoff, "Blacks and Jews: An Interview with Julius Lester," *Evergreen Review*, Apr. 1969, 22. Although Lester converted to Judaism and repudiated many of his opinions, he steadfastly believed that the UFT unjustly vilified Campbell to further a racist campaign against community control. Julius Lester, *Lovesong: Becoming a Jew* (New York: Henry Holt, 1988), 49–50, 56–7.

25. Will Maslow, "Negro-Jewish Relations in America," *Midstream* 12 (Dec. 1966): 63; Harris and Swanson, *Black-Jewish Relations*, 28, 109–111, 210, 205, 211, 216.

26. Simon, *Public Opinion*, 91; Harris and Swanson, *Black-Jewish Relations*, 119–122.

27. Lokos, *The New Racism*, 342.

28. Harris and Swanson, *Black-Jewish Relations*, 201.

29. Ferretti, "Black Anti-Semitism Scare," 20–21.

30. Irving Spiegel, "Jews Are Advised Not to Exaggerate Animosity of Negro," *New York Times*, 10 Sept. 1968, 73; Ferretti, "Black Anti-Semitism Scare," 20–21; Kovach, "Racist and Anti-Semitic Charges;" Simon, *Public Opinion*, 93.

31. See Daniel Perlstein, "American Dilemmas: Education, Social Science, and the Limits of Liberalism," in *The Global Color Line: Racial and Ethnic Inequality and Struggle From a Global Perspective*, Pinar Batur-VaderLippe and Joe Feagin, eds. (Stamford, CT: JAI Press, 1999), 357–79.

32. The over-representation of Jews among white supporters of the twentieth century civil rights movement has been widely noted. Philanthropist Julius Rosenwald donated millions of dollars to black schools in the South. Joel and Arthur Springarn served as presidents of the NAACP. In the 1920, one third of the Urban League's board of directors were Jewish, as was Edwin R. A. Seligman, its first chairman. Jack Greenberg headed NAACP Legal Defense Fund head, and the two white activists killed during Mississippi's 1964 Freedom Summer were Jews. In addition, many Jewish organizations took an active interest in civil rights.

33. David Levering Lewis, "Parallels and Divergences: Assimilationist Strategies of Afro-American and Jewish Elites from 1910 to the Early 1930s," *Journal of American History*, 71 (1984): 543–564.

34. Arthur Hertzberg, *The Jews in America: Four Centuries of an Uneasy Encounter: A History* (New York: Simon and Schuster, 1989), 323–27, 357. The element of self-service in Jewish support did not go unnoticed among blacks. See Kenneth Clark, "Candor About Negro-Jewish Relations," *Commentary*, Feb. 1946, 13.

35. Reassessment Committee of the National Jewish Community Relations Advisory Council, *The Public Schools and American Democratic Pluralism—the Role of the Jewish Community: report of a conference, May 1-May 3, 1971* (New York: Author, 1972), 27.

36. Roger Kahn, *The Passionate People: What It Means To Be a Jew in America* (Greenwich, CT: Fawcett, 1968), 92. See also Albert Arent, "Forward," *Schools and American Democratic Pluralism*, 5.

37. Markowitz, *My Daughter, the Teacher*, 61–64, 80–82, 155, 161–69; Perlstein, "American Dilemmas," 362–63.

38. Wolfe, *A Life In Two Centuries*, 43–4. When Wolfe applied to become a teacher in 1916, because the Board of Examiners employed tongue twisters and verse to make sure that applicants were "free from Brooklynese." Irving Howe was dissuaded from teaching in part by the oral examinations used eliminate Jewish applicants. Irving Howe, *A Margin of Hope: an Intellectual Autobiography* (New York: Harcourt Brace Jovanovich, 1982), 10. Wolfe's students included Marxist philosopher and John Dewey protégé Sidney Hook. History teacher and Teachers Guild leader Abraham Lefkowitz won his student Max Shachtman to Marxism at De Witt Clinton High School in the Bronx. Shachtman in turn became the political mentor of Al Shanker and others in the UFT inner circle. Peter Drucker, *Max Shachtman and His Left: A Socialist's Odyssey through the "American Century"* (Atlantic Highlands, NJ: Humanities Press, 1994), 1, 13, 268–269.

39. Howe, *Margin of Hope*, 14, 30. Howe spoke Yiddish better than English when he entered elementary school, but after being humiliated for using a Yiddish word in his first class, he resolved never again to speak the language to his parents. (Moore, *At Home in America*, 104.)

40. Perlstein, "American Dilemmas," 364.
41. Richard Wright, *Black Boy* (Harper & Row, 1966 [originally published in 1937]), 70–71.
42. L.D. Reddick, "Anti-Semitism Among Negroes," *Negro Quarterly*, Summer 1942, 113–114; Carl Offord, "Slave Markets in the Bronx," *Nation*, 29 June 1940, 780–81; Claude McKay, *Harlem: Negro Metropolis* (New York: Harcourt Brace Javanovich, 1968 [originally published 1940]), 187, 196.
43. Roi Ottley, *"New World A-Coming": Inside Black America* (Boston: Houghton Mifflin, 1943), 122–23, emphasis in original.
44. Chandler Owen, "Negro Anti-Semitism: Cause and Cure," *National Jewish Monthly*, Sept. 1942, 14. Echoing Owens' argument at the time of the conflict over community control, black writer James Baldwin excoriated black activists who "take refuge in the most ancient and barbaric of the European myths" at a time when "we should be storming capitols." James Baldwin, "Anti-Semitism and Black Power," *Freedomways*, Spring 1967, 77.
45. Louis Harap, "Anti-Negroism Among Jews," *Negro Quarterly*, Summer 1942, 105–106.
46. Stuart Svonkin, *Jews Against Prejudice: American Jews and the Fight for Civil Liberties* (New York: Columbia University Press, 1997), 67, 70, 75, 85.
47. Barbara Grizzuti Harrison, "Women and Blacks and Bensonhurst, Memories Evoked By a Racial Killing," *Harper's Magazine*, Mar. 1990, 75, 77.
48. Adina Back, "Blacks, Jews and the Struggle to Integrate Brooklyn's Junior High School 258: A Cold War Story," *Journal of American Ethnic History* (Winter 2001): 49.
49. James Hicks, "Polier Decision," *Amsterdam News*, 26 Oct. 1963; James Hicks, "The Polier Decision," *Amsterdam News*, 2 Nov. 1963; Justine Wise Polier, *Juvenile Justice in Double Jeopardy: The Distanced Community and Vengeful Retribution* (Hillside, NJ: Lawrence Erlbaum, 1989), 9.
50. Shad Polier, "Jews and the Racial Crisis, *Amsterdam News*, 8 Aug. 1964, 1, 46.
51. "One Down and Two To Go," *Jewish Teachers Association Bulletin*, Nov. 1954, 1.
52. Gerald Horne, "Why N.A.A.C.P. Won't Disown Nation of Islam," *New York Times*, 19 Jan. 1994, 20; Gerald Horne, "'Myth' and the Making of 'Malcolm X,'" *American Historical Review* 98 (1993): 442–43.
53. Claude Brown, *Manchild in the Promised Land* (New York: Macmillan, 1965), 287. See also Clark, "Candor," 8.
54. Rosenberg and Howe, "Are American Jews Turning To the Right," 72.
55. Richard B. Moore, "Criticism Is Not Anti-Semitism," *Liberator*, July 1963, 14. On the use of accusations of black anti-Semitism to discredit critics of Jewish labor unions, see Herbert Hill, "Black-Jewish Conflict in the Labor Context," in V. P. Franklin et al., eds, *African Americans and Jews in the Twentieth Century: Studies in Convergence and Conflict* (Columbia: University of Missouri Press, 1998), 269–75.
56. Howe, *A Margin of Hope*, 275.
57. Alfred Kazin, "New York Jew," in *Creators and Disturbers: Reminiscences by Jewish Intellectuals of New York*, Bernard Rosenberg and Ernest Goldstein, eds. (New York: Columbia University Press, 1982), 169, 206.
58. Lucy Dawidowicz, *On Equal Terms: Jews in America, 1881–1981* (New York: Holt, Rinehart and Winston, 1982), 132.
59. Arthur Liebman, "The Ties That Bind: The Jewish Support for the Left in the United States," *American Jewish Historical Quarterly* 66 (1976): 290; Berson, *Negroes and the Jews*, 296. Jews were not alone in rediscovering religious education. Between 1950 and 1960, years when blacks

were pushing for school integration, the number of white students in New York City parochial schools jumped from 307,000 to 415,000. Hertzberg, *Jews in America*, 357.

60. Riv-Ellen Prell, *Fighting to Become Americans: Jews, Gender and the Anxiety of Assimilation* (Boston: Beacon, 1999), 175; Eli Lederhendler, *New York Jews and the Decline of Urban Ethnicity, 1950–1970* (Syracuse: Syracuse University Press, 2001), 100–103.

61. Svonkin, *Jews Against Prejudice*, 69. Many Jewish groups soon grew disenchanted with the Judeo-Christian celebrations. Jonathan Zimmerman, *Whose America? Culture Wars in the Public Schools* (Cambridge: Harvard University Press, 2002), 159.

62. Kahn, *Passionate People*, 98–99; Ferretti, "Black Anti-Semitism Scare," 107. The classic imagined passage through "psychopathic" black identity in asserting Jewish masculinity is Norman Mailer, *Advertisement for Myself* (New York: Putnam, 1959), 337–39, 344.

63. Israel's military successes reinforced American Jews new feelings of assertiveness, The 1967 Six-Day War offered Irving Howe "a thrill of gratification" after "centuries of helplessness," and American Jews bought tens of thousands of posters portraying Israeli general Moshe Dayan as Superman. Howe, *A Margin of Hope*, 277; Lenora Berson, *Negroes and the Jews*, 299; Murray Polner, "Who Is A Jew?" *Nation*, 15 June 1992, 829. See Paul Breines, *Tough Jews: Political Fantasies and the Moral Dilemma of American Jewry* (New York: Basic Books, 1990).

64. Dawidowicz, *On Equal Terms*, 151.

65. Rabbi Meir Kahane, *The Story of the Jewish Defense League* (Radnor, PA: Chilton Book Co., 1975), 95, 134–5; Nathan Glazer and Daniel Patrick Moynihan, *Beyond the Melting Pot: The Negroes, Puerto Ricans, Jews, Italians, and Irish of New York City*, second edition (Cambridge, MA: M.I.T. Press, 1970), 176. Charges of Jewish timidity had the perceived failure of Jews to resist the Holocaust as a subtext. Before the school conflict, Jewish intellectuals and activists tended not to invoke the Holocaust in discussions of American anti-Semitism. Only when Jews felt a sense of collective power could the impotence of European Jewry be invoked or confronted. Interest in the Holocaust also reflected the decline of Jewish radicalism. In undermining Jews' claims to have assimilated, the Holocaust reinforced Jewish intellectuals' retreat from proletarian internationalism. Whereas in 1948, Soviet machinations in Czechoslovakia left Irving Howe feeling that "the world today is in far worse state than ten years ago when Hitler over-ran Europe," by the early 1950s, when he no longer considered himself a revolutionary, Howe mused that Marxism, for all its power, was unable to illuminate the meaning of Auschwitz. Irving Howe, "The New York Intellectuals" (1968), in *Selected Writings, 1950–1990* (New York: Harcourt Brace Jovanovich, 1990), 264; Irving Howe, *A Margin of Hope: An Intellectual Autobiography* (New York: Harcourt Brace Jovanovich, 1982), 247, 250. Although Howe's dismissive view of the Holocaust was extreme, it was by no means unique. See Edward Alexander, "Irving Howe and the Holocaust: Dilemmas of a Radical Jewish Intellectual," *American Jewish History* 88 (2000): 95–113; Kazin, "New York Jew," 208–9; Alan Wald, *The New York Intellectuals: The Rise and Decline of the Anti-Stalinist Left from the 1930s to the 1980s* (Chapel Hill: University of North Carolina Press, 1987), 276, 321; Alexander Bloom *Prodigal Sons: The New York Intellectuals and Their World* (New York: Oxford University Press, 1986), 138–9. See however Gail Malmgreen, "Labor and the Holocaust: The Jewish Labor Committee and the Anti-Nazi Struggle," *Labor's Heritage* 3 (Oct. 1991): 25–27.

66. Richard D. Alba, *Ethnic Identity* (New Haven: Yale University Press, 1990), 317. See also William Kornblum and James Beshers, "White Ethnicity: Ecological Dimensions," in Jon Mollenkopf, ed., *Power, Culture, and Place: Essays on New York City* (New York: Russell Sage, 1988), 213.

67. Richard Piro, *Black Fiddler* (New York: William Morrow, 1971), 132–33.

68. Hertzberg, *The Jews in America*, 361.

69. In the millennium preceding the Emancipation of European Jewry, the usual Jewish attitude was not one of liberalism but rather of political detachment. Religious American Jews have been less liberal than those who are not religious. Lawrence Fuchs, *The Political Behavior of American Jews* (Glencoe: Free Press, 1956); Charles Liebman, *The Ambivalent American Jew* (Philadelphia: Jewish Publication Society of America, 1973); William Toll, "Pluralism and Moral Force in Black-Jewish Dialogue," *American Jewish History* 77 (1987): 88–92; Ben Halpern, "The Roots of American Jewish Liberalism," *American Jewish Historical Quarterly* 66 (1976), 196; Werner Cohn, "The Sources of American Jewish Liberalism," in *The Jews: Social Patterns of an American Group*, Marshall Sklare, ed. (Glencoe: Free Press, 1958), 614–26.

70. Harris and Swanson, *Black-Jewish Relations*, 36, 60, 77, 135.

71. Alba, *Ethnic Identity*, 317.

72. Karen Brodkin, *How Jews Became White Folks and What That Says About Race* (New Brunswick: Rutgers University Press, 1998), 151.

73. Berson, *Negroes and the Jews*, 73, 119, 178, 218, 228, 425. See also Harris and Swanson, *Black-Jewish Relations*, 98, 119, 178, 218, 228.

74. Piro, *Black Fiddler*, 90. See also Galamison, "Ghost of McCarthy," 17; Berson, *Negroes and the Jews*, 325.

75. Vorspan, "Blacks and Jews," 198; Harris and Swanson, *Black-Jewish Relations*, 156–157.

76. Harris and Swanson, *Black-Jewish Relations*, 110, 226. Jews accurately assessed the views of non-Jewish whites.

77. Weisbord and Stein, *Bittersweet Encounter*, 153.

78. Ferretti, "Black Anti-Semitism Scare," 25.

79. "An Open Letter From B'nai B'rith" (advertisement), *New York Times*, 24 Oct. 1968, 51.

80. Jay Kaufman, "'Thou Shalt Surely Rebuke Thy Neighbor,'" in *Black Anti-Semitism and Jewish Racism*, 43–44.

81. Stern, "'Scab' Teachers," 21.

82. Meir Kahane, *Never Again! A Program for Survival* (Los Angeles: Nash, 1971), 102.

83. Kahane, *Jewish Defense League*, 91–92, 108–09. In 1970, the JDL demonstrated at UFT headquarters, protesting the union sponsored tours to the USSR. Ibid., 24. Noting the JDL's militant antipathy toward black radicals, the FBI fed Meier Kahane information, some of it "embellished" in order to encourage JDL opposition to the Black Panthers. SAC, New York to Director, Federal Bureau of Investigations, 10 Sept. 1969, p. 2 SAC, New York to Director, 21 May 1970, p. 2.

84. Herman Mantell, "President's Message," *Morim*, Feb. 1969, 2.

85. Herman Mantell, "President's Message," *Morim*, Sept. 1969, 1. The Council of Jewish Civil Service, headed by Mantell, is the only organization identified by Lionel Lokos as supporting the JDL. (Lokos, *The New Racism*, 335.)

86. "J.D.L.," *Morim*, Jan. 1970, 3.

87. Michael Leinwand, "Changing Priorities," *Morim*, Jan. 1972, 1. See also Herman Mantell, "President's Message," *Morim*, Sept. 1969, 2; Statement by Faculty-Hillel Associates on Anti-Semitism," *Morim*, Feb. 1969, 3; "The Blacks and the Jews: A Falling Out of Allies," *Time*, 31 Jan. 1969, 57; Kovach, "Racist and Anti-Semitic Charges;" Janet Dolgin, *Jewish Identity and the JDL* (Princeton: Princeton University Press, 1977), 4.

88. Leinwand, "Changing Priorities," 1.

89. "Merit; Mind; Political Muscle: Multiple Themes of JTA Luncheon," *Morim*, May 1972, 1; "Editorial: An Open Letter to the UFT," *Morim*, May 1972, 2; Lester Weinberg, UFT Chapter Chairman, et al., Letters to the Editor, *Morim*, May 1972, 2; Kahane, The *Jewish Defense League*, 249.

90. Isaacs, "A J.H.S. 271 Teacher," 76.

91. Harris and Swanson, *Black-Jewish Relations*, 124.

92. Ferretti, "Black Anti-Semitism Scare," 26–27; "Union on Alert Status to Combat Attacks Against Schools, Teachers," *United Teacher*, 4 Dec. 1968, 2. On October 25 1968, in the midst of the school conflict, Wallace staged a Madison Square garden rally at which 17,000 supporters screamed, "White Power!" and "Down with niggers!" David Caute, *Sixty-Eight: the Year of the Barricades* (London: Hamilton, 1988), 411.

93. Vorspan, "Blacks and Jews," 191. In a more nuanced argument, historian Joel Carmichael suggested that black anti-Semitism both expressed broader anti-white feelings and mimicked white attitudes. Although this argument rejects the view that black anti-Semitism is simply the expression of Christian views, it also suggests that improved race relations and the inculcation of tolerance will eliminate both sources of blacks' bias. Joel Carmichael, "Negro-Jewish Relations in America," *Midstream* 12 No. 10 (Dec. 1966): 8.

94. Alan Miller, "Black Anti-Semitism—Jewish Racism, in *Black Anti-Semitism and Jewish Racism*, 111.

95. Vorspan, "Blacks and Jews," 220–21; Scott Cline, "Jewish-Ethnic Interactions: A Biographic Essay," *American Jewish History* 77 (1987): 138, 149–50. On the history of American anti-Semitism, see John Higham, *Strangers in the Land* (New Brunswick: Rutgers University Press, 1955); Leonard Dinnerstein, *Uneasy at Home*; Morris Schappes, *A Documentary History of the Jews in the United States, 1654–1875* (New York: Citadel Press, 1950). The role of Jewish discussions of black identity in expressing Jews' own concerns was manifest in a symposium on black-Jewish published by the Jewish journal *Midstream* in 1966. Only 2 of 27 essays were by blacks. Jewish literary critic Leslie Fiedler rationalized that it was "incumbent on the Jewish writer to re-imagine the Negro . . . since the current crop of Negro novelists is fumbling the job." Leslie Fiedler, "Negro-Jewish Relations in America," *Midstream* 12 No. 10 (Dec. 1966): 22.

96. Vorspan, "Blacks and Jews," 220. White anti-Semites, unlike blacks, have exerted significant influence in American history. In the 1930s and 1940s, Gerald L. K. Smith won national fame as a riveting speaker, close associate of Huey Long and defender of Adolf Hitler. Following World War II, American Nazi Party Führer George Lincoln Rockwell mentored such influential white supremacists as *Turner Diaries* author William Pierce. Although George Wallace did not rely on anti-Semitism in his 1968 presidential bid, the campaign was a magnet for both white supremacists and anti-Semites. Lawrence Powell, "When Hate Came to Town: New Orleans' Jews and George Lincoln Rockwell," *American Jewish History* 85 (1997): 393–419; Glen Jeansonne, *Gerald L. K. Smith: Minister of Hate* (Baton Rouge: Lousiiana State University Press, 1997).

97. Levels of anti-Semitism in the United States had been declining since the late 1930s. Rita James Simon, *Public Opinion in America: 1936–1970* (Chicago: Rand McNally, 1974), 87–88, 91. See also Charles Stember, *Jews in the Mind of America* (New York: Basic Books, 1966).

98. Lokos, *New Racism*, 359; Arthur Liebman, *Jews and the Left* (New York: Wiley, 1979), 9.

99. *Jewish Teachers Association Bulletin*, 1961–1967, *passim*; *Morim*, 1967–1977, *passim*.

100. Fred Malek, who had supplied President Nixon with a list of Jews at the Labor Department, was George Bush's campaign manager in 1992. Anti-Semitic statements by Patrick Buchanan did not preclude respectful treatment of his 1992 by Bush, much of the media and political establishment. All of this occurred, as writer Micah Sifry, notes "with hardly a word of public protest

from the professional anti-anti-Semitic world." In more recent elections as well, links between Republican leaders and anti-Semitic groups have generated little outrage. Micah Sifry, "Anti-Semitism in America," *Nation*, 25 Jan. 1993, 92–6; "Rep. Bob Barr to ADL: Council of Conservative Citizens' White Supremacy Views Are Repugnant," Press Release, Anti-Defamation League, New York, 22 Dec. 1998; "Pat Buchanan's Poison," *Nation*, 18 Oct. 1999.

101. See A.M. Rosenthal, "On Black Anti-Semitism, *New York Times*, 11 Jan. 1994, 21.

102. Arthur A. Goren, *The Politics and Public Culture of American Jews* (Bloomington: Indiana University Press, 1999).

103. Seth Forman, "The Unbearable Whiteness of Being Jewish: Desegregation in the South and the Crisis of Jewish Liberalism," *American Jewish History* 85 (1997): 122.

Chapter 4: Teachers for Community Control

1. Angelina Grimke, "Human Rights Not Founded on Sex": Letter to Catharine Beecher, *Liberator*, 1837.

2. Bob Couche, et al., "Teachers and Parents Must Stand Together" (advertisement), *New York Times*, 27 June 1968, 37; Bob Couche, et al., Press Release, 24 June 1968; Annie Stein Papers, Public Education Association, New York City (hereafter, Stein Papers). The ad, which identified no organizational sponsor, appeared in *The Amsterdam News* and *El Diaro* on Sept. 21, 1968, and one activist remembers it running in the *New York Post* as well. Untitled note, Teachers Action Caucus Papers, Box 1, folder 3, Tamiment Institute Library, New York University (hereafter TAC Papers); Paul Becker, interview, Rockville Center, NY, 7 Sept. 1990.

3. Couche, et al., Press Release.

4. William Cutler, *Parents and Schools: The 150-Year Struggle for Control in American Education* (Chicago: University of Chicago Press, 2000).

5. Bob Couche, interview, New York City, 5 Oct. 1991; *United Teacher*, 21 May 1964, 1; P. Becker interview.

6. Couche, et al., Press Release.

7. Zippy Bauman, interview, New York City, 5 Sept. 1990.

8. Bob Greenberg, interview, New York City, 10 Sept. 1990; Bauman, P. Becker interviews.

9. Greenberg interview.

10. Bob Couche, et al., "Vote No Strike," no date (c. September 4, 1968), 1–3, Stein Papers.

11. Ted Bassett and Philip Bonosky, "Protest wave hits 3d Shanker strike," *Daily World*, 15 Oct. 1968, 5.

12. Bauman interview.

13. Ibid.

14. See Chapter V.

15. Bauman interview.

16. Filardo interview.

17. P. Becker interview.

18. Ibid.

19. Greenberg interview; "School Board Says It will Ask Court ... " *New York Times*, 23 Oct. 1968, 1, 32.

20. Introduction, TAC Papers, Box 1, folder 1.

21. Bauman interview; "Flash!" *Teachers for Community Control Newsletter*, Apr. 1969, 1, news bulletin file, TAC Papers.

22. *Teachers for Community Control Newsletter*, Feb. 1969, 4; newsletter file, TAC Papers. UFT Pres. Shanker created considerable controversy when he had the authors' names removed from a UFT book of African American history lesson plans that Paul Becker and Zippy Bauman helped write. Executive Board Minutes [transcripts], 29 Sept. 1969, Sub-group B, Exec. Admin. Records, Series 1, Minutes, UFT Papers.

23. Filardo interview.

24. "The Crisis in New York's High Schools," *TAC Newsletter*, Mar. 1970, 2, newsletter file, TAC Papers.

25. N. Becker interview.

26. Filardo, Greenberg interviews.

27. "TCC Records Its First Year," *Teachers for Community Control Newsletter*, Sept. 1969, 3, news bulletin file, TAC Papers. The name change was not a strictly local affair. In March 1968, a rank-and-file caucus bearing the name Teachers Action Caucus had been organized in the Chicago AFT local. ("Chicago Teachers' Union Curbing . . . Slates," *The Worker*, 3 Mar. 1968, 13.)

28. *Teachers for Community Control Newsletter*, Oct. 1969, 3, news bulletin file, TAC Papers; Bauman, Greenberg interviews; Tim Wheeler, "Community issue facing teacher meet," *Daily World* 14 Aug. 1968, 5. See Chapter V for an alternative perspective on the founding of TAC.

29. "TAC Statement: When Reform Is Not Reform," *TAC Newsletter*, Dec. 1969, 1, news bulletin file, TAC Papers.

30. Filardo interview.

31. Greenberg interview.

32. N. Becker interview; *TAC Newsletter*, Oct. 1970, 1, news bulletin file, TAC Papers.

33. Bauman, Filardo, P. Becker interviews; Ann Matlin, interview, New York City, 5 Sept. 1990.

34. Filardo interview. TU and then TCC member Nettie Becker was also very active in WSP. Nettie Becker, interview, Rockville Center, NY, 7 Sept. 1990. For accounts of segregation within open enrollment schools similar to that reported by Filardo, see Lisa Yvette Waller, "The Pressures of the People: Milton A. Galamison, The Parents' Workshop, and Resistance to School Integration in New York City, 1960–1963," *Souls* 1 (Spring 1999):39

35. John Theobald, "Education," in Lyle Fitch and Annmarie Hauck Walsh, *Agenda for a City: Issues Confronting New York* (Beverly Hills: Sage, 1970), 177.

36. Filardo interview.

37. P. Becker interview.

38. N. Becker interview. The length of time Becker took off from teaching to raise her children is itself a reflection of the changing lives of teachers. In 1930s, New York teachers rarely took child-care leaves beyond the one-and-a-half to two years mandated by the Board of Education. Rather, female relatives who lived with or near teachers cared for children. As suburbanization divided extended families and the ideology of motherhood gained force in the years following the Second World War, longer child-care leaves became more common. Ruth Jacknow Markowitz, *My Daughter, the Teacher: Jewish Teachers in the New York City Schools* (New Brunswick: Rutgers University Press, 1993), 144–46.

39. P. Becker interview; Filardo interview.

40. Bauman, Filardo interviews.

41. Bauman, Filardo, Greenberg, P. Becker interviews.

42. Greenberg interview.

43. N. Becker, Greenberg interviews.

44. P. Becker, N. Becker, Greenberg, Matlin interviews.

45. Filardo, Greenberg, Bauman interviews.

46. Jewish Currents, according to David Hacker, established editorial independence from the Communist Party in the late 1950s but maintained a "correct relationship with the CP and generally support[ed] Soviet foreign policy." Then, Soviet and American Communist Party opposition to Israel during the 1967 Six Day War, the rise of official anti-Semitism in the Soviet Union and Eastern Europe, and the Soviet invasion of Czechoslovakia led the journal and the party "to go their separate ways." David Hacker, "Jewish Life/Jewish Currents," in The Encyclopedia of the American Left, Mari Jo Buhle et al., eds. (New York: Garland, 1990), 391.

47. Editorial Board, Introduction to Rachel Levy, "N.Y. Teachers Strike—For What?" Jewish Currents, Dec. 1968, 5.

48. "Dissenting Views," The Worker, 23 May 1968, 4. See also Veteran Reader to editor, Daily World, 22 Aug. 1968, 7; B.A. to editor, Daily World, 21 Sept. 1968, 7; P.B. to editor, Daily World, 24 Sept. 1968, 7; Bert to editor, Daily World, 8 Nov. 1968, 7.

49. P. Becker interview; Teachers Action Caucus (TAC) Newsletter, Feb. 1970, 2, news bulletin file, TAC Papers.

50. Si Gerson, "What's behind the school strike?" Daily World, 26 Oct. 1968, 9.

51. Greenberg interview.

52. Bauman and Becker served on the TU executive Board. Bauman coordinated TU's annual conferences, and Becker was on the editorial staff of the TU newspaper. Ann Matlin was Co-Chairman of the Teachers Union Anti-Discrimination Committee. P. Becker and Bauman interviews; "Active TU'ers at End-Term Party," NY Teacher News, 18 June 1960, 3.

53. Greenberg interview.

54. Cedric Belfrage, The American Inquisition, 1945–1960: A Profile of the "McCarthy Era" (New York: Thunder's Mouth, 1989), 21.

55. Bauman interview.

56. Matlin interview. See also Irving Adler interview, New York City, 10 July 1986, UFT Oral History Project, United Federation of Teachers Collection, Robert F. Wagner Labor Archives, New York University; Celia Lewis Zitron, The New York City Teachers Union, 1916–1964: A Story of Educational and Social Activism (New York: Humanities Press, 1968), 30.

57. Quoted in Zitron, Teachers Union, 86–7.

58. Markowitz, My Daughter, the Teacher, 154, 158, 169. See Zitron, Teachers Union, 34; and Robert Iversen, The Communists & The Schools (New York: Harcourt, Brace and Co., 1959), 32–58.

59. Zitron, Teachers Union, 85–89; Mark Naison, Communists in Harlem During the Depression (Urbana: University of Illinois Press, 1983), 215–16.

60. George Charney, A Long Journey (Chicago: Quadrangle Books, 1968), 99; see also Zitron, Teachers Union, 88–9.

61. Alice Citron interview, 6 Jan. 1981, Oral History of the American Left Collection, Tamiment Institute Library, New York University; Naison, Communists in Harlem, 216; Matlin and Bauman interviews.

62. Adler Oral History; Zitron, Teachers Union, 106–08.

63. Zitron, Teachers Union, 101, 104, 240.

64. Ibid., 98–100; P. Becker and Bauman interviews.

65. Anna Matlin, "Teacher Likes Apple," *Amsterdam News*, 4 July 1964, 45.

66. Zitron, *Teachers Union*, 91–93.

67. James W. Ford, "The Struggle for the Building of the Modern Liberation Movement of the Negro People," *Communist*, Sept. 1939, 822; William Z. Foster, *The Negro People in American History* (New York: 1954), 463; Harry Haywood, *Black Bolshevik: Autobiography of an Afro-American Communist* (Chicago: Liberator Books, 1978), 230; Naison, *Communists in Harlem*, 11, 17–18; Theodore Draper, *The Rediscovery of Black Nationalism* (New York: Viking, 1969), 63.

68. Earl Browder, *What Is Communism?* (New York: Workers Library, 1936), 139. See also Joseph R. Starobin, *American Communism in Crisis, 1943–1957* (Berkeley: University of California, 1972), 131.

69. *The Communist Position on the Negro Question* (1934) in Naison, *Communists in Harlem*, 19.

70. The belief that "minority rights would be secured through the function of trade unions which guaranteed equality," Philip Bonosky argued, had driven "yesterday's men and women of good will" into a defense of white privilege and reactionary racial backlash. Philip Bonosky, "Get with it, teach," *Daily World*, 27 Sept. 1968, 6.

71. Browder, *What Is Communism?* 143; Resolution of the Communist Party in Ford, "Struggle for the Building of the Modern Liberation Movement," 822.

72. Mark Solomon, *The Cry Was Unity: Communists and African Americans, 1917–1936* (Jackson: University of Mississippi Press, 1998), p. 14, 74–5; Mark Solomon, *Red and Black: Communism and Afro-Americans, 1929–1935* (New York: Garland, 1988), 82. See also Philip Foner and James Allen, Introduction, *American Communism and Black Americans: A Documentary History, 1919–1929* (Temple University press, 1987), viii–ix; Naison, *Communists in Harlem*, 5.

73. Solomon, *Red and Black*, 106, 163. See also William Maxwell, *New Negro, Old Left: African-American Writing and Communism Between the Wars* (New York: Columbia University Press, 1999).

74. John Hudson Jones, "Parents, Pupils Fight for Victims of School Witchhunt," *Daily Worker*, 8 May 1950, 4.

75. Matlin interview.

76. Matlin, Bauman interviews; Citron Oral History. See Chapter V for a discussion of the appeal of anti-racist activity among Jews.

77. Markowitz, *My Daughter, the Teacher*, 151, 168, 178. See also Charney, *Long Journey*, 204.

78. Charney, *Long Journey*, 204; Zitron, *Teachers Union*, 234–5, 242–4; Adler Oral History; Carey McWilliams, *Witch Hunt: The Revival of Heresy* (Boston: Little, Brown and Co., 1950), 199; Belfrage, *American Inquisition*, 157, 226.

79. Belfrage, *American Inquisition*, 90–1; Zitron, *Teachers Union*, 210; Markowitz, *My Daughter, the Teacher*, 168; Bauman, Filardo, Matlin interviews; Dorothy Healey and Maurice Isserman, *Dorothy Healey Remembers: A Life in the American Communist Party* (New York: Oxford University Press, 1990), 152–54.

80. Adina Back, "Blacks, Jews and the Struggle to Integrate Brooklyn's Junior High School 258: A Cold War Story," *Journal of American Ethnic History* (Winter 2001): 52; Zitron, *Teachers Union*, 224–5.

81. Back, "Blacks, Jews," 43.

82. Back, "Blacks, Jews," 53; Zitron, *Teachers Union*, 91–93; Markowitz, *My Daughter, the Teacher*, 165–66.

83. Herbert Aptheker, "Integrated Education Requires Integrated Texts," *Political Affairs*, June 1964, 47.

84. Mike Davidow, "For First-Class Integrated Education," *Political Affairs*, Apr. 1965, 35; see also 34, 39.

85. On the optimism about white attitudes implicit in Communist support for independent black organizing, see James E. Jackson, "National Pride, Not Nationalism," *Political Affairs*, May 1967, 44.

86. Filardo interview.

87. Henry Winston, "Forge Negro-Labor Unity," *Political Affairs*, Feb. 1967, 9.

88. Betty Gannett, "Automation and the Negro Worker," *Political Affairs*, Aug. 1964, 80–1, 84–5, 88.

89. New York Communist Party, "Ditching the Public Housing Program," *Political Affairs*, Nov. 1964, 22–28.

90. Kenneth Jackson, *Crabgrass Frontier: The Suburbanization of the United States* (New York: Oxford University Press, 1985), 234.

91. William Allen, "Black teacher runs for AFT head," *Daily World*, 21 Aug. 1968, 3. On Shanker's support of the AFL-CIO's pro-Vietnam war policy, see "Executive Board Dissents from AFL-CIO Vietnam Policy," *United Teacher*, 15 Mar. 1967, 2; Albert Shanker to Ed Gottlieb, *United Teacher*, 5 May 1967, 4; Executive Board Minutes, 1 March 1967, in *United Teacher*, 5 May 1967, 23; Albert Shanker to Editor, *United Teacher*, 5 May 1967, 4. For a response to Shanker, see Paul Becker to Editor, *United Teacher*, 16 June 1967, 10.

92. Bauman interview.

93. P. Becker interview; Bernard Gordon, Paul Becker, Sydelle Dominitz, and Norma Becker, "It Is the United States That Is the Foreign Invader," *United Teacher*, 5 Nov. 1965, 7.

94. Bob Greenberg's peace activism dated from his student days at Brooklyn College in the late 1950s, where he was one of fifty-four students suspended for refusing to participate in an air-raid drill. After college, he was arrested during an anti-bomb protest at the Soviet mission to the United Nations.

95. P. Becker interview.

96. Bauman interview.

97. The police took seriously the power of Becker's ideas. An undercover cop sat in on his Afro-American history class. James Wechsler, "A High School Spy Story," *New York Post*, 13 Feb. 1970.

98. Herbert Aptheker, "Anti-Semitism and Racism," *Political Affairs*, Apr. 1969, 39.

99. Filardo interview.

Chapter 5: Up Against the Leviathan

1. Students for a Democratic Society, *Port Huron Statement of the Students for a Democratic Society* (New York: Author, 1962), 2–3.

2. Alexis de Tocqueville, *Democracy in America*, v.2, part 3, ch. 21, 639.

3. Liz (Fusco) Aaronsohn, personal communication to author, July 1993.

4. Liz (Fusco) Aaronsohn, interview, Willamantic, CT, 12 Sept. 1990.

5. Aaronsohn, personal communication.

6. See Daniel Perlstein, ""Minds Stayed on Freedom: Politics, Pedagogy, and the African American Freedom Struggle," *American Educational Research Journal* 39 (2002): 249–277.

7. "Teachers Who Give a Damn," *Time*, 4 Oct 1968, 50.

8. James Wechsler, "Those Who Care," *New York Post*, 26 Sept. 1968, 53.

9. Charles Isaacs, "A J.H.S. 271 Teacher Tells It Like He Sees It," *New York Times Magazine*, 24 Nov. 1968, 64; Aaronsohn interview; John Casey (pseudonym), interview, 22 Oct. 1990; Paul Baizerman, interview, Brooklyn, NY, 9 Sept. 1990.

10. Bruce Fuller, *Inside Charter Schools: the Paradox of Radical Decentralization* (Cambridge: Harvard University Press, 2000), 1–11.

11. Maurice Isserman, *If I Had a Hammer . . . The Death of the Old Left and the Birth of the New Left* (New York: Basic Books, 1987).

12. Wini Breines, *Community and Organization in the New Left: 1962–1968, The Great Refusal* (New York: Praeger, 1982), 58. Lynd had preceded Fusco as director Mississippi's Freedom Schools in 1964. Daniel Perlstein, "Teaching Freedom: SNCC and the Creation of the Mississippi Freedom Schools," *History of Education Quarterly* 30 (1990): pp. 297–324. On New Left ideology, see Richard Flacks, "On the Uses of Participatory Democracy," *Dissent*, Dec. 1969; George Vickers, *The Formation of the New Left* (Lexington, MA: Lexington Books, 1975); Isserman, *If I Had a Hammer*; Todd Gitlin, *The Sixties: Years of Hope, Days of Rage* (New York: Bantam, 1987). On the role of the Mississippi Freedom Summer in the development of the New Left, see Doug McAdam, *Freedom Summer* (New York: Oxford University Press, 1988).

13. See Ruth Dropkin and Arthur Tobier, eds. *Roots of Open Education in America: Reminiscences and Reflections* (New York: City College Workshop Center for Open Education, 1976). On race and Deweyan pedagogy, see Perlstein, "Community and Democracy in American Schools: Arthurdale and the Fate of Progressive Education," *Teachers College Record* 97 (1996): pp. 625–650; and Perlstein, "Minds Stayed on Freedom."

14. Although 1968 is widely portrayed as a pivotal moment in the history of the New Left, scholars have focused on student activists rather than on efforts to bring campus sensibilities to adult careers. See for instance Stephen Good, *Affluent Revolutionaries: A Portrait of the New Left* (New York: Franklin Watts, 1974), 1; George Katsiaficas, *The Imagination of the New Left: A Global Analysis of 1968* (Boston: South End Press, 1987), 27; Paul Buhle, "Remembering the Sixties," *Oral History Review* 17 (1989): 141; Jim Miller, *"Democracy Is In the Streets": From Port Huron to the Siege of Chicago* (New York: Simon and Schuster, 1987).

15. Liz Fusco (Aaronsohn), "To Blur the Focus of What You Came Here to Know: a letter containing notes on education and freedom schools," undated [spring 1966], 2; Student Nonviolent Coordinating Committee Papers, microfilm edition (hereafter SNCC Papers), A:VIII:122.

16. Aaronsohn interview; Liz (Fusco) Aaronsohn, "Learning to Teach for Empowerment," unpublished paper, 1990, 2.

17. Aaronsohn interview, personal communication.

18. Fusco, "To Blur the Focus;" Aaronsohn interview; Liz Fusco (Aaronsohn), "Freedom Schools in Mississippi, 1964," [fall 1964], 1, 3, 5; SNCC Papers, A:XV:165.

19. Aaronsohn, "Learning to Teach for Empowerment," 5.

20. Aaronsohn interview.

21. Fusco, "To Blur the Focus," 1. See also Perlstein, "Teaching Freedom."

22. Aaronsohn, "Learning to Teach," 7; Fusco, "To Blur the Focus," 1, 15.

23. Aaronsohn, interview; Aaronsohn personal communication.

24. Liz Fusco (Aaronsohn), "School Teaching: The Success of the System," *R.I.P. Newsletter*, Fall 1968, in *Movement*, 276.

25. Aaronsohn interview.

26. Ibid.

27. Ibid.

28. Ibid.

29. Bill Kovach, "Teachers Working on J.H.S. 271 Staff Feel a 'Vibrance,'" *New York Times*, 21 Oct. 1968, 42.

30. Isaacs, "A J.H.S. 271 Teacher," 72; Susan Brownmiller, "Touring an Open School: Dashikis, 2As, & Ties," *Village Voice*, 3 Oct. 1968, 55. "The New York teachers," SDS leader Todd Gitlin echoed, "built a union to safeguard their guild status and they now insist, brandishing their normal school certificates, that they and only they know what and how and even why to teach." The Teachers Incorporated, a non-profit group working with "cadres of teachers" willing to live in the urban neighborhoods in which they taught and to become active in community affairs, recruited only liberal-arts students. Todd Gitlin, "The Liberation of Bronx H.S. of Science," *San Francisco Express Times*, 13 Nov. 1968, reprinted as "Bringing A Lot of It Back Home," *High School Independent Press (HIP) Service*, No. 8 (18 Nov. 1968), B1; in *The Movement Toward a New America*, Mitchell Goodman, ed. (Philadelphia: Pilgrim Press, 1970), 287; Advertisement, [1968–69], in *Movement*, 732.

31. Joseph Featherstone, "Ocean Hill Is Alive, and, Well . . . ," *New Republic* 19 April 1969, 23.

32. "Teachers Who Give a Damn," 50.

33. New York's 60,000 person teaching staff included 7,200 new teachers in September 1968. Many of those who entered teaching in 1968 did not identify with the New Left but others who had already been teaching at the start of the school conflict were new leftists. *The Public Schools of New York Staff Bulletin*, 24 Sept. 1968, 1.

34. Robert Rossner, *The Year Without an Autumn: Portrait of a School in Crisis* (New York: Richard W. Baron, 1969), 7, 15, 38, 114.

35. Isaacs, "A J.H.S. 271 Teacher," 70; "Teachers Who Give a Damn," 50.

36. Metz interview.

37. Metz interview.

38. Metz, Stromberg, Baizerman interviews. For a history of the Student Peace Union, see Vickers, *Formation of the New Left*, 51–61.

39. Isaacs, "A J.H.S. 271 Teacher," 53; "Teachers Who Give a Damn," 50. New Left teachers' desire to undermine their classroom authority in part reflected naivete about their own privileged place in society. "What we didn't realize," Liz Aaronsohn notes, "was that . . . here . . . as in Mississippi, we were undermining the structure they had to live under once we inevitably left." (Aaronsohn, personal communication). Students were perhaps more aware of the real status differences in the classroom. Charlie Isaacs found that "many children found it impossible to take advantage of this familiarity."

40. Gitlin, "Liberation of Bronx H.S.," 289. Evocative of the French student-led revolt in May 1968, the "Imagination" slogan suggests the Bronx Science students' cosmopolitanism, as does the name of one of the school's underground newspapers, the Sans-culottes.

41. Rossner, *The Year Without an Autumn*, 190–91.

42. Kovach, "J.H.S. 271 Staff Feel a 'Vibrance,'" 42.

43. Kovach, "J.H.S. 271 Staff Feel a 'Vibrance,'" 42. For a discussion of the relationship of bureaucratic centralization to the unionization of teachers, see Marjorie Murphy, *Blackboard Unions* (Ithaca, NY: Cornell University Press, 1990).

44. Sol Stern, "'Scab' Teachers," *Ramparts*, 17 Nov. 1968, 21.

45. Rossner, *The Year Without an Autumn*, 38.

46. Rossner, *The Year Without an Autumn*, 147.

47. Stern, "'Scab Teachers," 19.

48. Dave Silver, interview, New York City, 6 Sept. 1990.

49. Isaacs, "A J.H.S. 271 Teacher," 70.

50. Rossner, *The Year Without an Autumn*, 90, 213–14.

51. Stern, "Scab Teachers," 19.

52. Rossner, *The Year Without an Autumn*, 3–5.

53. Margie Stamberg, "NY Schools Erupt," *Guardian*, 7 Dec. 1968, 6.

54. Diane Divoky, "The Way It's Going To Be," 101.

55. De Rivera, "Jumping the Track," 54.

56. "Free the New York City 275,000," *New York Herald Tribune*, March 1970, 1. Hoover Archives, New Left Collection, Box 28. "It all began," the underground paper recounted, "during the teachers strike, when students set up their own liberation schools."

57. Maurice Berube, "'Democratic Socialists' and the Schools," *New Politics*, Summer 1969, 62. See also Frances Fox Piven, "Militant Civil Servants," *Transaction* 7 (Nov. 1969), reprinted in Richard Cloward and Frances Fox Piven, *The Politics of Turmoil: Poverty, Race, and the Urban Crisis* (New York, 1975); Marilyn Gittell, *Participants and Participation* (New York, 1967). On the political impact of efforts to "professionalize" teaching, see also Stephen Cole, *The Unionization of Teachers: A Case Study of the UFT* (New York, 1969).

58. Rossner, *The Year Without an Autumn*, 90, 213–14.

59. Brownmiller, "Touring an Open School," 55.

60. Stephen Bloomfield, "Radical Teachers: What Role?" *Urban Underground*, May 1970, 8; Hoover Archives, New Left Collection, Box 44, Stanford, CA.

61. Gitlin, "Liberation of Bronx H.S.," 289.

62. Martin Arnold, "P.S. 178: Study in Disrepair," *New York Times*, 28 Feb. 1968, 41.

63. Isaacs, "A J.H.S. 271 Teacher," 79. See also Charles Hightower, "Brownsville Seeks Control of Schools," *Guardian*, 25 May 1968, 10.

64. Rossner, *The Year Without an Autumn*, 124–25, 134, 182–3. See also "Donovan Misses His Check as a Result of City Caution," *New York Times*, 16 Nov. 1968, 26.

65. Vivian Stromberg, interview, Brooklyn, NY, 11 Sept. 1990.

66. Hechinger, "Defiance and Enthusiasm Spark Ocean Hill;" Isaacs, "A J.H.S. 271 Teacher," 76.

67. Casey interview; Aaronsohn, personal communication, emphasis in original.

68. Rossner, *The Year Without an Autumn*, 154, 158.

69. Casey interview.

70. Murray Kempton, "The Busting of Rhody McCoy," *New York Post*, 1 Oct. 1968; Fred Hechinger, "Defiance and Enthusiasm Spark Ocean Hill Schools," *New York Times*, 23 Oct. 1968, 1; Featherstone, "Ocean Hill Is Alive," 21–22; Isaacs, "A J.H.S. 271 Teacher," 53.

71. Isaacs, "A J.H.S. 271 Teacher," 74.

72. Rossner, *The Year Without an Autumn*, 201–202.

73. Newman, et al., "Conference of Faculty Members," 1.

74. Casey interview.

75. Pasha Brant, "Are You Willing to Be a Nigger Again?" *High School Independent Press (HIP) Service*, 18 Nov. 1968, A6.

76. Casey interview.

77. Pearl Newman, et al., "Conference of Faculty Members," 22 Nov. 1968 (transcript), 2–3, copy in author's possession. Ironically, Rutberg's action was in fact legal, and the principal's action supporting strike was not.

78. Stromberg interview.

79. In Fusco's case, almost two decades elapsed before she became a professor. Vivian Stromberg stayed in teaching, but she directed little of her energy on teacher politics. Instead, she focused on such efforts as the Angela Davis defense committee and later became a leader of Madre, an international solidarity organization.

80. These teachers were not alone. In 1968, New York teachers resigned from their jobs at five times the normal rate. Mark Maier, *City Unions: Managing Discontent in New York City* (New Brunswick: Rutgers University Press, 1987), 131.

81. Joseph R. Starobin, *American Communism in Crisis, 1943–1957* (Berkeley: University of California, 1972), xiv.

82. See for instance John Chubb and Terry Moe, *Politics, Markets, and America's Schools* (Washington, DC: Brookings Inst., 1990).

83. Christopher Jencks, "Private Schools for Black Children," *New York Times Magazine*, 3 Nov. 1968, 140.

84. Albert Shanker, "A Whirlpool of Failure," in Stanley Wanat and Michael Cohen, eds., *Before the Fall: A Discussion of Schools in Conflict with Community* (Ithaca: Cornell University, 1969), 11. The recent history of mental health policy suggests the obstacles that confront visions of deinstitutionalization. Dan A. Lewis, et al., "After Deinstitutionalization: the present and future of mental health long-term care policy," *The Journal of Social Issues* 45 (1989), 1–15.

85. Robert Lowe and Harvey Kantor, "Bureaucracy Right and Left: Thinking About the One Best System," in Larry Cuban and Dorothy Shipps, eds., *Reconstructing the Common Good in Education: Coping with Intractable American Dilemmas* (Stanford, CA: Stanford University Press, 2000), 138–9.

86. Adickes, "Woman Power at Whitehall ST," *East Village Other*, June 15–July 1, 1967, 17.

Chapter 6: The Case Against Community

1. Homer, *The Iliad*, Richard Lattimore, trans. (Chicago: University of Chicago Press, 1951), Book 14, line 80.

2. John D'Emilio, "Homophobia and the Trajectory of Post-War American Radicalism: The Case of Bayard Rustin, *Radical History Review* No. 62 (1995): 82.

3. Bayard Rustin to Charles Cogen, 16 Aug. 1968, Bayard Rustin Papers, microfilm edition (hereafter BRP) reel 21, 1227; Victor Gotbaum, interview, New York City, 18 June 1991; Thomas Brooks, "A Strategist Without a Movement," *New York Times Magazine*, 16 Feb. 1969, 24–5; Maurice Carroll, "Giant City Hall Rally Backs Teachers," *New York Times*, 17 Sept. 1968, 1.

4. Among those directly influenced by Rustin is William Julius Wilson. Bayard Rustin and Norman Hill to William Julius Wilson, 21 Sept. 1982, BRP, 17, 507; William Julius Wilson, *The Bridge Over the Racial Divide: Rising Inequality and Coalition Politics* (Berkeley: University of California Press, 2001).

5. Bayard Rustin, "Integration Within Decentralization," speech on receiving the United Federation of Teachers' John Dewey Award, 6 Apr. 1968, in *Down the Line: the Collected Writings of Bayard Rustin*, Bayard Rustin, ed. (New York: Quadrangle, 1971), 213–14.

6. Ibid., 215, 218-220.

7. See Bayard Rustin, "Education?" 55, c. 1967, BRP, 17, 862.

8. Rustin, "Integration Within Decentralization," 215-16.

9. Ibid.

10. Bayard Rustin, "The Mind of the Black Militant," speech delivered at the Conference on the Schoolhouse in the City, Stanford University, 10 July 1967, in *Down The Line*, 209.

11. Although Rustin opposed judging workers on the basis of race, he supported targeted efforts to recruit and train greater numbers of black teachers. Bayard Rustin, "Ethnics: A New Separatism," *AFL-CIO Federationist* (Dec. 1974), BRP, 17, 962; Bayard Rustin, speech to the Plenary Session of the National Jewish Community Relations Advisory Council, June 30-July 3, 1968, in Robert Browne and Bayard Rustin, *Separatism or Integration; Which Way for America?* (New York: A. Philip Randolph Educational Fund, Oct. 1968), 30.

12. Rustin, "'Black Power' and Coalition Politics," 155.

13. Bayard Rustin, "A Word to Black Students" (Tuskegee Institute commencement address, 31 May 1970), *Dissent*, Nov.-Dec. 1970, 496.

14. Bayard Rustin et al., "Where Is the Negro Movement Now? A Conversation with Bayard Rustin," *Dissent*, Nov.-Dec. 1968, 491.

15. Rustin, "The Mind of the Black Militant," 211.

16. Brooks, "A Strategist Without a Movement," 104. See also Rustin, "The Mind of the Black Militant," 211; Rustin, "'Black Power' and Coalition Politics," *Commentary* Feb. 1967, in *Down the Line*, 157.

17. Rustin to Robert Curvin, 9 Oct. 1968, BRP, 6, 193-4.

18. Bayard Rustin, "The Alienated: The Young Rebels of Today . . . and Why They're Different," Speech to the International Labor Press Association, 1967, 1, BRP, 17, 827.

19. Bayard Rustin, "The Failure of Black Separatism," *Harper's Magazine*, Jan. 1970, in *Down the Line*, 297-99.

20. Bayard Rustin, "Separatism Repackaged," *New Leader*, 12 June 1972, 11.

21. Rustin, "Integration Within Decentralization," 219-20.

22. Bayard Rustin, "A Way Out of The Exploding Ghetto," *New York Times Magazine*, 13 Aug. 1967, 62.

23. Rustin, "A Way Out of The Exploding Ghetto," 54.

24. Rustin, "'Black Power' and Coalition Politics," 155.

25. Rustin to Robert Curvin.

26. Rustin, "Where Is the Negro Movement Now?" 494-5. Advocates of separate black development, Rustin warned, would discover that "the Negro businessman will ultimately be a businessman before he is a Negro." Still, Rustin's critique is inaccurate and unfair. While black support of community control did increase with income and educational attainment, blacks of all classes opposed the UFT and supported community control. Advocates of community control included activists such as Sonny Carson and Oliver Leeds, whom Rustin would label lumpenproletarian and proletarian. Furthermore, non-proletarians have been among the leaders of virtually all social movements, and the presence of black ministers did not preclude Rustin's support of the Montgomery Movement. Finally, to charge that black teachers are middle class undermines Rustin's claim that white UFT teachers could lead a labor-civil rights alliance. Rustin, "Where Is the Negro Movement Now?" 497; Louis Harris and Bert Swanson, *Black-Jewish Relations in New York City* (New York: Praeger, 1970), 133.

27. A Philip Randolph Institute, "An Appeal to the Community from Black Trade Unionists" (advertisement), *New York Post*, 19 Sept. 1968, 31.

28. Rustin, "The Mind of the Black Militant," 211. See also Rustin, "Where Is the Negro Movement Now?" 493; Rustin, "'Black Power' and Coalition Politics," 157; and Sandra Feldman, "N.Y. City Decentralization," *New America*, 31 Mar. 1968, 5.

29. Rustin to Robert Curvin.

30. Bayard Rustin, "The Negroes, the Cops, the Jews," *Dissent*, Mar.–Apr. 1967, 172–3.

31. Rustin, "A Word to Black Students," 583.

32. Daniel Levine, *Bayard Rustin and the Civil Rights Movement* (New Brunswick, NJ: Rutgers University Press, 2000), 10–11.

33. Martin Duberman, *Paul Robeson* (New York: Knopf, 1988), 238; Levine, *Bayard Rustin*, 16–17; "An Interview With Bayard Rustin," 6.

34. Bayard Rustin, *Strategies for Freedom: The Changing Patterns of Black Protest* (New York: Columbia University Press, 1976), 9–10; Jervis Anderson, A. *Philip Randolph: A Biographical Portrait* (New York: Harcourt Brace Jovanovich, 1973), 275; Taylor Branch, *Parting the Waters: America in the King Years, 1954–63* (New York: Simon and Schuster, 1988), 168–171.

35. Anderson, *Randolph: A Biographical Portrait*, 6.

36. Levine, *Bayard Rustin*, 23–33–34, 47.

37. Rustin, *Strategies for Freedom*, 17; Paula Pfeffer, A. *Philip Randolph, Pioneer of the Civil Rights Movement* (Baton Rouge: Louisiana State University Press, 1990), 228.

38. Pfeffer, A. *Philip Randolph, Pioneer*, 181–88.

39. Ibid., 152–55, 187–92; Anderson, *Randolph: A Biographical Portrait*, 274, 281; August Meier and Elliott Rudwick, *CORE: A Study in the Civil Rights Movement, 1942–1968* (New York: Oxford University Press, 1973), 11–15.

40. Bayard Rustin, "From Protest to Politics: The Future of the Civil Rights Movement," *Commentary* (Feb. 1965), in *Down The Line*, 111. The essay was a revision of a speech urging MFDP leaders to drop their demands at the Atlantic City convention.

41. Rustin, speech to the National Jewish Community Relations Advisory Council, 20.

42. Rustin, "From Protest to Politics," 113.

43. Rustin, "The Negroes, the Cops, the Jews," 172–3.

44. Anderson, *Randolph: A Biographical Portrait*, 324; Meier and Rudwick, *CORE*, 224; Pfeffer, A. *Philip Randolph, Pioneer*, 247, 266.

45. Meier and Rudwick, *CORE*, 224; Pfeffer, A. *Philip Randolph, Pioneer*, 234, 245–47, 266.

46. Rustin, "The Alienated," 8.

47. Rustin, "From Protest to Politics," 117, 120.

48. Terry Ferrer and Joseph Michalack, "44.8 Per Cent Absent, Pickets Brave Weather," *New York Herald Tribune*, 4 Feb. 1964, 7; "Negroes Mapping School Boycotts in 3 Cities," *New York Times*, 25 Feb. 1964; Noel Day, interview, San Francisco, CA, 23 Feb. 1988.

49. Marianne Cole, "We Want Respect, Not Love, Declares Dick Gregory Here," *New York World-Telegram*, 3 Feb. 1964, 2.

50. Ferrer and Michalack, "44.8 Per Cent Absent," 1.

51. Milton Galamison to Charles Cogen, BRP, 5, 505; Joseph Michalack, "School Plan—A Loud No and Boycott," *New York Herald Tribune*, 30 Jan. 1964, 1; "Executive board minutes," *United Teacher*, 24 Jan. 1964, 7. One newspaper claimed that although more than 3,000 teachers participated in the boycott, teacher attendance was actually higher than was normal for a Monday. The union organized a broad range of supporters to prevent the Board of Education from taking

action against the teachers. (Alfred Robbins and Donald Flynn, "School Boycott Peaceful: Many Teachers Absent, Most Teachers In," *New York Journal American*, 3 Feb. 1964, 1; "Quick and Solid Action By Union Squashes Board of Ed 'Blacklist,'" *United Teacher*, 5 Mar. 1964, 1; AdCom Minutes, 11 Mar. 1964, in *United Teacher*, 23 Apr. 1964, 8.)

52. Oliver Leeds to Bayard Rustin, 10 Aug. 1968, BRP, 23, 1258; Albert Vann, "The Agency Shop" (Position Paper), Afro-American Teachers Association, 6 May 1969, in *What Black Educators Are Saying*, Nathan Wright, Jr., ed. (New York: Hawthorn, 1970), 235. See also Miriam Wasserman, *The School Fix, NYC, USA* (New York: Outerbridge & Dienstfrey, 1970), 315-6.

53. Jimmy Breslin, "The Boycotters," *New York Herald Tribune*, 31 Jan. 1964, 1; "A Boycott Solves Nothing," *New York Times*, 31 Jan. 1964, 26; Diane Ravitch, *The Great School Wars, New York City, 1805–1973: A History of the Public Schools as Battlefield of Social Change* (New York: Basic Books, 1974), 275.

54. Leonard Buder, "Split Threatens Boycott Leaders," *New York Times*, 11 Feb. 1964, 1; Leonard Buder, "Galamison Foes Drop Ouster Bid," *New York Times*, 12 Feb. 1964, 25; Statement of Frederick Jones, Education Chairman, New York State Conference of NAACP Chapters, 17 Feb. 1964, BRP, 11, 630; Statement by Frederick Richmond, President of the New York Urban League, 9 Feb. 1964, BRP, 11, 634.

55. Leonard Buder, "Third CORE Group Will Aid Boycott," *New York Times*, 5 Mar. 1964, 27; James Hicks, "O Ye of Little Faith," *Amsterdam News*, 21 Mar. 1964, 11; Simon Anekwe, "Powell, Galamison Call Boycott Big Victory, Especially in Brooklyn," *Amsterdam News*, 21 Mar. 1964, 27; Levine, *Bayard Rustin*, 275; Meier and Rudwick, *CORE*, 231.

56. Milton Galamison, Letter to the Editor, *New York Times*, 19 May 1964; Peter Obi, "Many Negro Leaders In Thick of March," *Amsterdam News*, 21 Mar. 1964, 27; Meier and Rudwick, *CORE*, 254.

57. Kenneth Gross, "School March Will Support State Report," *New York Post*, 14 May 1964, 3.

58. Woody Klein, "Galamison Promises to Aid School Protest," *New York World Telegram*, 11 May 1964, 12.

59. Bayard Rustin to friend, 9 May 1964, BRP, 12, 279.

60. Gross, "School March," 3.

61. "Our Purpose," no date, BRP, 12, 273.

62. "Partial List of Sponsors—March for Democratic Schools," no date, BRP, 12, 218; Press Release, "Jewish Labor Committee Announces Support for May 18th School Demonstration," BRP, 12, 351. Other organizations cool to the school boycott had included the Anti-Defamation League and the Catholic Interracial Council. Richard Montague and Alfred Hendricks, "The Battle for the Schools," *New York Post*, 2 Feb. 1964, 22.

63. Gross, "School March," 3.

64. Terry Smith, "Pickets, School Boycott, Rally—Rights Protest Falls Short," *New York Herald Tribune*, 19 May 1964, 1.

65. Bayard Rustin, "Reverberations: Why I Support the UFT," *New York Amsterdam News*, 23 Sept. 1967, 16.

66. Rustin, "Integration Within Decentralization," 218.

67. Ben Stahl to Bayard Rustin, 1 Jan. 1965, BRP, 4, 572; Rolland Dewing, "Teacher Organizations and Desegregation," *Phi Delta Kappan*, 49 (Jan. 1968): 257-60.

68. Press Release, "Randolph and Rustin Support UFT Agreement—Breakthrough for Ghetto School," 28 Sept. 1967, BRP, 5, 859.

69. "A Meeting for Shachtman," *New America*, 31 Dec. 1972, 8; "APRI, Statement of Income and Expenses," c. Aug. 1965, BRP, 21, 467; Herbert Hill, "Black Protest, Union Democracy & UFT," *New Politics*, Fall 1970, 35; Pfeffer, A. *Philip Randolph, Pioneer*, 281; Anderson, *Randolph: A Biographical Portrait*, 314. Daniel Levine stresses the role of Shachtman and AFL-CIO official Don Slaiman in creating the APRI. Levine, *Bayard Rustin*, 175.

70. Sandra Feldman to Al Shanker, Memorandum, 9 Feb. 1968, BRP, 5, 891–92.

71. "Back UFT Then Rent Office Space," *Amsterdam News*, 5 Oct. 1968, p. 1; Pfeffer, A. *Philip Randolph, Pioneer*, 293.

72. Meier and Rudwick, *CORE*, 125–6, 182–3.

73. Bayard Rustin to Priscilla Berry, 14 July 1964, BRP, 21, 018.

74. Fred Shapiro and James Sullivan, *Race Riots: New York, 1964* (New York: Thomas Crowell, 1964).

75. Photograph, *Amsterdam News*, 25 July 1964, 1. See also George Todd, "James Powell's Funeral," *Amsterdam News*, 25 July 1964, 30.

76. Shapiro and Sullivan, *Race Riots*, 80; Levine, *Bayard Rustin*, 163.

77. Federal Bureau of Investigation, surveillance, 28 July 1964, 30 July 1964, in Kenneth O'Reilly and David Gallen, ed., *Black Americans: The FBI Files* (New York: Carroll & Graf, 1994), 393, 394–95; Bayard Rustin to Whitney Young, 29 July 1964, BRP, 21, 021; Rochelle [Horowitz] to Bayard, 24 July 1964; BRP, 21, 025; Shapiro and Sullivan, *Race Riots*, 80; Jackie Robinson, "Home Plate: Goldwater Ammunition," *Amsterdam News*, 1 Aug. 1964, 19; Levine, *Bayard Rustin*, 164. King explained to black New Yorkers that he had intervened because "New York City is the center of the Negro struggle for equality," and "What happens here affects the whole country—from the share croppers of Mississippi longing for freedom to the followers of Barry Goldwater hoping to discredit liberalism." *Amsterdam News*, 8 August 1964. Ironically, the school at which James Powell was shot was named in honor of Robert Wagner Sr.

78. Bayard Rustin, "Nonviolence on Trial," *Fellowship*, July 1964, 5–7.

79. Peter Drucker, *Max Shachtman and His Left: A Socialist's Odyssey through the "American Century"* (Atlantic Highlands, NJ: Humanities Press, 1994), 268.

80. "The Leaders Who Would Curb Election Demonstrations," *Amsterdam News*, 8 Aug. 1964, 43.

81. Rustin to A.J. Muste, 28 Jan. 1965, BRP, 21, 265; Rustin to Muste, 16 Nov. 1965, BRP, 21, 454; Staughton Lynd to Rustin, 19 Apr. 1965, BRP, 21, 346; Rustin to Neil Haworth, 17 Nov. 1964, BRP, 21, 455; Norman Thomas to Rustin, 31 Aug. 1966, BRP, 13, 228; Floyd McKissick to Rustin, 10 Oct. 1966, BRP, 13, 617; David McReynolds to Rustin, 2 July 1970, BRP, 14, 613; Eleanor Holmes Norton to Bayard Rustin, 4 Jan. 1968, BRP, 21, 997; Oliver Leeds to Bayard Rustin, 7 June 1968, BRP, 21, 1161. See also *NOtes* (June 1983); Jacqueline Trescott, "Bayard Rustin: Contradiction of a Legendary Leader," *Washington Post* 21 Aug. 1983, 6; Brooks, "A Strategist Without a Movement," 107.

82. John Lewis, *Walking With the Wind: A Memoir of the Movement* (New York: Simon & Schuster, 1998), pp. 286–88, 291.

83. Federal Bureau of Investigation, 6 Aug. 1964, 14 Aug. 1964, 25 Aug. 1964, 29 Sept. 1964, in *Black Americans*, 397–402; Levine, *Bayard Rustin*, 122, 168–69.

84. Federal Bureau of Investigation, 16 Dec. 1966, in *Black Americans*, 414.

85. Federal Bureau of Investigation, 16 Dec. 1966, in *Black Americans*, 415.

86. Just before the 1963 March on Washington, segregationist Senator Strom Thurmond took to the floor of the Senate and denounced Rustin as a homosexual. Branch, *Parting the Waters*,

861–2. See also Bayard Rustin, "In Answer to Senator Thurmond," in *Down the Line*, 109; "An Interview With Bayard Rustin," *Open Hands: Journal of the Reconciling Congregation* 2 No. 3 (1988): 5.

87. John Swomley to Glenn Smily, 1 Mar. 1956, BRP, 4, 237; Branch, *Parting the Waters*, 172.

88. Branch, *Parting the Waters*, 265, 314–15, 329.

89. John O'Neil, interview, in *Schools Against Children: The Case for Community Control*, Annette Rubinstein, ed. (New York: Monthly Review Press, 1970), 180; David Selden, *The Teacher Rebellion* (Washington: Howard University Press, 1985), 15, 29; Maurice Berube, "'Democratic Socialists' and the Schools," *New Politics*, Summer 1969, 58; Israel Kugler, "A Life in the Workmen's Circle," *Labor Heritage*, Oct. 1991, 36–49.

90. See Chapter II for a fuller discussion of social democratic notions of race. In the famous phrase of leader Eugene Debs, "The Socialist Party is the Party of the whole working class, regardless of color" and therefore had "nothing special to offer the Negro." "As a longtime Socialist" Rustin looked "upon the failure of the Socialist Party to make that special appeal as a tragic error" except for which it "might have changed the whole course of the civil rights movement." Still, Rustin's claim that the elimination of Jim Crow made civil rights protest anachronistic implies that Debs erred in stressing the exclusivity of class relations a half-century too soon. Anderson, *Randolph: A Biographical Portrait*, 148–9; Rustin, *Strategies for Freedom*, 8.

91. Rustin, speech to the National Jewish Community Relations Advisory Council, 16.

92. Bayard Rustin, "The Case of LeRoi Jones," *Amsterdam News*, 27 Jan. 1968, 14.

93. Richard Cloward, et al., "Educating the Children of the Welfare Poor: A RECORD Symposium," 3 Nov. 1967, in *Teachers College Record* 69 (1968): 304.

94. Rustin, "The Mind of the Black Militant," 209.

94. Rustin, "Educating the Children of the Welfare Poor," 305. Detroit school superintendent Norman Drachler made a similar critique, arguing that "The Kerner Commission on Civil Disorders listed several major recommendations to save large city school systems. One of the seven was community participation; the other six cost money." Norman Drachler, "The Public Schools and American Democratic Pluralism," in *The Public Schools and American Democratic Pluralism—the Role of the Jewish Community: report of a conference, May 1-May 3, 1971* (New York: Reassessment Committee of the National Jewish Community Relations Advisory Council, 1972), 16.

96. Brooks, "A Strategist Without a Movement," 104.

97. Bayard Rustin, Remarks, World Without War Conference, 3 May 1968; BRP, 21, 1184.

98. Frank Karelsen to Bayard Rustin, 5 Apr. 1965, BRP, 21, 341. See also Staughton Lynd to Bayard Rustin, 19 Apr. 1965, BRP, 21, 346.

99. Rustin to Irving Howe, 10 Nov 1966, BRP, 13, 115; Rustin to Robert Paehlke, 15 Mar. 1967, BRP, 13, 278. For a critique of the Rustin's assertion that military spending in Vietnam need not affect the funding of anti-poverty programs, see Norman Thomas to Bayard Rustin, 31 Aug. 1966, BRP, 13, 226; Seymour Melman, "Great Society Priorities," *Commonweal*, 5 Aug. 1966, 494–97.

100. Thomas to Bayard Rustin, 31 Aug. 1966; McReynolds to Rustin, 2 July 1970; Stokely Carmichael to Bayard Rustin, 16 Aug. 1966, BRP, 13, 226; McKissick to Rustin, 10 Oct. 1966. See also Trescott, "Rustin: Contradiction of a Legendary Leader," 6.

101. Ralph Poynter to Bayard Rustin, 2 Apr. 1968, BRP, 5, 893; Ad Hoc Committee Against Racism, "Join the Freedom Picket Line," (undated), BRP, 5, 894.

102. Pfeffer, A. *Philip Randolph, Pioneer*, 198; Anderson, *Randolph: A Biographical Portrait*, 259–60.

103. Herbert Hill, "Black Dissent in Organized Labor," in *Seasons of Rebellion: Protest and Radicalism in Recent America,* Joseph Boskin, ed. (Washington, DC: University Press of America, 1980), 74–5. See also Richard Parrish, "The New York City Teacher Strikes: blow to education, boon to racism," 1, 4, mimeographed leaflet, reprinted from *Labor Today,* May 1969.

104. "Spanish-Speaking and Black Unionists Move for School Solution," *Daily World,* 29 Oct. 1968, 5; Statement Adopted at a Meeting of 200 Black and Spanish-Speaking Labor Leaders, 28 Oct. 1968, 1–2, Richard Parrish Papers, Other Organizations file: UFT correspondence and papers, Schomburg Center for Research in Black Culture, New York Public Library, New York City. See also "Negro Unionists Threaten a City Labor Revolt," *New York Times,* 14 Nov. 1968, 1; "Shanker Is Called 'Racist' by Labor Leaders Here," *New York Times,* 14 Nov. 1968, 39.

105. Early in the twentieth century, members of the African Blood Brotherhood broke with the Socialist Party, stressing the centrality of race as well as class to progressive African-American politics, and American Communists had long combated racism as well as economic issues. Anderson, *Randolph: A Biographical Portrait,* 120; Mark Naison, *Communists in Harlem During the Depression* (Urbana: University of Illinois Press, 1983).

106. W. E. B. DuBois, "Marxism and the Negro Problem," *Crisis,* May 1933, 104.

107. Walter A. Jackson, "The Making of a Social Science Classic," *Perspectives on American History* New Series 2 (1985): 241–44.

108. Gerald Horne, "Why N.A.A.C.P. Won't Disown Nation of Islam," *New York Times,* 19 Jan. 1994, 20. See also Gerald Horne, "'Myth' and the Making of 'Malcolm X,'" *American Historical Review* 98 (1993): 442–48.

109. Nat Hentoff, *The New Inequality* (New York: Viking, 1964), 100–105.

110. The construction job protests are discussed in chapters 7 and 9.

111. Harris and Swanson, *Black-Jewish Relations,* 160.

112. Rustin, "Integration Within Decentralization," 215.

Chapter 7: Milton Galamison and the Integrationist Ideal

1. Martin Luther King, Jr., "Letter from Birmingham Jail—April 16, 1963," in *Afro-American Religious History: A Documentary Witness* (Durham: Duke University Press, 1985) Milton Sernett, ed., 435.

2. M.A. Farber, "Galamison Named With Four Others to School Board," *New York Times,* 15 July 1968, 1; Jitu Weusi (Leslie Campbell), interview, New York City, 21 Dec. 1990; Carlos Russell, "Rev. Milton A. Galamison: Man of Action," *Liberator,* May 1963, 19.

3. "Some City Schools Held Segregated," *New York Times,* 25 Apr. 1954; "Education Board Sets a Bias Study," *New York Times,* 9 May 1955, 25; "Civic Unit Pushes School Bias Study," *New York Times,* 18 Jan. 1956; Benjamin Fine, "Schools Get Plan to Wipe Out Bias," *New York Times,* 17 May 1956, 33.

4. Milton Galamison, oral history transcript, 14 Feb. 1970, 2, Moorland-Spingarn Research Center, Howard University, Washington DC.

5. NAACP Brooklyn Branch Education Committee, *Annual Report,* 29 Nov. 1956, in Milton Galamison Papers (hereafter NY Galamison Papers), Box 11, folder 98, Schomburg Center for the Study of Black Culture, New York City Public Libraries Galamison Papers.

6. "Integrate JHS 258 Now" (editorial), *Amsterdam News*, 2 June 1956, 12; Galamison, "Promises, Promises," 7; Harold X. Connolly, *A Ghetto Grows in Brooklyn* (New York: New York University Press, 1977), 93, 214-15; "Hint of Violence Scored By Clergy, Parent, Negro Groups," *New York Teacher News*, 17 Nov. 1956, 2. A few years after the school crisis, Judge Jack Weinstein confirmed what activists had charged. He ruled that between 1963 and 1973, "decisions of school officials" about zoning had left Coney Island's JHS 239 half-empty and largely non-white. Hart v. the Community School Board of Brooklyn, New York School District # 21 [28 Jan. 1974].

7. "School Segregation Here?" (editorial), *New York Times*, 8 Nov. 1955, 30; Leonard Buder, "City Schools Cleared In Segregation Study," *New York Times*, 7 Nov. 1955, 1; "Segregation Laid to Schools Here," *New York Times* 10 Nov. 1955, 39; Clarence Taylor, *Knocking*, 66.

8. Galamison oral history transcript, 4-5; "Judge, 2 Other Officials Of NAACP Quit in Row," *New York World-Telegram and Sun*, 30 Jan. 1957; Galamison, "Promises, Promises," 7, 9-11; Taylor, Knocking, 68. .

9. Galamison, "Promises, Promises," 7; Milton Galamison to Pastor Francois Akoa, 13 Dec. 1955; Milton Galamison Papers, State of Wisconsin Historical Society, Madison, WI (hereafter WI Galamison Papers), folder 1; MG to Bruce Rigdon, 7 Dec. 1955, WI Galamison Papers, folder 1.

10. Carl Bernstein, *Loyalties: A Son's Memoir* (New York: Simon and Schuster, 1989), 92-98, 165, 175-76, 208; "C.I.O. Expels Union of Public Workers," *New York Times*, 17 Feb. 1950, 5. Other Truman Loyalty hearing questions included, "Do you ever entertain Negroes in your home?" "What magazines do you read?" "Do you read a good many books?" "Is it not true that you lived next door to and therefore were closely associated with a member of the IWW?" "Have you ever discussed the subject of dance in Russia?" and "Did you ever write a letter to the Red Cross about the segregation of blood?" (Bernstein, *Loyalties*, 195, 198, 205).

11. Meier and Rudwick, *CORE*, 51-2; Constance McLaughlin Green, *The Secret City: A History of Race Relations in the Nation's Capital* (Princeton: Princeton University Press, 1967), 297; Gladys Byram Shepperd, *Mary Church Terrell: Respectable Person* (Baltimore: Human Relations Press, 1959), 50.

12. Clarence Taylor, *Knocking at Our Own Door: Milton Galamison and the Struggle to Integrate New York City Schools* (New York: Columbia University Press, 1997), 57.

13. Adina Back, "Blacks, Jews and the Struggle to Integrate Brooklyn's Junior High School 258: A Cold War Story," *Journal of American Ethnic History* (2001): 45.

14. Olivia Taylor, interview, New York City, 19 Dec. 1990; and Mary Ellen Pfeiffer, interview, New York City, 23 Dec. 1991.

15. Milton Galamison to Rose Russell, 25 Nov. 1959; WI Galamison Papers, file 33; "Rev. Galamison, NYC Civil Rights Leader, to Address TU Conference," *Teacher News*, 19 Mar. 1960, 1.

16. Lisa Yvette Waller, "The Pressures of the People: Milton A. Galamison, The Parents' Workshop, and Resistance to School Integration in New York City, 1960-1963," *Souls* 1 (Spring 1999): 33.

17. Milton Galamison to John Theobald, 12 June 1959, MG Papers, file 2, Carita Roane to MG, 8 June 1958; John Theobald to Milton Galamison, 21 Mar. 1960, 14 June 1960, WI Galamison Papers, folder 2; Ida Posner, interview, New York City, 21 Dec. 1990; Connolly, *A Ghetto Grows in Brooklyn*, 215-16.

18. James Allen to Milton Galamison, 9 June 1959; Milton Galamison to John Theobald, 12 June 1959, WI Galamison Papers, file 2; Galamison oral history transcript, 2.

19. Galamison, interview, in *Why Teachers Strike*, 298; Galamison oral history transcript, 6; Waller, "Pressures of the People,"35-36.

20. Theobald to Galamison; Taylor interview. See also New York City People's Board of Education, Press Release, 26 Dec. 1966, Annie Stein Papers, Public Education Association, New York City; and Annie Stein, "Strategies for Failure," *Harvard Education Review* 41 (1971): 171.

21. Galamison oral history transcript, 6–8; Galamison to Silver, 26 Apr. 1961, WI Papers; Galamison to Silver, 2 May 1961, *News from the Parents Workshop*, May 1961.

22. Joseph Noethen to Milton Galamison, 29 June 1961, WI Galamison Papers, folder 2.

23. Taylor, *Black Churches*, 146.

24. Taylor, *Black Churches*, 143–144.

25. Oliver Leeds to MG, 12 Aug. 1963, WI Galamison Papers, folder 3; Clarence Taylor, "'Whatever the Cost, We Will Set the Nation Straight': The Ministers' Committee and the Downstate Center Campaign," *Long Island Historical Journal* 1 (1989): 136–146; Meier and Rudwick, *CORE*, 231, 237; Dave Silver, interview, New York City, 16 Dec. 1990.

26. Taylor, *Knocking*, 117.

27. Gertrude Wilson, "The Will and the Way of Boycotters," *Amsterdam News*, 8 Feb. 1964, 4; "Executive board minutes," *United Teacher*, 24 Jan. 1964, 7; Joseph Michalak, "School Plan—A Loud No," *Herald Tribune*, 30 Jan. 1964, 1. Among the many white liberals condemning the boycott were Jimmy Breslin, "The Boycotters," Herald Tribune, 31 Jan. 1964, 1; and "A Boycott Solves Nothing," *New York Times*, 31 Jan. 1964, 26.

28. Transcript, WCBS, "Newsmakers," 19 Jan. 1964, NY Galamison Papers, Box 13, folder 92; *New York Times*, 3–4 Feb. 1964.

29. Bernard Bard, "Boycott Chiefs Say 50,000 Will Stay Out," *New York Post*, 2 Feb. 1964; Sue Reinert, "At Boycott Headquarters, A Hard But Happy Day," *New York Herald Tribune*, 4 Feb. 1964; "Malcolm Nash Reports: Headquarters of Harlem Boycott," *Amsterdam News*, 8 Feb. 1964, 7; Gertrude Wilson, "The Will and the Way of Boycotters," *Amsterdam News*, 8 Feb. 1964, 4.

30. Robert Walsh and Sidney Kline, "Third of Pickets Out in Peaceful Boycott," *Daily News*, 4 Feb. 1964, 19; Henry Hillson, "The Negro History and Culture Club," *High Points*, Dec. 1943, 19–23; James Booker, "JHS 103, PS 194 and City Hall," *Amsterdam News*, 8 Feb. 1964, 1; "What Board and Gross Say of the Picketing," *Daily News*, 4 Feb. 1964.

31. Leonard Buder, "Galamison Foes Drop Ouster Bid," New York Times, 12 Feb. 1964, 25; *New York Times*, 27 Feb. 1964. Chicago's school boycotts witnessed the same division between moderates and militants as New York's. Alan Anderson and George Pickering, *Confronting the Color Line: the Broken Promise of the Civil Rights Movement in Chicago* (Athens : University of Georgia Press, 1986), 130–31.

32. Galamison, *Why Teachers Strike*, 300–301; Galamison oral history, 10–11; Milton Galamison, "The Hooky Party," undated [c. 1969], 19, NY Galamison Papers, Box 12, folder 75; "Galamison Plans A Work Stoppage for April 22," *New York Times*, 14 Mar. 1964, 10; Peter Goldman, *The Death and Life of Malcolm X* (New York: Harper & Row, 1973), 143–5. As late as 1968, 90% of teachers were white, and only 5 of 865 principals were black, and only 12 of 1500 assistant principals were black or Puerto Rican. Galamison, "View From the Eleventh Floor," undated [c. 1969], 28–31, NY Galamison Papers, Box 12, folder 75; Milton Galamison, "The Ocean Hill-Brownsville Dispute," *Christianity and Crisis*, 14 Oct. 1968, 239.

33. Milton Galamison, "Statement Pertaining to the Upgrading of Negro teachers to Supervisory and Administrative Positions in the New York City School System," July 1964, author's personal copy; Galamison, "The Hooky Party," 25–27; Milton Galamison to parents, 4 Feb. 1965, Equal Papers, Milbank Library, Teachers College, Columbia University, folder 3; "Integration

Group Splits on Merits of School Boycott," *Long Island Press*, 16 Dec. 1964, 2; *New York Times*, 24 Nov. 1964; Galamison, *Why Teachers Strike*, 303.

34. Lenora Berson, *The Negroes and the Jews* (New York: Random House, 1971), 289; Diane Ravitch, *The Great School Wars, New York City, 1805–1973: A Brief History of the Public Schools as Battlefield of Social Change* (New York: Basic Books, 1974), 307.

35. Ravitch, *The Great School Wars*, 308; Henry Hampton and Steve Fayer, *Voices of Freedom: An Oral History of the Civil Rights Movement from the 1960s Through the 1980s* (New York: Bantam, 1990), 487–88; New York City People's Board of Education, Press Release, 26 Dec. 1966, 1, 3, author's personal copy.

36. Milton Galamison, "If Blaine Amendment is Repealed," *African-American Teachers Forum*, Sept.–Oct. 1967, 1, 4.

37. Galamison, "The Ghost of McCarthy," 34.

38. Galamison, "Ocean Hill-Brownsville Dispute," 240.

39. Bernard Bard and Alfred Hendricks, "Battle for the Schools, The Man Behind the Boycott," *New York Post*, 28 Jan. 1964, 23.

40. Pfeiffer interview.

41. Galamison, *Why Teachers Strike*, 309; M.A. Farber, "New School Plan Gaining Support," *New York Times*, 20 May 1968, 1, 36; Weusi interview.

42. Milton Galamison, "The Ghost of McCarthy," 34, NY Galamison Papers, Box 12, folder 73; Galamison, *Why Teachers Strike*, 304–5, 313.

43. Galamison, "View From the Eleventh Floor," 6.

44. Galamison, *Why Teachers Strike*, 305; Galamison, "The Ghost of McCarthy," 1, 29.

45. "OIC Job Training Center "Sign In" Started Monday," *Amsterdam News*, 11 Nov. 1967, 25; Daphne Sheppard, "Kings Diary," *Amsterdam News*, 11 Nov. 1967, 22; George Todd, "BSRC Funds OIC," 9 Dec. 1967, 25; Weusi interview.

46. Galamison, "Color Me Black," 23.

47. Milton Galamison, "Color Me Black," undated [c. 1969], 7, 10, NY Galamison Papers, Box 12, folder 72; Fred Powledge, *Free At Last? The Civil Rights Movement and the People Who Made It* (Boston: Little, Brown, 1991), 551.

48. MG to Bruce Rigdon, 7 Dec. 1955, WI MG Papers, folder 1; Russell, "Man of Action," 20; Waller, "The Pressures of the People," 34.

49. Taylor, *Knocking*, 30, 35, 223.

50. Powledge, *Free At Last*, 552.

51. Galamison, "Promises, Promises," 4–6.

52. Russell, "Man of Action," 20.

53. Milton Galamison, "The Period of the Pendulum," undated, 11, Galamison Papers, Box 12, file 73. Like many black intellectuals of his day, Galamison considered classical European culture a part of his birthright. He played Bach and considered Socrates, Plato, Aristotle, Kant, Darwin, and Shakespeare "the great thinkers of civilization," and he quoted such authors as John Stuart Mill and Maxwell Anderson in his sermons. Milton Galamison, "Educational Values and Community Power," *Freedomways*, Fall 1968, 312; Milton Galamison, sermons, 2 June 1968, 21 July 1968, and 15 Sept. 1968, NY Galamison Papers, Box 6, folder 33.

54. Milton Galamison, sermon, 6 Oct. 1968, NY Galamison Papers, Box 6, folder 33.

55. Bernard Bard and Alfred Hendricks, "Battle for the Schools, The Man Behind the Boycott," *New York Post*, 28 Jan. 1964, 23.

56. Galamison, "Color Me Black," 15, 21.

57. Bernard Bard and Alfred Hendricks, "Battle for the Schools, The Man Behind the Boycott," *New York Post*, 28 Jan. 1964, 23.

58. Milton Galamison, "Order Out of Chaos" (sermon), 27 Oct. 1968, NY Galamison Papers, Box 6, folder 33.

59. Galamison, "Ocean Hill-Brownsville Dispute," 329–240.

60. Bernard Bard and Alfred Hendricks, "Battle for the Schools, The Man Behind the Boycott," *New York Post*, 28 Jan. 1964, 23.

61. Connolly, *A Ghetto Grows in Brooklyn*, 67, 89, 93, 113–116, 150, 171–74, 199–200, 228.

62. King, "Letter from Birmingham Jail," 435; James Farmer, "Some Views on the Relationships Between Decentralization and Racial Integration in Large City School Systems," in *Decentralization and Racial Integration*, Carroll Johnson and Michael Usdam, eds. (New York: Teachers College, Columbia University, 1968), 186–87. Brooklyn activist and future member of the House of Representatives Major Owens also saw no contradiction between community control and a commitment to integration. (Major Owens, interview, Chicago, 5 Apr. 1991.)

63. C. Herbert Oliver, interview, in Melvin I. Urofsky, *Why Teachers Strike*, 222.

64. Eugenia Kemble, "U.F.T. Debate, Dissent Greet Bundy Report" [1967] in *The Community and Racial Crisis* 2nd edition, Barbara Flicker, ed. (New York: Practicing Law Institute, 1969), 73.

65. Bill Kovach, "School Crisis Helps Ocean Hill in Its Search for a Community Identity," *New York Times*, 31 Oct. 1968, 51.

66. Taylor interview. White women could ally themselves with black activists, but living in communities where most of their neighbors opposed the movement for black equality, they could rarely be an organic part of it. Al Lurie to Robert Morris, 22 Oct. 1979, Guide to Ellen Lurie Papers, Teachers College.

67. Kovach, "School Crisis Helps Ocean Hill."

68. Education Action Program, Brownsville Community Council, "Memorandum to Isaiah Robinson, Re: Proposed Resolution for Board of Education Action on the Construction of Schools in Brownsville," Isaiah Robinson Papers, series 378, box 17 folder 2, Teachers College, Columbia University.

69. Taylor interview.

70. Taylor interview; Bill Kovach, "How Ocean Hill Spread the Word: Communications Network Keeps People Informed," *New York Times*, 9 Nov. 1968, 20.

Chapter 8: From Community Organizing to Community Control

1. Julius Lester, *Look Out, Whitey! Black Power's Gon' Get Your Mama* (New York: Grove Press, 1968), ix.

2. William L. Van Deburg, *New Day in Babylon: The Black Power Movement and American Culture, 1965–1975* (Chicago: University of Chicago Press, 1992), 197.

3. Mwlina Imiri Abubadika (Sonny Carson), *The Education of Sonny Carson* (New York: Norton, 1972), 157.

4. Carson retained his commitment to an independent black politics for decades. See Peter Noel, "What Black Vote?" *Village Voice*, Sept. 11, 2001.

5. Daisy Bates, *The Long Shadow of Little Rock* (New York: David McKay, 1962), 103–147; Frye Gaillard, *The Dream Long Deferred* (Chapel Hill: University of North Carolina Press, 1988), 8.

6. Abubadika, *The Education of Sonny Carson*, 188.

7. Abubadika, *The Education of Sonny Carson*, 304, 310; Leonard Buder, "CORE 'River Rats' Stress Militancy," *New York Times*, 14 Mar. 1964, 11.

8. Abubadika, *The Education of Sonny Carson*, 157, 11–12.

9. Abubadika, *The Education of Sonny Carson*, 14, 23.

10. Abubadika, *The Education of Sonny Carson*, 23, 38–39. On the extreme abuse of teachers in ghetto schools see also Jim Haskins, *Diary of a Harlem Schoolteacher* (New York: Grove Press, 1969), 52; Jean Anyon, Ghetto Schooling: A Political Economy of Urban School Reform (New York: Teachers College Press, 1997), 29–30.

11. Abubadika, *The Education of Sonny Carson*, 32, 36–40.

12. Abubadika, *The Education of Sonny Carson*, 57.

13. Abubadika, *The Education of Sonny Carson*, 60, 80, 109–110.

14. Oliver Leeds to Milton Galamison, 12 Aug. 1963, Milton Galamison Papers, file 3: Civil Rights, 1961–64, Wisconsin State Historical Society; Clarence Taylor, "'Whatever the Cost, We Will Set the Nation Straight': The Ministers' Committee and the Downstate Center Campaign," *Long Island Historical Journal* 1 (1989): 136–146; Abubadika, *The Education of Sonny Carson*, 114, 304, 310; Buder, "CORE 'River Rats.'"

15. Abubadika, *The Education of Sonny Carson*, 31, 37, 49, 102.

16. Abubadika, *The Education of Sonny Carson*, 121–22.

17. Abubadika, *The Education of Sonny Carson*, 122.

18. Peter Kihss, "School Leaders See Bias in Bids to Oust Principals," *New York Times*, 22 May 1967, 34; Abubadika, *The Education of Sonny Carson*, 133–34, 137.

19. Abubadika, *The Education of Sonny Carson*, 135–36; Peter Kihss, "Donovan Seeks More Community Help to Schools, *New York Times*, 25 May, 1967, 34; Kihss, "School Leaders See Bias."

20. Clarence Funnye, "Bundy and Black Power: A Retreat to Reality," *Village Voice*, Apr. 1967, quoted in Feldman, "N.Y. City Decentralization," 5.

21. Abubadika, *The Education of Sonny Carson*, 175–76.

22. Abubadika, *The Education of Sonny Carson*, 141–43; Edward Baneal, "Student's Access to Lawyer Backed," *New York Times*, 11 Apr. 1967, 39; Kathleen Teltsch, "Educators Score Discipline Ruling," *New York Times*, 12 Apr. 1967, 49; Maurice Carroll, "Progress Hinted in Teacher Talks," *New York Times*, 28 Aug. 1967, 29; Milton Galamison, oral history transcript, 14 Feb. 1970, 7–8, Moorland-Spingarn Research Center, Howard University. These developments were not unique to New York. See Paul Peterson, *School Politics Chicago Style* (Chicago: University of Chicago Press, 1976), 174; Roger Biles, *Richard J. Daley: Politics, Race, and the Governing of Chicago* (DeKalb: Northern Illinois University Press, 1995), 142; Adam Cohen and Elizabeth Taylor, *American Pharaoh: Mayor Richard J. Daley: His Battle for Chicago and the Nation* (Boston: Little, Brown, 2000), 335–37.

23. "14 Civic Groups Charge Pupils Are Often Unfairly Suspended," *New York Times*, 6 Apr. 1967, 33; C. Gerald Fraser, "Workshop Is Held in Brooklyn to Teach Parents How to Teach," *New York Times*, 9 Sept. 1967, 18.

24. Thomas Johnson, "2 Schools Sought to Aid Disruptive," *New York Times*, 21 Sept. 1967, 52.

25. Abubadika, *The Education of Sonny Carson*, 169.

26. Abubadika, *The Education of Sonny Carson*, 170–74.

27. Johnson, "2 Schools Sought to Aid Disruptive;" Thomas Johnson, "Schools for Disruptive Children Proposed to Donovan by CORE," *New York Times*, 10 Nov. 1967, 16.

28. *New York Post*, 23 Jan. 1968; *Amsterdam News*, letter, 16 Jan. 1968; *New York Times*, 11 Jan. 1968, 1; Miriam Wasserman, *The School Fix, NYC, USA* (New York: Outerbridge & Dienstfrey, 1970), 340; Abubadika, *The Education of Sonny Carson*, 170–74.

29. Abubadika, *The Education of Sonny Carson*, 125, 129, 170; Johnson, "2 Schools Sought to Aid Disruptive."

30. Lawrence Levine, *Black Culture and Black Consciousness: Afro-American Folk Thought from Slavery to Freedom* (Oxford: Oxford University Press, 1977), 407–420; Ronald Butchart, "'Outthinking and Outflanking the Owners of the World': A Historiography of the Afro-American Struggle for Education," *History of Education Quarterly* 28 (1988): 333.

31. Piri Thomas, *Down these Mean Streets* (New York: Alfred A. Knopf, 1967), 64, 68.

32. Claude Brown, *Manchild in the Promised Land* (New York: Macmillan, 1965), 18, 21.

33. Paul Chevigny, *Cops and Rebels: A Study of Provocation* (New York: Pantheon, 1972), 69–70. Among the members of the Tilden Afro-American Club was long-time New York City activist Al Sharpton. Michael Klein, *The Man Behind the Sound Bite: The Real Story of the Rev. Al Sharpton* (New York: Castillo International, 1991), 70, 77–78.

34. Kuwasi Balagoon, et al., *Look For Me in the Whirlwind: The Collective Autobiography of the New York 21* (New York: Vintage Books), 126–28.

35. Abubadika, *The Education of Sonny Carson*, 119. See also James Baldwin, "A Report From Occupied Territory" *Nation*, 11 July 1966; Nat Hentoff, "Blacks and Jews: An Interview with Julius Lester," *Evergreen Review*, Apr. 1969, 74; Truman Nelson, *The Torture of the Mothers* (Boston: Beacon Press, 1968 [1965]). Radical black nationalist poet Don L. Lee recommended Nelson's book to those seeking to understand white supremacy in America. Don L. Lee, *From Plan to Planet: Life Studies: The Need for Afrikan Minds and Institutions* (Chicago: Broadside, 1973), 155. Networks established to defend the Six also served to promote school integration and then black community control of ghetto schools. Annette Rubinstein, "Freedom School in Manhattan," *The Call to Conscience* [newsletter of the Charter Group for a Pledge of Conscience], Feb.–Mar. 1965, 3; Jane McManus, "Lessons in Freedom," *National Guardian*, 27 Feb. 1965, 10; Larry Fosburgh, "'Harlem Four' Are Freed After Manslaughter Pleas," *New York Times*, 5 Apr. 1973, 55.

36. Junius Griffin, "Harlem: The Tension Underneath—Youths Study Karate, Police Keep Watch and People Worry," *New York Times*, 29 May 1964, 1.

37. "3 Youths Seized in Harlem Killing: A Racial Motive in Recent Assaults Is Investigated," *New York Times*, 1 May 1964; "Suspect Gives Up in Harlem Death: Negro Youth Is Third Accused in Shopkeeper's Murder," *New York Times*, 5 May 1964; "6 Youths Indicted in Harlem Slaying," *New York Times*, 26 May 1964, 28.

38. Griffin, "Harlem: The Tension Underneath."

39. The *Times*'s fantasies reflected wider white sentiments and not specific events. Following the Harlem riot of the summer of 1964, reporters Fred Shapiro and James Sullivan claimed as fact that in Harlem, "rape and assault and murder and theft and addiction are a part of life. . . . There seem to be no rules, no discipline, nothing but a vast, heaving anarchy." Fred Shapiro and James Sullivan, *Race Riots: New York, 1964* (New York: Thomas Cromwell, 1964), 29.

40. Griffin, "Harlem: The Tension Underneath," 1; Nelson, *Torture of the Mothers*.

41. Nelson, *Torture of the Mothers*, 71, 81, 103. Their court-appointed lawyers were political appointees, who were paid a set fee for each case. Such lawyers frequently visited their clients only to urge plea-bargains, and they were deeply distrusted.

42. Malcolm X, *Malcolm Speaks: Selected Speeches and Statements* (New York: Pathfinder, 1965), 65.

43. Nelson, *Torture of the Mothers*, 60–1, 65.

44. Abubadika, *The Education of Sonny Carson*, passim.; Jitu Weusi (Leslie Campbell), Interview, Brooklyn, 21 Dec. 1990; Nelson, *Torture of the Mothers*, 98; Chevigny, *Cops and Rebels*, 45; Haskins, *Diary of a Harlem Schoolteacher*, 55, 86.

45. Bill Kovach, "How Ocean Hill Spread the Word: Communications Network Keeps People Informed," *New York Times*, 9 Nov. 1968, 20.

46. Abubadika, *The Education of Sonny Carson*, 134.

47. Nell Irvin Painter, "Malcolm X Across the Genres," *American Historical Review* 98 (1993): 436.

48. Michele Wallace, *Black Macho and the Myth of the Superwoman* (New York: Dial, 1978), 36.

49. Myrna Katz Frommer and Harvey Frommer, *It Happened in Brooklyn: An Oral History of Growing Up in the Borough in the 1940s, 1950s, and 1960s* (New York: Harcourt Brace & Co., 1993), 214.

50. Queen Mother Moore, "We Refused to Be Programmed Anymore," in Stanley Wanat and Michael Cohen, eds., *Before the Fall: A Discussion of Schools in Conflict with Community* (Ithaca: Cornell University, 1969), 20; Audley Moore, Oral History Interview, 6 and 8 June 1978, in *The Black Women Oral History Project from The Arthur and Elizabeth Schlesinger Library on the History of Women in America, Radcliffe College* (Vol. VIII), Ruth Edmonds Hill, ed. (Westport: Meckler, 1991), 116, 142, 176–8.

51. Balagoon, et al., *Look For Me in the Whirlwind*, 271.

52. Abubadika, *The Education of Sonny Carson*, 157.

53. See for instance Roi Ottley, *"New World A-Coming"* (Boston: Houghton Mifflin, 1943), 101–103; Sterling Stuckey, *Slave Culture: Nationalist Theory and the Foundations of Black America* (New York: Oxford University Press, 1987); Tony Sewell, *Garvey's Children: the Legacy of Marcus Garvey* (Trenton, NJ: Africa World Press, 1990).

54. Lawrence Levine, *Black Culture and Black Consciousness: Afro-American Folk Thought from Slavery to Freedom* (Oxford: Oxford University Press, 1977), 407–420. The African American folklore figure Stagolee, Black Panther Bobby Seale argued, represented the "bad nigger off the block" who "didn't take shit from nobody. All you had to do was organize him" and "make him politically conscious." Bobby Seale, *Seize the Time: the Story of the Black Panther Party and Huey P. Newton* (New York: Vintage, 1970), 4.

55. On the impact of deindustrialization, see William Julius Wilson, *When Work Disappears* (New York: Knopf, 1996).

56. John Devine, *Maximum Security: the Culture of Violence in Inner-City Schools* (Chicago: University of Chicago Press, 1996).

57. This chapter builds on the work of scholars such as Paul Willis, who have demonstrated how the oppositional stance of subordinated students simultaneously challenges and reproduces social hierarchies, and on the work of scholars such as John Ogbu, Signithia Fordham, and Ann Ferguson, who have illuminated how such tensions pervade the experience of African American students. See Paul Willis, *Learning to Labor: How Working Class Kids Get Working Class Jobs* (New York: Columbia University Press, 1981); John Ogbu, "Understanding Cultural Diversity and Learning," *Educational Researcher* (Nov. 1992): pp. 5-15; Signithia Fordham, "Racelessness as a Factor in Black Students' School Success: Pragmatic Strategy or Pyrrhic Victory," *Harvard Educational Review* (1988): 54–84; and Ann Ferguson, *Bad Boys: Public School in the Making of Black Masculinity* (Ann Arbor: University of Michigan Press, 2000).

58. Richard Slotkin, *Gunfighter Nation: the Myth of the Frontier in Twentieth-Century America* (Norman: University of Oklahoma Press, 1998).

59. Frank B. Williams, "Thousands Flock to Funeral for Eazy-E," *Los Angeles Times*, 8 Apr. 1995, B-1.

60. James Wechsler, "Those Who Care," *New York Post* 26 Sept 1968, 53; Joseph Lelyveld, "Negro-White Friction Is Eroding Teacher-Student Relations in City's High Schools," *New York Times*, 9 Feb 1970.

61. Signithia Fordham, "Those Loud Black Girls": (Black) Women, Silence, and Gender 'Passing' in the Academy," *Anthropology and Education Quarterly* 24 (1993): 3-32. See also Anne Campbell, *The Girls in the Gang* (Cambridge, MA: Blackwell, 1991).

62. Milton Galamison, "A Grand and Awful Time," undated [c. 1969], 24, Milton Galamison Papers, Schomburg Center for the Study of African American Culture, Box 12, folder 72.

63. Sanyika Shakur, *Monster: the Autobiography of an L.A. Gang Member* (New York: Atlantic Monthly Press, 1993), 219, 276, 306; Rovell Patrick Solomon, *Black Resistance in High School: Forging a Separatist Culture* (Albany: State University of New York Press, 1992).

Chapter 9: Visible Men

1. Horace Mann Bond, "Main Currents in the Educational Crisis Affecting Afro-Americans," Freedomways, Fall 1968, p. 308.

2. Randall Robinson, *The Debt: What America Owes to Blacks* (New York: Penguin, 2000), 7.

3. Alex Poinsett, "Battle to Control Black Schools," *Ebony*, May 1969, 45.

4. Kenneth D. King, "Attitudes on School Decentralization in New York's Three Experimental School Districts," (dissertation, Teachers College, 1971), 57.

5. Leslie Campbell, "The Difference," *Afro-American Teachers Forum* (second quarter, 1968), reprinted in *What Black Educators Are Saying*, Nathan Wright, Jr., ed. (New York: Hawthorn, 1970), 25.

6. W. E. B. DuBois, "Education and Work" [1930], in *The Education of Black People: Ten Critiques, 1906-1960, by W.E.B. DuBois*, Herbert Aptheker, ed. (New York: Monthly Review Press, 1973), 64.

7. Benjamin Mays, *Born to Rebel* (Athens: University of Georgia Press, 1987), 26.

8. Ralph Ellison, *Invisible Man* (New York: Vintage, 1980), 3-4.

9. Martin Luther King, Jr., "Letter from Birmingham Jail—April 16, 1963," in *Afro-American Religious History: A Documentary Witness*, Milton Sernett, ed. (Durham, NC: Duke University Press, 1985), 435.

10. David Spencer and Charles Wilson, "The Case for Community Control" (1968), in *The Community and Racial Crisis* 2nd edition, Barbara Flicker, ed. (New York: Practicing Law Institute, 1969), 69.

11. This chapter builds on a growing body of scholarship on the work and thought of black educators. See Gloria Ladson-Billings, *The DreamKeepers: Successful Teachers of African American Children* (San Francisco: Jossey-Bass, 1994); Michele Foster, *Black Teachers on Teaching* (New York: The New Press, 1997); V.P. Franklin, "They Rose and Fell Together": African American Educators and Community Leadership, 1795-1954," *Journal of Education* 172 (1990): 39-64; Michael Fultz, "African American Teachers in the South, 1890-1940: Powerlessness and the Ironies of Expectations and Protest," *History of Education Quarterly* 35 (1995): 401-422; Emily V. Siddle-Walker, "Caswell County Training School, 1933-1969: Relationships between Community and School," *Harvard Educational Review* 63 (1993): 161-82.

12. Although women outnumbered men among New York's black teachers, men played the leading role in shaping black educational thought and activism in the late 1960s. While nationalist

thought and activism contained patriarchal elements, one should not reduce nationalist politics to a vehicle for women's victimization. Women activists as well as men noted the special burdens that American racism had placed on black men, and celebrations of black manhood repudiated the "nobodiness" felt by black women as well as black men. See for instance Audley (Queen Mother) Moore, Oral History Interview, in *The Black Women Oral History Project from The Arthur and Elizabeth Schlesinger Library on the History of Women in America*, Radcliffe College Vol. VIII, Ruth Edmonds Hill, ed. (Westport: Meckler, 1991), 176–177.

13. Joyce Elaine King, "Culture-Centered Knowledge: Black Studies, Curriculum Transformation, and Social Action," in James A. Banks, ed., *Handbook of Research on Multicultural Education* (New York: Macmillan, 1995), 265–266.

14. William Watkins, "Black Curriculum Orientations: A Preliminary Inquiry," *Harvard Educational Review* 63 (1993): 229–30.

15. Jonathan Kaufman, *Broken Alliance: the Turbulent Times Between Blacks and Jews in America* (New York: Scribner, 1988), 132 ; Diane Ravitch, *The Great School Wars: a History of the New York City Public Schools* (New York: Basic Books, 1988), 322.

16. Rhody McCoy, Interview, in *Why Teachers Strike: Teachers' Rights and Community Control*, Melvin Urofsky, ed. (Garden City: Doubleday, NY, 1970), 112–13. On racism in the assignment of students to 600 schools, see Bernard Mackler, "The '600' Schools: Dilemmas, Problems, and Solutions," *Urban Review* 1 (June 1966): 8–14.

17. Henry Hampton and Steve Fayer, *Voices of Freedom: An Oral History of the Civil Rights Movement from the 1960s through the 1980s* (New York: Bantam, 1990), 491–92.

18. On race and civic capacity in school reform, see Jeffrey Henig et al., eds., *The Color of School Reform: Race, Politics, and the Challenge of Urban Education* (Princeton: Princeton University Press, 1999).

19. Robert B. Westbrook, "Schools for Industrial Democrats: the Social Origins of John Dewey's Philosophy of Education," *American Journal of Education* 100 (1992): 401–419.

20. See for instance Herb Goro, *The Block* (New York, Vintage, 1970), 42, 31, 44.

21. Rhody McCoy, "The Formation of a Community-Controlled School District," in *Community Control of Schools*, Henry Levin, ed. (Washington: Brookings Inst., 1970), 169 (emphasis added).

22. McCoy, Interview, 138–39.

23. Rhody McCoy, Preface, "A Plan for An Experimental School District: Ocean Hill-Brownsville," Aug. 1967, Board of Education Papers, Rose Shapiro Collection, Milbank Library, Teachers College, Columbia University, Box 8, Jerald Podair, *Like Strangers: Blacks, Whites, and New York City's Ocean Hill-Brownsville Crisis, 1945–1980* (Ph.D. dissertation, Princeton University, 1997), 111–112; Rhody McCoy, "The Year of the Dragon," in *Confrontation at Ocean Hill-Brownsville* Maurice Berube and Marilyn Gittell, eds. (New York: Praeger, 1969), 52.

24. McCoy, Interview, 118.

25. Joshua Freeman, *Working Class New York: Life and Labor Since World War II* (New York: New Press, 2000), 143, 168.

26. Joseph Featherstone, "Ocean Hill Is Alive, and, Well . . . ," *New Republic* 19 Apr. 1969, 23. The imperialist architecture of New York's new ghetto schools was in part a legacy of Cold War fantasies that windowless schools would offer shelter in case of nuclear war. (JoAnne Brown, "'A Is for Atom, B Is for Bomb': Civil Defense in American Public Education, 1948–1963," *Journal of American History* 75 [1988]: 88–89.)

27. McCoy, "The Year of the Dragon," 53–55.

28. McCoy, "The Formation of a Community-Controlled School District," 180; Rhody McCoy, "Why Have an Ocean Hill-Brownsville?" in Wright, *What Black Educators Are Saying*, 255.

29. McCoy, "The Year of the Dragon," 52.

30. Kaufman, *Broken Alliance*, 157.

31. McCoy, "The Year of the Dragon," 54–55.

32. McCoy, "Why Have an Ocean Hill-Brownsville?" 253.

33. McCoy, "Analysis of Critical Issues and Incidents," xi, 1, 52, 72, 78.

34. McCoy, "Analysis of Critical Issues and Incidents," xi, 59–62, 151–53.

35. Hampton and Fayer, *Voices of Freedom*, p. 508.

36. Roy Wilkins (1901–1981) served as Executive Secretary of the NAACP from 1955 to 1977. Whitney Young, Jr. (1921–1971) served as president of the National Urban League from 1961 through 1971.

37. Emanuel Perlmutter, "Principal's Bail Raised to $100,000," *New York Times*, 28 Feb. 1968, 50. Shabazz was the widow of Malcolm X.

38. Herman Ferguson, "A black survival curriculum," *Guardian*, 9 Mar. 1968, 16. See also Homer Bigart, "Ferguson Gives Plan For Schools," *New York Times*, 14 Mar. 1968, 36.

39. Ferguson, "black survival curriculum." Although Ferguson's shooting range proposal was considered extremist, shooting ranges have been quite common in American schools. See Reserve Liaison and Training Branch, United States Marine Corps, *Adventures in Leadership: A Text for U.S. Marine Corps Junior ROTC* (Quantico, VA: Author, 1973); "Student Rifle Teams In Spotlight Amid Recent Spate of School Shootings," *San Francisco Chronicle*, 27 Nov. 1999, A12.

40. Ferguson, "black survival curriculum;" C. Gerald Fraser, "Workshop Is Held in Brooklyn to Teach Parents How to Teach," *New York Times*, 9 Sept. 1967, 18. On banking pedagogy and black radicalism, see Daniel Perlstein, "Minds Stayed on Freedom: Politics, Pedagogy, and the African American Freedom Struggle," *American Educational Research Journal*, Summer 2002.

41. Garry Wills, "The Second Civil War," *Esquire*, Mar. 1968, 80, 140, 144; "Ferguson Convicted," *New York Times* 15 June 1968, 7; "Ferguson, Guilty, Is Freed on Bail," *New York Times*, 16 June 1968, 48.

42. Herman Benjamin Ferguson, "Speech at Sentencing on Bail Jumping Charge, June 28, 1990," (New York City: Committee to Free Herman Ferguson, n.d.), 15.

43. "Firebrand or Educator? Herman Benjamin Ferguson," *New York Times*, 28 Feb. 1968, 50. See also Leonard Buder, "Hundreds of Pupils Rampage at Brooklyn School," *New York Times*, 3 Feb. 1968, 1.

44. Ferguson's father was the Superintendent of the Sunday school at Evens Metropolitan A.M.E.Z. Church and the only male president of the North Carolina Congress of Colored PTAs. His mother was a state PTA leader, the vice-president of the Fayetteville chapter of the Urban League, and founder of the James Walker Hood "Negro Branch" of the Fayetteville public library. Hood was the founding father of the AMEZ Church in North Carolina and a civil rights leader who served as North Carolina's assistant superintendent of public instruction during Reconstruction. The line from Hood to Ferguson epitomizes the vibrant African American political culture that developed in the shadow of the racial caste system. "Ferguson Elementary School" (Fayetteville, NC: Ferguson-Easley Elementary School, Nov. 1978); Sandy D. Martin, *For God and Race: The Religious and Political Leadership of AMEZ Bishop James Walker Hood* (Columbia: University of South Carolina Press, 1999).

45. Herman Ferguson, Interview, New York City, Dec. 1991. Similarly, in the segregated elementary school of his Kansas City childhood, of civil rights activist Julius Lester studied Paul Robe-

son, W. E. B. DuBois, Booker T. Washington, and Mary McLeod Bethune. Raised in a small, segregated Oklahoma town, Charles Columbus Thomas attended a school named after Toussaint l'Ouverture. A large portrait of the Haitian revolutionary leader hung in the entrance, and students were taught of Toussaint's achievements. As a teacher in New York, Thomas was "very shocked" when he encountered black students who lacked a "coherent sense of themselves" and had "learned to be less ambitious, willing to give up despite their intelligence." (Charles Columbus Thomas, Interview, New York City, 13 Sept. 1990; Julius Lester, *Lovesong: Becoming a Jew* [New York: Henry Holt, 1988], 22.)

46. Ferguson, Interview.
47. Ferguson, Interview.
48. Ferguson, Interview.
49. "A 'Slow Burning' School Aide is Among Terrorist Suspects," *New York Times*, 22 June 1967, 25.
50. George Breitman, ed., *Malcolm X Speaks* (New York: Grove Press, 1965), 50. "Black people of the world (darker races, black, yellow, brown, red, oppressed peoples)" asserted the Revolutionary Action Movement, a radical black organization in which Ferguson was active, were all "enslaved by the same forces." Martin Staniland, *American Intellectuals and African Nationalists, 1955–1970* (New Haven: Yale University Press, 1991), 197.
51. Ferguson, "Speech at Sentencing," 1, 3, 4, 9, 11; Ferguson, Interview; Federal Bureau of Investigation, Organization of Afro-American Unity Case File, NY 100-153308, pp. 15, 44–45, Feb.–Mar. 1965, *FBI File on the Organization of African-American Unity, Microfilm Edition* (Wilmington, DE: Scholarly Resources, 1996), Sec. 3, No. 0573, 0599-0600); William W. Sales, Jr., *From Civil Rights to Black Liberation: Malcolm X and the Organization of Afro-American Unity* (Boston: South End Press, 1994), 114, 120–121.
52. Simon Beagle, "Analyzes Various Problems Facing 'More Effective Schools' Program," *United Teacher*, 18 Feb. 1965, 7; "UFT Proposals Focus on Ghetto Education," *United Teacher*, 6 Jan. 1967, 2–3; "A 'Slow Burning' School Aide." Educator Herb Kohl witnessed MES while teaching in New York. Echoing Ferguson's critique, Kohl would recall decades after the school conflict that because teachers were awarded MES assignments according to seniority, many of the most cynical teachers were hired. "Teachers who screamed at their classes during the school day screamed at groups of four or five children after school." MES, Kohl concluded, was "a crazed parody of education." Herbert Kohl, *The Discpline of Hope: Learning from a Lifetime of Teaching* (New York: Simon and Schuster, 1998), 105.
53. Fraser, "Workshop Is Held in Brooklyn."
54. The FBI had initiated surveillance of Ferguson when he worked with the OAAU Education Committee. Only two decades after Ferguson's 1968 conviction were his defenders able to document Hoover's orders to anonymously convince Ferguson that another black radical was conspiring to kill him. (Federal Bureau of Investigation, Organization of Afro-American Unity Case File, NY 100-153308, Cover page C, Feb.–Mar. 1965, 0553; Harold Jamison, "Ferguson Returning Home on April 15 to Face the Music, *Amsterdam News*, 1 Apr. 1989, 6. See also Ken Bailey and Tim Wheeler, "RFK's Name Inserted in Frameup of Ferguson," *The Worker*, 11 June 1968, 8.)
55. M. A. Farber, "Board of Education Creates Post of Demonstration School Principal in 3 Districts," *New York Times*, 25 Aug. 1967, 21.
56. Leonard Buder, "Negroes Urged at I.S. 201 To Arm for 'Self-Defense,'" *New York Times*, 22 Feb. 1968, 1; Perlmutter, "Principal's Bail Raised to $100,000."

57. Leonard Buder, "I.S. 201 Panel Told to Oust Ferguson," *New York Times*, 2 Mar. 1968, 4.

58. "Ferguson Convicted;" "Ferguson, Guilty, Is Freed on Bail."

59. Subcommittee on Investigations of the Senate Committee on Government Operations, *Riots, Civil and Criminal Disorders*, Part 20, 26, 30 June 1969, 4253–55; Ferguson, "Speech at Sentencing," 1, 3, 4, 7, 11. "Black control," Republic of New Africa leader Brother Imari made clear, "includes Puerto Ricans."

60. Ferguson, Interview.

61. Keith Baird, "The Meanings of Black Nationalism," 1973, John Henrik Clarke Papers, Schomburg Library, New York City, Box 5, folder 4; *Amsterdam News*, 22 Mar. 1969, p. 25.

62. Baird, Interview.

63. "Curriculum Changes Planned Quietly in Ocean Hill," *New York Times*, 18 Sept. 1968, 32.

64. Keith Baird et al., "Minutes of Document Committee Meeting," CORE Independent School District, 16 Nov. 1967, 2, copy in author's possession.

65. Keith Baird, Interview, Atlanta, 3 Oct. 1991.

66. The editors, "Education for Social Change," *Freedomways*, Fall 1968, 301.

67. Fabianism takes its name the Fabian Society, founded in Britain in 1884. Fabians believed that by using research and reason to influence those in power they could gradually promote a modest version of socialism, while avoiding class conflict.

68. Born in Jamaica in 1887, Marcus Garvey organized the Universal Negro Improvement Association, whose program of black economic and cultural self-determination won it millions of members in the 1920s, until internal divisions and government harassment undermined the movement.

69. Baird, Interview.

70. Like Baird, poet Claude McKay also contrasted Caribbean and American race relations. When McKay entered the United States in 1912, it was "the first time I had ever come face to face with such manifest, implacable hatred of my race." Quoted in Joyce Moore Turner, "Richard B. Moore and his Works," in W. Burghardt Turner and Joyce Moore Turner, eds., *Richard B. Moore, Caribbean Militant in Harlem* (Bloomington: Indiana University Press, 1988), 29.

71. A settled question among linguists, the legitimacy of African-American language patterns resurfaced as a hot political topic when the Oakland, California school board endorsed classroom use of Ebonics in 1996. See Theresa Perry and Lisa Delpit, *The Real Ebonics Debate: Power, Language, and the Education of African-American Children* (Boston: Beacon Press, 1998). On Weinrich, see Eli Lederhendler, *New York Jews and the Decline of Urban Ethnicity, 1950–1970* (Syracuse: Syracuse University Press, 2001), 30.

72. Rogers, black journalist Roi Ottley noted in 1943, was "the most widely read pamphleteer in black America." Although he was "rarely heard beyond the Negro world, and "orthodox historians frown upon his work, Rogers' pamphlet *100 Amazing Facts About the Negro*, then in its eighteenth edition, was "the 'Bible' of soapbox speakers and lecturers throughout the country." Roi Ottley, *"New World A-Coming"* (Boston: Houghton Mifflin Co., 1943), 101–103.

73. Mark Solomon, *Red and Black: Communism and Afro-Americans, 1929–1935* (New York: Garland, 1988), 82. See also Philip Foner and James Allen, Introduction, *American Communism and Black Americans: A Documentary History, 1919–1929* (Philadelphia: Temple University Press, 1987), viii–ix; Mark Naison, *Communists in Harlem During the Depression* (Urbana: University of Illinois Press, 1983), 5.

74. Knight, "Introduction," 9. On the wider campaign to eliminate the word "Negro," see Robert Harris, Nyota Harris, and Grandassa Harris, eds., *Carlos Cooks and Black Nationalism from Garvey to Malcolm* (Dover, MA: Majority Press, 1992), xviii.

75. Keith E. Baird, "Semantics and Afro-American Liberation," *Social Casework* 51 (May 1970): 265–67.

76. Baird, Interview. See also Richard B. Moore, *The Name "Negro"—Its Origin and Evil Use* in *Richard B. Moore*, 225, 231.

77. Baird, "Semantics and Afro-American Liberation," 266. See also Moore, *The Name "Negro,"* 237.

78. Baird, "Semantics and Afro-American Liberation," 265–66. Again the influence of Richard B. Moore is unmistakable: "The names "Black Man" or "Black Race" . . . [are] loose, racist, color designations which have no basic, obvious or unmistakable linkage with land, history and culture." (Moore, *The Name "Negro,"* 237.)

79. John Henrik Clarke, Richard B. Moore, and Keith Baird, *Africa Lost and Found: a Dialogue* (New York: WCBS-TV and Columbia University, motion picture recorded 1964; Released by Holt, Rinehart and Winston, 1969.

80. Kenneth Clark, *Dark Ghetto: Dilemmas of Social Power* (New York: Harper & Row, 1965), 50.

81. "Minutes of Instructors Conference," no date, Clarke Papers, Box 21, folder 15; KB to Nathan Burnett, 22 Mar. 1967; KB to Laura Pires, 11 July 1966; KB to Dorothy Orr, 31 July 1967; KB to Laura Pires, 16 Dec. 1965, Clarke Papers, Box 21 folder 17; KB to Laura Pires, 24 May 1966, KB to Dorothy Orr, 29 May, 1967, Clarke Papers, Box 21, folder 20.

82. Baird, "The Meanings of Black Nationalism."

83. KB to Douglas Pugh, 29 Dec. 1965, Clarke Papers, Box 21, folder 10.

84. KB to Pugh.

85. Program Announcement, Clarke Papers, Box 21, folder 40.

86. Tina Harris to John Henrik Clarke, 3 Mar. 1966, Clarke Papers, Box 21, folder 6; William Ware to John Henrik Clarke, 18 June 1966, Clarke Papers, Box 21, folder 4; John Henrik Clarke to Dorothy Orr, 1 Sept. 1967, Clarke Papers, Box 21 folder 48.

87. See for instance Martin P. Deutsch, "The Disadvantaged Child and the Learning Process," in A. Harry Passow, ed., *Education in Depressed Areas* (New York: Teachers College Press, 1965), 170.

88. Keith Baird, Speech to AFT Conference, American Federation of Teachers Collection, Human Rights and Community Relations Department—AFT Series I. Folder 10, Walter P. Reuther Library of Labor & Urban Affairs, Wayne State University. See also Racism in Education Conference, *United Teacher*, 20 Jan 1967, 6–8; *American Teacher*, Apr. 1967, 13.

89. Nan Robertson, "Teacher Opposes the Term 'Negro,'" *New York Times*, 10 Dec. 1966; Gerald Grant, "1300 Teachers Debate Textbook Negro Image," *Washington Post*, 10 Dec. 1966, A3. Among those influenced by Moore's pamphlet was Kwanzaa creator Mualana Karenga, a cultural nationalist who defined self-determination ("Kujichagulia") as the ability to "define ourselves, name ourselves, and speak for our selves." Mualana Karenga, Interview, no date, 1–2, Clarke Papers, Box 5, folder 68.

90. Baird interiew.

91. Baird's "council of humanity" metaphor recalls Horace Kallen's classic 1915 pluralist claim that society is an orchestra in which ethnic groups are the instruments that "make up the symphony of civilization," Horace Kallen, "Democracy versus the Melting Pot," *Nation* 18 Feb. 1915, 191–4, and 25 Feb. 1915, 217–20. On the history of cultural pluralism in African American educational thought, see Johnny Washington, *Alain Locke and Philosophy A Quest for Cultural Pluralism* (Westport: Greenwood, 1986).

92. "Curriculum Changes Planned Quietly in Ocean Hill." *New York Times*, 18 Sept. 1968, 32.

93. Angelina Reyes et al. to the City of New York, 12 Nov. 1969, Isaiah Robinson Papers, Box 17,

folder 8, Milbank Library, Teachers College, Columbia University; Mario Fantini, Marilyn Git-tell, and Richard Magat, *Community Control and the Urban School* (New York: Praeger, 1970), 223.

94. John Kifner, "Substitute Word for 'Negro' Argued," *New York Times*, 11 Dec. 1966.

95. Harold Cruse, *The Crisis of the Negro Intellectual* (New York: William Morrow, 1967), 255. See also See Alan Wald, *The New York Intellectuals: The Rise and Decline of the Anti-Stalinist Left from the 1930s to the 1980s* (Chapel Hill: University of North Carolina Press, 1987), 29; Jennifer Jordan, "Cultural Nationalism in the 1960s: Politics and Poetry," in Adolph Reed, Jr., ed., *Race Politics, and Culture: Critical Essays on the Radicalism of the 1960s* (Westport, CT: Greenwood, 1986), 33–35. On the appeal of Garveyism among working-class black New Yorkers did not have Caribbean roots, see Irma Watkins-Owens, *Blood Relations: Caribbean Immigrants and the Harlem Community, 1900–1930* (Bloomington: Indiana University Press, 1996).

96. Clark, *Dark Ghetto*, 219.

97. *New York Times*, 10 June 1967.

98. Christine Sleeter and Carl Grant, "An Analysis of Multicultural Education in the United States," *Harvard Educational Review* 57 (1987): 421–444.

99. Jitu Weusi, "The East Legacy," *Journal of Community Advocacy and Activism* I (1996).

100. "The East: A Model of Nationhood," *Imani*, Aug.-Sept. 1971, 32; Weusi, "Legacy."

101. Weusi, "Legacy."

102. "The East," 28–29.

103. Steven Mufson, "A Dream Deferred: Ocean Hill-Brownsville Remembers," *Village Voice*, 6 June 1989, 29–30; "The East," 30, 32; Alton Rison, "How to Teach Black Children," *BlackNews*, Jan. 1973, 36; Podair, *Like Strangers*, 297.

104. Jitu Weusi [Leslie Campbell], Interview, Brooklyn, 21 Dec. 1990. A lawyer who defended the "Scottsboro Boys" and represented Harlem on the New York City Council, Benjamin Davis was one of the 11 Communist leaders indicted under the Smith Act trial. Campbell's high school activism led the FBI to open a file on him, one that would grow to hundreds of pages.

105. Weusi, Legacy, Interview.

106. Weusi, Interview; Daisy Bates, *The Long Shadow of Little Rock* (New York, David McKay, 1962).

107. Weusi, Interview.

108. Weusi, Interview.

109. Weusi, Interview.

110. Weusi, Interview, Weusi, "Legacy."

111. Weusi, Interview.

112. Leslie Campbell, "The Devil Can Never Educate Us," *Afro-American Teachers Forum*, Nov. 1968, reprinted in Wright, *What Black Educators Are Saying*, 29.

113. Leonard Buder, "Teacher Ousted Over I.S. 201 Show," *New York Times*, 28 Feb. 1968, 50.

114. See for instance "Incitement and Assaults reported," *United Teacher*, 1 May 1968, 4; "Another View of the 271 Scene," *United Teacher*, 1 May 1968, 4.

115. Charles Isaacs, "A J.H.S. 271 Teacher Tells It Like He Sees It," *New York Times Magazine*, 24 Nov. 1968, 72.

116. Hampton and Fayer, *Voice's of Freedom*, 492.

117. Arnold Forster to Editor, *Columbia Journalism Review*, Spring 1970, 61; Nat Hentoff, "Blacks and Jews: An Interview with Julius Lester," *Evergreen Review*, Apr. 1969, 22; Julius Lester, *Lovesong: Becoming a Jew* (New York: Henry Holt, 1988), 49–50, 56–7; Henry Raymont, "Teachers Protest Poem to F.C.C.," *New York Times*, 16 Jan. 1969, 48; "UFT Raps Anti-Semitic Poem,"

United Teacher 22 Jan. 1969, 9; Julius Lester, "A Response," in *Black Anti-Semitism and Jewish Racism*, Nat Hentoff, ed. (New York: Richard W. Baron, 1969), 229–232; Rabbi Meir Kahane, *The Story of the Jewish Defense League* (Radnor, PA: Chilton Book Co., 1975), 91–92, 108–09.

118. Podair, *Like Strangers*, 303.
119. Weusi, Interview, Hampton and Fayer, *Voices of Freedom*, 502–03.
120. Weusi, "Legacy."
121. Kalonji Lasana Niamke, "The Legacy of "The East": An Analysis of a Case Experience in Independent Institution and Nation(alist) Building, 1969–1986," masters thesis Cornell University, 1999; Kierna Mayo, "Independents' Day," *City Limits Monthly*, Jan. 1997; "Profile on Jitu Weusi," Bedstuyonline, *http://bedstuyonline.com/People/Profiles/jweusi/jweusi.htm*; M.A. Farber, "An 'African Centered' School: How the Idea Developed and Why It May Fail," *New York Times*, 8 Feb. 1991, A13.
122. Julius Lester, "Reactionary Aspects of Black Power," in *Revolutionary Notes* (New York: Richard Baron, 1969), 104–5.
123. James Baldwin, Introduction, in Robert Campbell, *The Chasm: The Life and Death of a Great Experiment in Ghetto Education* (Boston: Houghton Mifflin, 1974), xi–xii.
124. Adolph Reed, Jr., Introduction, in Adolph Reed, Jr., ed., *Race Politics, and Culture: Critical Essays on the Radicalism of the 1960s* (Westport, CT: Greenwood, 1986), 5.
125. James Baldwin, *The Fire Next Time* (New York: Dial Press, 1963), 132.

Chapter 10: Schools and Social Justice in the Post-Liberal City

1. David B. Tyack, "Q. 'What Do You Think About Education in Harlem?' A. 'I Think It Would Be a Good Idea,'" unpublished manuscript, no date [1967], 1.
2. Mark Maier, *City Unions: Managing Discontent in New York City* (New Brunswick, NJ: Rutgers University Press, 1987), 127. See also Maurice Berube and Marilyn Gittell, eds., *Confrontation at Ocean Hill-Brownsville: The New York School Strikes of 1968* (New York: Praeger, 1969), v.
3. McCoy, "Analysis of Critical Issues and Incidents," xi, 1, 52, 72, 78.
4. *A Summary of the 1969 School Decentralization Law for New York City* (New York: Office of Educational Affairs, no date).
5. Naomi Levine, *Ocean Hill-Brownsville: Schools in Crisis* (New York: Popular Library, 1969), 5; Milton Galamison, interview, in *Why Teachers Strike: Teachers' Rights and Community Control*, Melvin Urofsky ed. (Garden City, NY: Doubleday, 1970), 305. On activists' critique of the "decentralization" law, see also Gary Huth et al., Ad Hoc Committee of the Lower East Side Concerned with School District Boundaries for District #1, to Joseph Monserrat and Isaiah Robinson, 31 Oct. 1969, Isaiah Robinson Papers, Box 17, Folder 2, Teachers College, Columbia University. See also Community Action for Education; "Think the New School Bill Will Help Your Johnny Read? Our Communities Say No!" undated, Robinson Papers, Box 19, folder 40; Evelina Antonetty, "Why We Are Not Participating in the Local School Board Elections," Bronx United Parents, Jan. 1970, copy in author's possession; *New York Times* 1 May 1969, 1; David Bresnick, "Legislating New York City School Decentralization" (Ph.D. dissertation, Columbia University, 1972); Annie Stein, "Strategies for Failure," *Harvard Educational Review* 41 (1971): 171.
6. Melvin Zimet, *Decentralization and School Effectiveness: A Case Study of the 1969 Decentralization Law in New York City* (New York: Teachers College Press, 1973), 46.

7. Jim Gelbman, "Evolution of District 12: The Implementation of Public Policy in a Decentralized New York City School District, 1969–1982," Ph.D. dissertation, Fordham University, 1984, 254.

8. Brownsville and Ocean Hill Coalition for Community Control, "Some Questions About This Fraudulent Election of 1970," no date, Robinson Papers, Box 19, folder 27, series 378; Edward Fiske, "Community-Run Schools Leave Hopes Unfulfilled," New York Times, 24 June 1980, 1.

9. Jonathan Rieder, Canarsie: The Jews and Italians of Brooklyn Against Liberalism (Cambridge, 1985), 2, 209, 225.

10. Jerald Podair, "Like Strangers: Blacks, Whites, and New York City's Ocean Hill-Brownsville Crisis, 1945–1980" (Ph.D. dissertation, Princeton University, 1997), 9.

11. "Excerpts from the President's Message to Congress on Education Reform," New York Times, 4 Mar. 1970, 28. The conservative potential of community control did not come as a surprise to Bayard Rustin, who noted the ironic alliance of Brooklyn CORE leader Roy Innis and segregationist stalwart Lester Maddox. Bayard Rustin, Strategies for Freedom: The Changing Patterns of Black Protest (New York: Columbia University Press, 1976), 20. See also Robert Allen, Black Awakening in Capitalist America (New York, 1969).

12. Michael Katz, Class, Bureaucracy and Schools: The Illusion of Educational Change in America (New York: Praeger, 1971), 40.

13. Marjorie Murphy, Blackboard Unions: The AFT and the NEA, 1900–1980 (Ithaca: Cornell University Press, 1990), 236–8.

14. Classic accounts of urban renewal, highway construction and suburbanization include Robert A. Caro, The Power Broker: Robert Moses and the Fall of New York (New York: Vintage, 1975); Kenneth T. Jackson, Crabgrass Frontier: The Suburbanization of the United States (New York: Oxford University Press, 1985); Herbert Gans, The Levittowners (New York: Pantheon, 1967). As Jackson argues, suburbanization was not the result of bankers' manipulating unsuspecting upwardly (and outwardly) mobile urbanites but represented a coincidence of their interests, at the expense of the urban poor (216–17). The years of the community control conflict were a time when many teachers on both sides of the dispute moved to the suburbs. Paul Becker, interview, Rockville Center, NY, 7 Sept. 1990; Paul Burkowsky, interview, Brooklyn, NY, 10 Sept. 1990.

15. Ira Rosenwanke, Population History of New York City (Syracuse: Syracuse University Press, 1972); Susan Fainstein and Norman Fainstein, "Economic Change, National Policy and the System of Cities," in Restructuring the City: the Political Economy of Urban Redevelopment rev. ed., Susan Fainstein et al., eds. (New York; Longman, 1987); Margaret Weir, "The Federal Government and Unemployment: The Frustration of Policy Innovation from the New Deal to the Great Society," in Politics of Social Policy, Margaret Weir et al., eds. (Princeton: Princeton University Press, 1988), 149–190.

16. Steve Zeluck, "The UFT Strike," Phi Delta Kappan, 1968, 253–54; Allen Ornstein, Metropolitan Schools: Administrative Decentralization vs. Community Control (Metuchen, NJ, 1974), 181; Samuel Freedman, Small Victories: The Real World of a Teacher, Her Students & Their High School (New York, 1990), 109–110; Eric Lichten, Class, Power and Austerity: the New York City Fiscal Crisis (South Hadley: Bergin & Garvey, 1986), 154. Freedman reports that in 1968 teachers left the school system at five times the usual rate.

17. Catherine Gewertz, "N.Y.C. Mayor Gains Control Over Schools," Education Week, 19 June 2002.

18. Clarence Stone, et al., Building Civic Capacity: The Politic of Reforming Urban Schools (Lawrence: University of Kansas Press, 2001), 1.

19. Stone, *Building Civic Capacity*.

20. Jeffrey R. Henig, Richard C. Hula, Marion Orr, and Desiree S. Pedescleaux, *The Color of School Reform: Race, Politics and the Challenge of Urban Education* (Princeton: Princeton University Press, 1999).

21. Marion Orr, *Black Social Capital: The Politics of School Reform in Baltimore, 1986–1998* (Lawrence: University of Kansas Press, 1999).

22. James Traub, "A Lesson in Unintended Consequences," *New York Times Magazine*, 6 Oct. 2002.

23. David Alison, *Searchlight: An Expose of New York City Schools* (New York: Teachers Center Press, 1951), 1–21.

24. Jessica Kowal, "Rules for Schools: Bloomberg's Takeover Plan Would Shift Roles, Emphasize Results," *New York Newsday*, 28 May 2002.

25. Kenneth K. Wong, et al., "City and State Takeover as a School Reform Strategy," Paper Presented at the Research Conference of the Association for Public Policy Analysis and Management, 2000, 14; John Portz, Lana Stein, and Robin R. Jones, *City Schools and City Politics: Institutions and Leadership in Pittsburgh, Boston, and St. Louis* (Lawrence: University Press of Kansas, 1999), 82–105

26. Debra Viadero, "Big-City Mayors' Control of Schools Yields Mixed Results," *Education Week*, 11 Sept. 2002; James Cibulka, "Old Wine, New Bottles," *Education Next* 1 (Winter 2001): 28–35.

27. Michael Katz, *The Undeserving Poor: From the War on Poverty to the War on Welfare* (New York: Pantheon, 1990).

28. Christopher Jencks and Meredith Phillips, eds., *The Black-White Test Score Gap* (Washington: Brookings Institution Press, 1998).

29. See for instance Louis Hartz, *The Liberal Tradition in America: an Interpretation of American Political Thought Since the Revolution* (New York: Harcourt, Brace, 1955).

Index